and long life so that they may continue to help others. May His favor be upon them and a thousand generations and their family and their children and their children, and their children.
—Zendaya, MCF Beneficiary

I was a street boy back in the day. I have gotten here only because I went through MCF as a beneficiary of the works of Dr. Charles and Esther Mulli.

My story is told in this book, and it was my pleasure and honour to share it. I wanted to use it to touch the lives of many people who never made it to visit us. I wanted to show that restoration is possible.

The journey of my restoration has been long, spanning most of my life. The bigger part up to the age of about 24 was through MCF where I met Dr. Charles Mulli and Esther Mulli who became my dad and mum.

Their impact is permanent, and I can't begin to imagine all ways to give gratitude. I can only follow in their footsteps to pursue God's mission in my life and to bring hope and restoration in other people's lives.

Our stories will touch your life in a special way. Please enjoy reading the book.
—Karl, MCF Beneficiary

MULLY CHILDREN'S FAMILY

TRANSFORMATIONS

SEVEN CHANGED LIVES

PAUL H. BOGE
FOREWORD BY NDONDO MUTUA MULLI

For more information about Mully Children's Family please visit
www.MullyChildrensFamily.org.

MULLY CHILDREN'S FAMILY TRANSFORMATIONS
Copyright ©2024 Paul H. Boge

978-1-998815-25-8 Soft Cover
978-1-998815-26-5 E-book

Published by:
Castle Quay Books
Tel: (416) 573-3249
E-mail: info@castlequaybooks.com | www.castlequaybooks.com

Edited by Marina Hofman Willard PhD
Cover and book interior design by Burst Impressions

Library and Archives Canada Cataloguing in Publication
Title: Mully's Children Family transformations / by Paul H. Boge.
Other titles: Transformations
Names: Boge, Paul H., 1973- author.
Description: "Seven changed lives."
Identifiers: Canadiana (print) 20240467426 | Canadiana (ebook) 20240467434 | ISBN 9781998815258
   (softcover) | ISBN 9781998815265 (EPUB)
Subjects: LCSH: Mulli, Charles. | LCSH: Mully Children's Family. | LCSH: Street children—Kenya—
   Biography. | LCSH: Abandoned children—Kenya—Biography. | LCSH: Street children—Protection—Kenya.
   | LCSH: Abandoned children—Protection—Kenya. | LCSH: Christian biography—Kenya. | LCGFT:
   Biographies.
Classification: LCC HV887.K4 B64 2024 | DDC 362.7096762—dc23

CASTLE QUAY BOOKS

I appreciate Daddy Mulli for the great things he has done. I am thankful to him and Mamma Esther for receiving me as their son, for the trust they have given me, and for inviting me to be in their family. I am thankful to God for giving me loving brothers and loving sisters with whom we walk together with love, unity, and peace. We follow the footsteps of our father in transforming the youth to live a dignified livelihood in future.
—Saul, Mully Children's Family Beneficiary

Mully Children's Family Transformations presents the heartfelt accounts of extraordinary journeys of children who were otherwise condemned, abandoned, hopeless, and left to discover new levels of rock bottom. But they each got a turning point, a sliver of hope, and things were never the same. This book is not only a story, but a testament to the resilience, faith, and love that define Mully Children's Family and a manifestation of how God works through man to change destinies.

Sharing my story has been a profound experience, one that has deepened my appreciation for the incredible work of MCF. The unwavering commitment of one man who obediently followed his call to bring back life to a rather lifeless situation. Some of the stories, I dare say, might sound like fiction, but these stories, mine included, are real, and we have the scars to testify of our incredible journeys. We share our stories hoping that you, the reader, will be inspired and hopefully get touched to touch a life.

My admiration for Daddy and Mommy Mulli and their unwavering faith is boundless. Their selfless dedication and love have created a ripple effect of positive change that reaches far beyond the boundaries of MCF. Their example reminds us of the power of faith, love, and sacrifice in overcoming life's challenges.

I sincerely hope that you, dear reader, find as much joy and inspiration in this book as I and several other MCF beneficiaries found in sharing our stories. May it encourage you to believe in the power of love and faith to create lasting change.

Thank you for embarking on this journey with us. Your support and interest in *MCF Transformations* means the world. Hats off to the great author and friend of Mully Children's Family, Paul Boge.
—Keren, MCF Beneficiary

I am happy to share my story because I am grateful for what God has done for me through MCF. By sharing my story, I wish to encourage someone to never to give up in life no matter what. No situation is permanent. Just as God came through for me, He can come through for anyone. MCF is the best place and family to belong because God is doing wonders though MCF. I love our Dad and Mom because they have allowed God to use them to impact and transform

lives. By reading this book you are going to be blessed because every story is a real story of what God is doing in MCF through Daddy and Mamma. Enjoy.
—Moses, MCF Beneficiary

When I was young, there was no one to protect my rights as a child until I was rescued by Daddy Mulli.

I am happy to share my story so that God's work and miracles may be seen in my life. God has been faithful and loving to me since I was young up to now. He has guided me in every aspect of my life and has never forsaken me. I know and believe He will continue guiding me until I achieve the great plans He has for me (Jeremiah 29:11).

Daddy Mulli rescued me and fulfilled all my rights as a child. Mully Children's Family has been a great home for me. This is where I experienced parental love for the first time from Daddy Mulli and Mamma Esther. They have been my role model and encouraged me to keep pursuing my dreams. I thank them for transforming my life from nothing to something. I do not know where I would be if they had not rescued me. May Almighty God bless them abundantly.

My hope is that everyone who would get an opportunity to read this would be blessed and encounter God's greatness.
—Ruth, MCF Beneficiary

After I lost my parents to HIV/AIDS, I became a street boy. I met with Mrs. Esther Mulli in the street. She was sent by God. It was the moment my life turned around.

Daddy Mulli's love for me is indescribable. He never gave up on me even when I did so many bad things as a child. He kept feeding me, taking me to school, and rehabilitating me through the word of God. He counseled me, provided medical care, encouraged my entrepreneurial skills, and taught me how to live with dignity and confidence. Professor Charles Mulli was and still is a mentor, missionary, and leader, and the best choirmaster and coach I could ever hope for. I can not thank him enough. I am so grateful for Mully Children's Family.
—Muchoki, MCF Beneficiary

I express my heartfelt gratitude to Daddy Mully and Mamma Esther for their love, support, prayers, and encouragement. They entered my life during a difficult period, bringing light to my darkest moments. I thank God for working through them and am forever grateful. Their impact on my life has created a ripple effect, allowing me to bless others because I have been blessed. My heartfelt prayer is that God may keep and sustain them, grant them good health

Foreword

In the heart of Kenya, filled with striking landscapes and rich cultural heritage, lies a story of incredible resilience and compassion. *Mully Children's Family Transformations* by Paul H. Boge captures the journey of my father, Charles Mulli, who rose from poverty to create a legacy of hope and change.

As the fourth-born of Charles and Esther Mulli, I have had the privilege of seeing firsthand the seven children featured in this book who are now adults. They are a testament to the thousands of children rescued, rehabilitated, and reintegrated into the community. My parents, siblings, and I have witnessed the transformation of lives, one child at a time—an honour and privilege beyond words. The impact of Mully Children's Family (MCF) on these children's lives is a beacon of hope, showing that change is possible even in the most challenging circumstances.

This book delves into the heart-wrenching and inspiring narratives of the children rescued by the MCF. Each story powerfully reminds us of the harsh realities many face in Kenya and the profound impact one individual's vision and action can have on an entire community. From the bustling slums of Nairobi to the serene refuge provided by MCF, Boge paints a vivid picture of transformation, resilience, and redemption.

For instance, we meet a young boy who survived by stealing mangos to fend off hunger, only to find hope and a new direction in life through MCF. His journey out of a life of desperation into that of a hopeful student and soccer enthusiast encapsulates the life-changing power of MCF's intervention.

Another poignant story is that of a young girl who escaped domestic trouble and instability to find safety and purpose at MCF. Encouraged by the nurturing environment, she pursued her passion for nursing, ultimately becoming a healthcare professional and lecturer.

These examples illustrate the broader impact of MCF's work, showing how children from dire circumstances can achieve remarkable personal growth and contribute positively to society when given the proper support and opportunities.

Paul Boge has been a cherished friend of my parents for over twenty years. He wrote the first biography of my father, *Father to the Fatherless*, the sequel *Hope to the Hopeless*, the children's book *The Biggest Family in the World*, and *Hannah's Hope*. His dedication to our family and MCF is profound; he has steadfastly walked beside us through every challenge and triumph and currently serves as the board chair of MCF Canada. Paul's writing is meticulous, reflecting his exceptional talent and deep personal knowledge of the specific stories of the children featured in this book. His unwavering commitment to our cause is a source of inspiration for us all.

Paul's passion for children's lives is profound, and his love for them is evident in his work. His outstanding qualities and skills shine through in every word he writes. Remarkably, Paul writes about MCF without seeking profit, driven purely by his commitment to our cause. His contributions are invaluable, and his stories continue to inspire and uplift.

As you read these pages, you will encounter the harrowing experiences of children who once knew nothing but despair. You will walk alongside them as they journey from the brink of hopelessness to the embrace of a loving family. You will witness the remarkable changes brought about by education, mentorship, love, and the unwavering support of the MCF community.

Paul's dedicated documentation and heartfelt narration ensure that the legacy of my parents, Charles and Esther Mulli, and the transformative power of the Mully Children's Family model will continue to inspire generations. As you immerse in this book, may you be moved to reflect on the change you can bring to the world, no matter how small it may seem.

It is my prayer that this book will be a blessing to you, to know that it is never too late for God to transform a life to His purpose.

—Ndondo Mutua Mulli

PART 1
SAUL

The following are true accounts of children who have been rescued by Charles and Esther Mulli through Mully Children's Family. In certain places, names have been changed. Be blessed and encouraged.

CHAPTER 1

The blistering sun made the road feel endless.

Young Saul struggled in the unbearable Kenyan heat. How much further? A car drove past him, engulfing him in clouds of dust. He coughed. Wiped his red eyes.

When his vision cleared, he saw Hali waiting for him.

"This is a terrible idea," Hali said.

"You have a better one?"

"It's lunchtime," Hali replied, glancing behind him to make sure no one was listening. "The workers will be on break."

"Let's go."

Saul led them down the path to a large mango farm. The massive trees stretched out as far as they could see. Saul's dry mouth dropped open.

"I don't know about this, Saul. You know what can happen."

Saul crouched down and pulled Hali with him. "We have to be quick," Saul said. "In and out. Got it?"

Hali struggled. "Okay."

"No one's forcing you."

"Let's do this."

They snuck onto the farm. That felt strange. They suddenly sensed the strain on their nerves that came with trespassing. It all seemed so simple. Get in. Steal fruit. Run away. But the unbearable fear pounding through their veins made them wonder if they had made a mistake.

Saul and Hali each grabbed a handful of mangos from one of the forbidden trees. Sweat dripped from their foreheads—a combination of the sweltering heat and the stress of what might happen to them if they got caught.

Saul tried to push those thoughts from his mind. Stay focused. Nearly there. They turned to leave. No point in getting greedy. They could always come back for more. Saul breathed a sigh of relief.

But a sickening feeling in his stomach told Saul things would not go as planned.

They stopped. Did a branch break behind them?

Every sound felt as loud as an explosion, magnified by their panicked imaginations.

Hali shot him a nervous glance.

Saul motioned for them to return to the path. He looked ahead. They were in the clear.

Then, another sound. Definitely. Someone's footsteps.

"Run!" Saul whispered.

The boys bolted as if on a breakaway on the soccer pitch.

They dropped the mangos. Sprinted through the maze of trees.

Suddenly, a large male figure stood in Saul's path. "I caught you!" the man shouted as he lunged at Saul.

A painful burst of adrenaline shot through Saul. The shock of an impending beating ripped through his body. He faked one way and then ran in the other direction around the man.

Where's Hali? Did he make it?

Saul raced down a row between long lines of trees. He glanced to the side, looking for Hali in the forest of mango trees.

But his break in concentration proved to be his undoing.

Another man grabbed Saul's arm. Saul kicked and flailed away at him. The man gripped harder, deadening whatever hope of escape remained in Saul. He heard Hali shouting. The men brought the boys into a clearing.

"You boys are worthless!" the taller man shouted.

"We just need something to eat," Saul said. "Please—" He wanted to continue explaining. But out of the corner of his eye, he saw the man's hand poised to strike.

He hit Saul with such force that Saul spun to the ground. He felt disoriented. His vision blurred. Had he been knocked out? He struggled to his knees, then wondered if it would have been better to stay down on the ground.

The men beat the boys under the merciless blast of the noon sun. When they finished, they dragged Saul and Hali to the edge of the property and dropped their bruised bodies on the dry ground.

"You pathetic leeches! You are nothing! Don't ever come back!"

Saul heard their footsteps fade into the distance. He lay still, unable to move. Pain consumed his body. His head pounded with a deafening headache. He focused on breathing to help ease the shock. Short breath in. Short breath out. Every part of him throbbed in agony. Was anything broken? Could they stand?

"Hali?"

No response.

"Hali?"

"Yes," came a quiet reply.

Saul blinked. "Okay, maybe this wasn't such a good idea."

"Forget the mangos."

"Agreed. Your turn. Where are we going to eat?"

The boys struggled down the dusty road until they finally reached a small mosque. They entered. Got down on their knees. Pressed their faces down on the mats. And prayed for something good to happen. They ate a few bites of chicken. Felt their stomachs settle.

By late afternoon the boys recovered enough from their beatings to be able to pass the ragged soccer ball between them. There was no grass field to play on. Not for them. Instead, they played on an uneven dirt field. The simple rolling of a ball back and forth provided them with both connection and comfort.

"We have to get out of here," Saul said.

"Perfect. I have already booked the plane tickets. First class, too. And I have the reservations at the hotel all set to go."

Saul laughed. Hali too. That wasn't smart. The movement caused different muscles in their backs to hurt from the beating.

"I mean it," Saul said. "We're going nowhere."

"No kidding," Hali said. "I want out. You want out. Everybody *wants* out of here. The key is *finding* a way out."

The coastal area of Mombasa served as an ideal tourist destination for foreigners. They could come and go as they like. Stay in the fancy hotels. Sit on the pristine beaches. Enjoy Mombasa without being in the *real* Mombasa. Because there were *two* Mombasas. One for tourists. One for locals. And locals didn't see Mombasa as a dreamland. Poverty is poverty.

Even on a beach.

"Then we're going to be the ones to actually do it," Saul said.

"And what do we know better than everyone else? You have rich friends?"

"Plenty."

"Do you know someone in the government?"

"I'm best friends with the president."

Hali passed the ball to Saul. "We're the same as everyone else," he said.

"I don't believe that."

"Then find us a bird to fly us out of here," Hali said.

"Forget the birds. We don't need them."

"You don't like birds?"

"I like lions."

"Why?"

"Because of the attitude. They believe. They fight. They back down from no one."

"That's all fine, Saul," Hali said. "But we still don't have a way out of here."

"We're not trapped," Saul said.

"Then show me a way out."

"You need better friends," Saul's mother said in their small iron sheet hut.

"Hali is fine."

"He's not leading you in a good direction."

"It was my fault, Mom."

Mary sat down on the ground next to him as he lay down on a blanket. He noticed in his mother's eyes the look of a woman battered by the waves of life. Yet, she still exuded the ability to make her son feel loved without having to use words. She gazed into Saul with compassionate eyes that revealed the anguish of her soul.

There was no father around. Not since Saul was born. She sighed. It all felt too much. Saul sensed the tightening vise grips around her mind preventing her from thinking of a solution to life's increasingly complex and unsolvable problems. Food, safety, education, future. Was there reason for hope? Was there a path forward? She closed her eyes, exasperated. Her other children were no better off.

"It will be okay," Saul said.

She nodded. But they both knew better.

She managed a smile. Saul noticed the bags under her eyes. Had she had lost more weight? Was the stress of life chewing her alive?

He studied her eyes, deep in thought.

What to do? What to do?

Transferring Saul to the agricultural town of Homabay near Lake Victoria to live with relatives was Mary's last and only option. She wanted to keep him. Wanted to raise her son. But food is a cruel dictator.

And hunger drives decisions.

It pained him to wave goodbye to his mother. Which hurt more? His heart or his stomach? He boarded the bus and burned the image in his mind of her standing outside, hoping that whatever good she had offered him in his young life would somehow stick with him. As the bus drove off, he wondered when he would see her again.

When he arrived, Saul's uncle encouraged him to visit the local mosque. Saul integrated into daily life. Felt part of the family. Received enough food on most days.

One day, as he came home and entered the family village, he noticed everyone crying.

"What's wrong?" Saul asked. But they avoided the question, following a cultural tradition of not passing on bad news.

Saul found his uncle. "Why is everyone crying?"

Saul's uncle tried not to respond. But Saul saw the answer in his uncle's bewildered and empty eyes.

"We have lost your mother," he said at last.

The shock felt as if someone had pulled Saul's life right out of him. He stood there. Hollowed out. Feeling the unbearable desire to leave this terrible new reality but not having the power to do so.

Had he heard that correct?

No, no, no. This can't be happening.

But it *was* happening. And it was happening to him.

There would be no undoing this. No going back.

He thought of his last conversation with Mom. Her saddened face. Had she been sick then already? Had she known? He thought of the many times she would tuck him in at night in their small hut. He thought of the comfort he felt when she would come home. He loved seeing her. Loved her gentle smile. Her strong will. Her commitment to stay with the family despite insurmountable struggles.

He grieved his mother in silence, the way children do when they withdraw in an effort to use what little energy they have left to process their confusion. Her face stayed in his mind, exactly the way he trained it to remember her. He constantly thought of her. Her memory felt more real than he did.

If only there was a way to bring her back. One more hug. A long one. A never-ending one.

There was nothing more for him in Homabay. He told his uncle he would be leaving. His uncle objected. But Saul was the authority in his life now. At the ripe old age of eight, he returned to Kalifi. But this time he settled in the beaches of Mombasa.

The sand under his feet felt warm. He walked into the water, never deeper than his knees. He turned back to study the beach. Noticed all the tourists. So many foreigners. They wore nice clothes. Sat on nice chairs. Reading books. Sleeping. Looking out at the Indian Ocean through sunglasses that shielded them from the bright rays and the realities of the world around them.

Saul thought it through. Foreigners with money. Maybe this could work.

He waited on them. Refilling drinks. Selling lotions. Getting towels. Carrying luggage. Cleaning sunglasses. Living the life of a beach boy. Cooling off in the water when it got too hot. *How much can I earn? Maybe this can change my life.*

And at first it did. Money in his pocket made a difference. But it wasn't much. Certainly not enough. And the lack of getting ahead weighed on him one evening as the tourists left the beach. He watched them pack. Offered to help carry items for them. With the sinking sun came the sinking reality that this was never going to be a long-term solution.

A sudden chill ran through him. He struggled inside his mind to fight thoughts that hammered away at him like the crashing of the waves on the shore.

This is it, Saul. You will be a beach boy for life.

No. No, I can still make it.

Make it where? What reality are you living in?

I can … I can …

What? How many things can you carry for tourists? How much can you earn by doing this? You are barely surviving.

I can go to school.

School? Which one? They all cost money. Far more money than you can afford.

Saul swallowed. He reached into his pocket for money to buy food. He found nothing. *What? … Oh, right.* He had bought mango slices earlier in the day. Not much. Certainly not enough. He glanced up at the beachside restaurants filled with people. He noticed a waiter delivering food to a table. There was more on one plate than what he would eat in a week.

He looked down the endless beach. He turned around to see the shoreline stretch out in the other direction. He glanced out at the ocean. The vast expanse met the horizon somewhere in the far distance.

Saul, do you have money?

No.

Do you have a wealthy person who can help you?

No.

Do you have anyone who can help you?

He sighed.

This is it, Saul. This beach is the rest of your life. You will never leave. Tourists will come and go. But your future is as predictable as the sand on the beach and the water in the ocean. It will always be here. Just like you. Settle in, young boy. This is all there is for you.

Saul thought of his friend Hali. He wondered whatever became of him. He thought of his mother. He thought of soccer.

He walked down the beach, hearing the sounds of laughter and joy coming from the packed-out restaurants.

CHAPTER 2

A knock at the door sent a sudden shiver through Saul.

He walked to the window. The last rays of sunshine shone through the opening in the wall, illuminating the mesh covering. Saul strained his neck to catch a glimpse outside, hoping to find a reason to convince his heart to stop pounding.

Did I steal from a tourist? Have they tracked me down? How many of them are there?

Another knock. This one louder. The sound of the door rattling filled his one-room hut made of an iron sheet roof and mud walls.

"Hello," a male voice said.

Saul breathed. The voice didn't sound angry. It sounded altogether different to him.

What did this man want?

"Saul, are you in there?"

He didn't recognize the voice. Didn't recognize the tone either. *How does he know my name? Is this a trick? Have the police snuck up on either side of the hut? Are they coming to arrest me?*

A third knock.

Time to answer.

Saul edged closer. Braced himself. Opened the door.

And looked into the eyes of a stranger who looked oddly familiar.

"I didn't steal any mangos," Saul said.

The man smiled through his eyes. So bright. So clear. He wore a dress shirt and dress pants. Medium height with a kind face that put Saul at ease.

The man laughed. "I'm not here to see if you have stolen any mangos."

"I haven't done anything wrong."

That was accurate. Wasn't it? How far back did he have to remember? Had he taken something accidentally?

Another laugh from the man. Those eyes. Saul had never seen such light coming from *inside* a person.

"I have come to help you."

"Me?"

"I am from Mully Children's Family."

The name *Mully* was new. The word *family* felt so foreign to him, he had a hard time remembering what that was like.

"What's that?"

"A home for children who need help. There is a branch in Vipingo. Not far from here. There is also a home in Yatta. Where your sister lives."

"Velma?"

"She misses you."

"What is this home?"

"A six-year-old boy named Charles Mulli was abused by his father and abandoned by his family. He went from hut to hut begging for food. He was kicked out of school for not having enough fees. Later, he started a small taxi company. That grew bigger and bigger. As a young man, he branched out into oil and gas distribution, property management, real estate, and insurance and became extremely wealthy. Then one day, God called him to sell everything he had, go into the streets, and rescue destitute children."

Impossible. Mulli had to be the most fantastical story Saul had ever heard. And he would have thought it a crazy lie were it not for the sudden impact he felt in his soul.

"Your sister wants us to help you. We are inviting you to join the school here in Vipingo."

"I don't have the fees."

"Ah. Quite right. But his school is different. His school doesn't require fees."

"Free school?"

"And free food."

Saul pulled back. His mind tried to absorb this new reality. Hadn't he just been on the beach coming to terms with the rainy forecast on his life? How could life turn so quickly? Or worse, maybe it wasn't really turning around at all. Who gives an unknown child free food and free schooling? What's in it for them?

"I've never heard of this place," Saul said, taking another step back.

"There's no catch."

"I'm not sure it's for me."

"Your sister thinks it is," the man said. "Come and see."

"What do you want from me?"

The man smiled. "Want from you? I want nothing from you, Saul. I want to *give you* something. A chance at life. Real life."

"This place exists?"

"Of course."

The man indicated with a nod that he was about to leave. "It's a day program. Food and school and love during the day. Then you sleep here at your home at night. I'll be back tomorrow," he said. "Think about it."

Saul nodded. He closed the door.

And wondered how the man had managed to track him down.

Mully Children's Family Vipingo campus looked out of place compared with the surrounding poverty. Saul saw children in uniforms wearing huge smiles as they laughed from a place of joy inside their hearts that Saul could not immediately recognize. A man called out and all the children gathered together. They prayed. The children hurried to line up for food. The man introduced Saul to the teachers and made an announcement to the other students.

Saul watched as a woman dipped a large ladle into a pot of maize and beans called *githeri*. She scooped so much into a plate that the student could barely hold it.

Is that an overflowing plate of food? Isn't that just for tourists?

Saul stepped closer and saw the meal come within his reach. He noticed two white foreigners helping to hand out food. He broke his gaze away to take in the surroundings. School buildings. Teachers talking with students. Everyone looking so clean. So friendly.

Saul held out his plate. He felt the weight of food sag against his hands. He sat down next to other children his age. He ate too fast, the way impoverished children do when they don't know when their next meal will be coming. He noticed other children returning to the line for seconds. He hurried to join in. Another heap of food landed on his plate. Incredible. He sat down again and savoured the food as he finished his plate. When he was done, he felt what it was like to be full.

He sat down in math class, followed by Swahili. So much information so quickly, yet he sensed he would be able to keep pace. At recess, the boys raced off to play soccer. Only one other player wanted to be goalkeeper, so Saul offered to play in net on the opposing side. He studied the players as they set up in their format.

As soon as the game began, Saul suddenly saw with new eyes.

He felt as if someone had flicked a switch inside his brain. He noticed plays developing. He recognized, even predicted, how opponents would attack his net. His mind ignited in a way he'd never experienced before. Far more than when he and Hali kicked the ball after the beating. He planned when to rush to break up a play. When to charge to parry a corner kick and when to stay back.

The chains of poverty and worry began to come loose.

He felt himself come alive.

An unbearable burden lifted. He discovered the freedom to think without being weighed down with how to find food. He threw himself into the game without worrying about his future. A new world opened for him. He felt engrossed in the field of play, captivated by the physical, mental, and emotional demands of the game.

When the match ended, his teammates congratulated him. So did the opposing players, demonstrating a remarkable togetherness amongst brothers. They joked about convincing him to come play for their side next game. As they laughed on their way to the assembly area, Saul felt the peace of belonging.

The same teacher who knocked on his door yesterday led them in a devotional. He shared a story from the Bible followed by a word of encouragement. Saul paid little attention, preferring instead to talk with his new soccer friends.

But he *did* pay attention when it came time to sing. When the children stood and began a chorus, Saul felt a surge of power rise within him. Even more so than when he played soccer. The entire school sang with such conviction that it filled the evening air. Their strong, honest voices spoke to the deepest part of Saul, convincing him they had something he desperately wanted.

Each night as he walked home, he hummed the tunes they sang that evening. One night, he passed by a large church tent gathering. People sang and clapped, reminding him of the joy he felt at MCF Vipingo. He stepped inside the packed-out meeting and felt the same power he sensed when singing with his MCF siblings.

Why are all these Christians so happy?

The music stopped. An older man wearing a suit stepped onto the stage. He lifted his Bible onto the wooden lectern. Saul listened as the man spoke, then made his way back.

He opened the door to his hut, lay down on the ground and covered himself with a blanket.

His thoughts followed after him.

These Christians are different.

No different than anyone else. You are Muslim. Don't forget it.

But they are full of joy. The teachers. The students. Everyone.

What difference does it make? You can't change religions. You are what you are.

Who says I can't change?

You just can't. You are your religion for life. That's the way it goes. You can't change your skin color, can you? Some things are there forever.

But I sense something different when I am at MCF.

Of course you do. They provide food.

Something even deeper than that. The singing. It ... it ....

It what?

It feels right.

How can you say that? You never grew up with it. How could you possibly know what's right?

When I am singing, I have the most amazing feeling ... I feel ....

You feel an emotional high. It comes from singing. It's no big deal.

This isn't just emotional. It's more than that. I feel ....

You feel what?

I feel like I am connecting with God.

You already know what that's like.

Not like this. Saul wiped tears from his eyes. *The Christian God is different.*

Not true.

This God loves me.

Loves you? How could you possibly know that? You get free meals and get taught some math. That's all this is. Human beings are being kind to you. Don't attribute that to their religion. It's them. They are the ones who are impacting you.

It's in them, too. There is something about them.

What would your mother say? Would she approve?

He squished out his remaining tears. Turned over onto his back. Gazed up at the metal roof. He replayed the songs over in his mind. He sensed the same peace as when he was together with the others. As he drifted off to sleep, he thought about how it would only be a few short hours before he would see them again.

He thought about Charles Mulli, who made it out of poverty and then decided to help kids like him. What would make a man want to do something like that?

He thought about what made all his new siblings so different.

So joyful.

So content.

And he wondered if it was something he too could experience.

CHAPTER 3

The night sky looked both brilliant and simple.

Saul gazed up through the window as he rode the overnight MCF bus from Vipingo to Yatta. The dazzling display captivated his imagination. Stars shone with a unique African clarity, free of light pollution from distant cities. He observed so many stars. Clustered together. Uncountable. Yet each star stood out from all the others.

Sleep drifted into him. He closed his heavy eyelids, taking with him the detail and comfort of the night canvas. He woke to the squeaking of brakes as the bus came to a stop at Mully Children's Family Yatta branch.

When Charles and Esther Mulli first started rescuing children, they brought them to their home in Eldoret. When they outgrew it, they expanded to the semi-arid region at MCF Ndalani. Needing still more space, they started yet another property about forty minutes from Ndalani at Yatta. Later, they expanded to Vipingo and other areas.

Saul stepped off the bus. The massive property sprawled out as far as he could see. Solid, well-constructed buildings made of stone. Clean grounds. So many smiling faces to welcome him. He recognized a voice calling his name. He followed the sound to see his sister Velma. A flood of joy erupted inside him. Her eyes lit up. She smiled with such intensity that her face glowed. They ran to each other and hugged.

It had been such a long time. People change. Saul sensed something different in Velma. She exuded a vitality he had not seen in her before.

They talked. Shared. Felt the connection that binds siblings together when their decision to love each other is stronger than their blood connection.

Saul looked at the children eating lunch. What was the long green food they were eating?

"Why are people eating grass?" Saul asked.

Velma burst out laughing. "That's not grass," she said. "Those are French beans."

"French?" Saul asked. "Why can't you get them from Kenya?"

Velma laughed again. She shook her head as she took him to the kitchen. "We grow French beans here on our farms."

Saul took in his surroundings. Yatta looked far bigger than he imagined. Dormitories. Schools. Fields. How could all of this come about from one man?

"You will meet our father and mother."

"Mulli?"

"Yes," she said. "You will notice that our father shines."

"Shines?"

Velma nodded.

"How does he do that, exactly?" Saul asked.

MCF Yatta felt like a dream world for Saul. Food. Friends. Education. And, most importantly, soccer. Lots and lots of soccer. The soccer field stretched out longer and wider in Yatta than Vipingo. It allowed for more complicated plays to develop. Saul moved out of goal to defence to be part of developing and breaking up attacks. Playing with talent from all over Kenya improved his skills. He found himself thriving in a place where he could give everything he had.

After an early morning soccer match, he noticed a man in a hat leading a group of visitors around the property. The man led them to church for the Sunday morning service. Velma had invited Saul to go. And even though all of his teammates from school went to church, Saul declined.

Saul walked through the compound towards one of the massive reservoirs at Yatta. Mulli built the reservoirs to provide water for crops during droughts and to produce fish as a source of food for the children. Saul took a path that passed by the dormitories and through the wooded area. With hundreds of children on the property, a break from everyone became a welcome chance to enjoy quiet and time to think. As he neared the reservoir, he heard footsteps approaching. He turned to see the man with the hat. He wondered why a watchman would come down here this time of day.

"Hello," the man said.

Saul made no reply.

"What is your name?"

Why does this watchman want to know my name?

The man smiled and repeated. "What is your name?"

"Saul Anguka."

Saul turned and walked away.

TRANSFORMATIONS

That Friday evening, he found himself drawn to the gentle power of the choir practising in the chapel. The singing reminded him of Vipingo. He felt it surround him. Fill him.

Convict him.

He stood outside. Part of him wanted to go in. Part of him resisted and wanted to leave.

He listened as they sang a song called *Sauli*.

Mtu mmojo jina lake	There was once a man
Liitwa Sauli	His name was Saul
Alikuwa wakutishaa	He was terrible
Kutisha Sana	So terrible he was
Aliwaua wanafunzi	He killed many disciples
Wake Mungu	Disciples of God
Waliomcha mungubaba	Who worship and adored the Lord
Bila huruma	Without any mercy
Sauli Sauli wee	Saul, dear Saul!
Mbona unaniudhi	Why do you upset me?
Mimi ndimi Yesu wako	I am your Jesus
Simama uende	Stand up and go
Alipokuwa akisafiri	When he was on a journey
Kuelekea dameski	On his way to Damascus
Apomwangaza ukatokea	There then light appeared
Nuru toka mbinguni akanguko	Divine light came down
Kifundifudi kaskia sautiii	Then he heard a voice
Wanadamu waleo	Many people today
Ni kama Sauli	Are like you, Saul
Aliyekuwa muuaji	Who was a murderer
Wa watu wa Mungu	Of disciples of God
Mbona sasa wanadamu	Why then do humans
Wawatesa wengine	Persecute one another?
Mje kwake bwana Yesu	Let all come to the Lord Jesus
Awaokoe	To save you

The words gripped him. Pierced him. For the first time he felt music reach inside him to a place he didn't know existed. It touched the depth of his emptiness. What was happening to him? As he began to allow the music to fill his soul, an old acquaintance in his mind began to fight back.

Why are you listening to this music?

Because I love it.

Love it? You know nothing about it.

I know it impacts me.

You need to leave this place. This is not for you.

Why isn't it for me? Why do I sense such a connection to it if it is not for me?

Because you weren't raised with this music.

I want to go inside.

You? What for?

Maybe I could change.

Do you need to?

Maybe I could I be like the other Saul. Is this music my blinding light? Are my eyes being opened to become a Christian?

Don't be ridiculous. And don't overreact. This music is wrong.

Wrong? The food here is right. The education is right. The dormitories are right. The leaders are right. Everything here is right. But the music is wrong? That doesn't fit. It's not logical.

You can't change. You are who you are.

Saul stood in front of the entire congregation. People filled the church to capacity. He stood preaching. The congregation listened to his every word. When he finished, he said with a loud voice: "Amen!"

Saul woke. His friend Patrick in the next bunkbed woke too. Saul had spoken the word *amen* in both dreaming and waking worlds.

"Did you get whatever you were praying for?" Patrick asked, trying to control his laughter in the packed dormitory. Saul explained the dream.

Patrick reflected on the importance of it. "God is speaking something to you, my friend," he said.

"Are you sure?"

"You like the Sauli song, right?" he said, his voice becoming quieter to let the others sleep, and out of reverence for the gravity of what Saul experienced.

"I do."

"Let's sing it. Real quiet. Okay?"

He found a seat beside Velma at breakfast the next morning still trying to make sense of the impact the song had on him. It was more than music. Something had reached him. But what?

"Hello," Velma said with her trademark smile. "Are you still with us?" she joked as her brother broke from his stare out into nowhere.

"I'm here."

"You are thinking a lot," she said. Then she became serious, the way siblings do when they discern an expression in the eyes. "What's on your mind?"

That I am just like Saul in that song. Something is not right with me. And that song has figured out what it is.

Saul diverted his attention to the field. He saw the man in the hat.

"That man in the hat is everywhere. He is a very good watchman."

Velma laughed. "You think so?"

"Yes," Saul said. "This is a very large property. Yet, look how often you see him. That watchman is amazing."

"I am glad you approve," Velma said, trying to control her laughter.

"Why is that?"

"Because that watchman is your father."

"What? That humble man?"

Velma nodded.

"That's Mulli?" Saul asked.

"*Daddy* Mulli."

In spite of the honest and incredible laughter he heard from his sister, Saul felt an incredible rush of emotion rip through him. He felt as if he would collapse on the ground in a rush of tears.

The man—*his father*—turned down a road and walked into the distance out of sight.

Saul watched him leave, unable to respond. Velma picked up on it.

"It is him, isn't it," Saul whispered.

"It is."

Saul stood outside as the choir rehearsed the Sauli song. He gathered courage and walked to the door. He stopped at the entrance. To go in or not to go in?

What are you doing? This is not you! Turn around.

And go where?

You cannot turn your back on who you are.

Who I was.

You can't change. You can't leave who you are.

Sure I can. This is different.

Religion is religion. How is this different?

I'm loved.

Loved? Lots of teachers love their students.

Not just by them.

Then by whom?

By God.

You can't know that.

I can and I do.

Saul walked into the church. The choir took a break. After a brief conversation with Johnson the choir conductor, Saul asked if he could join the choir. Johnson agreed. Saul sang the Sauli song with the choir. Afterwards Johnson took Saul aside.

"You can really sing," Johnson said.

Saul laughed. "You don't have to say such things. I am not a singer."

"I mean it. You have a good voice," he said. "But there is something inside you. Something deep."

"You mean it?"

"I wouldn't say such things to you if I did not mean it, Saul. God has gifted you."

Before Saul had time to evaluate what was happening Pastor Murigi walked in, unaware of the song they had just finished singing.

The tall, gentle pastor opened his Bible to the book of Acts. He led a Bible study on the conversion of Saul.

"Saul persecuted the church," he said. "He did what he thought was right. His heart was at war with God. And yet, God reached out to him. Saul responded and became Paul.

"You can run from God. But God will not reject you. He will continue to love you. You may have stolen things. Done other bad things. The Bible calls this sin. When Adam and Eve sinned in the Garden of Eden, sin entered into the human race. Our sin separates us from God. There is nothing we can do to earn our way back to him. God had mercy on Saul. And God sent His Son Jesus to have mercy on us. The punishment that was due us, fell on Jesus. He died on the cross for your sins and mine. If you ask Jesus to forgive your sins, if you turn from them and put your trust only in Jesus Christ, He will live in you and grant you eternal life."

As Murigi continued talking, Saul repeated those words over in his mind. *Put my trust only in Jesus.*

Murigi noticed Saul paying close attention to him. After the Bible study, he approached Saul. "There is a baptism taking place soon at Ndalani. I want you to go."

"What is baptism?"

"Are you born again?" Murigi asked.

"What does it mean to be born again?"

The chapel cleared out. They sat down on a bench.

"A man named Nicodemus came to Jesus at night. Jesus told him he had to be born again. Many people believe in God. They can believe in Jesus. Even the Holy Spirit. But there is a difference between knowing about God and having God live inside of you."

"God wants to live inside of me?"

"That is what every human being on earth is designed for. We are all born physically. But we must be born again spiritually. We are born again through trusting in the forgiveness of sins by Jesus Christ's death on the cross and His resurrection from the dead to grant you eternal life."

"Even me?"

"What Jesus said to Nicodemus he says to you today—You *must* be born again."

Traitor. How can you do this?

I am loved. And I can be forgiven.

Big deal. Just work harder, and you can become a better person.

Just like Saul was trying to do what was right?

Don't bring him into this.

Jesus opened his eyes. Just like He is doing for me.

That is an unfair comparison. That's the Bible. You're just a beach kid.

Not according to God.

"All right," Saul said. "What do I do?"

Murigi bowed his head and led him in a prayer. Saul followed.

"Father, you are the creator of the world. You made me. You love me. I have sinned. You died to pay for my sins, Jesus. I ask forgiveness for my sins, I turn away from them, and I put my trust only in You. I ask You to make me your child and to give me everlasting life. Help me to follow You. Amen."

The thought of getting baptized initially interested Saul. But when he stood on the banks of the Thika River at Ndalani, the water concerned him. He watched others ahead of him being baptized. It seemed safe. The water wasn't that deep. Was it? Ironic that in spite of all his time on the beach, he never learned to swim.

The girl in front of him leaned back into the water, immersed in it, and came back up.

It was his turn.

He approached Mulli.

Saul recalled seeing Mulli the first time he arrived at Yatta. He remembered their first brief meeting at the reservoir.

"What is your name?" Mulli asked.

"Saul."

"Saul," Mulli said. "Now your name is going to change to Paul." Mulli took both his hands. "I baptize you in the name of the Father, the Son, and the Holy Spirit."

Mulli leaned Paul backwards into the water and fully submerged him, symbolizing the death of Christ and the death to self, and then brought Paul up out of the water, symbolizing the resurrection and new life in Christ.

As Paul opened his eyes, he saw an incredibly bright light that blinded him. Then, just as quickly as it came it disappeared again.

Paul joined the others in the chapel for communion.

He reintroduced himself to his sister.

This time as Paul.

He found the name change curious.

And wondered if the developments in his life were setting him up for something he could not previously have imagined.

CHAPTER 4

Considering how close the connection between a person's name and their identity can be, it surprised Paul how easily he adapted to his new designation. Ironically, his new name felt more fitting than his birth name. Like he wasn't leaving an old name behind, but rather stepping into the one he was always meant to have.

There were, however, times when his siblings called him by his new name, and he wouldn't immediately respond. They would throw a joke his way followed with *Hey, I'm talking to you.* Paul would nod and smile with the kind of contentment that comes to people who are free.

Each Sunday afternoon MCF ran internal soccer tournaments where each grade would form a team and play against another grade. But for those like Paul who adored soccer, they also played every day after classes. He would race out to the pitch at the school bell, play soccer, and then come late to supper.

After a particularly exciting game where Paul's team managed to shut out their opponent, he finished his supper and was about to return to his dorm when Mulli approached.

"Ooo-aye," Mulli said.

Mulli gave his signature MCF greeting when he started his work reaching street children in the slums. He gave two thumbs up and called out *Ooo-aye* as his own created word that came to mean "peace". Mulli used it to convince downtrodden street children that he could be trusted. The expression stuck and became synonymous with MCF greetings all over Kenya and beyond.

"Daddy Mulli!" Paul said, then wondered if maybe his ongoing lateness to supper might be the reason Mulli wanted to talk.

"Ooo-aye," he replied.

"How are you, Daddy?"

Mulli hugged him and let out a laugh that was so genuine and infectious that it reached into Paul. "I am so glad to see you, Paul," Mulli said, adding a special emphasis on his name. "You remember?" Mulli said with a laugh. Paul laughed, too. "Your name was changed from Saul to Paul. At your baptism. I think you remember that?"

Paul tried to control his laughter. "Yes, Daddy. I recall. I was the one you were baptizing."

Mulli closed his eyes and let out a loud laugh. He nodded. "You are making a very good point, my son. I tell you, you have remembered exactly."

A group of younger children ran by, talking and laughing on their way to their evening devotional. Mulli and Paul watched as their little legs hurried down the path. How many thousands of children had run that same way?

"You are a very talented soccer player," Mulli said.

"I know I came late to supper. I am sorry. I will do better."

Mulli became quiet. "You know, Paul, I did not come to ask you to shorten your soccer playing time."

"No?"

"I have watched you all these years. You are a very good player. You are gifted in soccer. Oh yes. I can see this."

"Thank you, Daddy."

"It is a great talent."

Paul turned to the side, embarrassed and unsure of whether he agreed. "It is only soccer, Daddy."

"You think so?"

"It's not real."

"Not real. What do you mean by that?" Mulli asked.

"It's not like being a doctor or a pastor or singing or something like that."

Mulli nodded, not so much as a sign that he agreed but that he understood what it meant to question the usefulness of talents a person possessed.

"Sometimes we think what we have been given is not as important as what someone else has been given. But God is the giver of *all* gifts. The Bible says the Holy Spirit distributes to each person just as He wills."

"Even soccer?"

"Of course."

"But what can I accomplish by playing soccer?"

"Very good that you should ask. The Bible says *a man's gift makes room for him and brings him before great men.* We seek to develop everyone's talent at MCF. Education, singing, agriculture, karate. Many, many talents. Even soccer."

"I love to play soccer. I am grateful to be playing here, but—"

"You are most welcome," Mulli said. "But you are not meant to simply play *here*."

Paul didn't follow. Where else? MCF Yatta down the road?

Mulli picked up on it and continued. "We are starting an official soccer team at MCF. We will play in a competitive league. I am looking to put the first team together. Are you willing to play?"

Had he heard correctly? Wasn't soccer a side activity that provided children with a short relief from their studies? Why wasn't Mulli pushing him to leave soccer altogether to focus on schooling?

But Paul felt the answer in his heart and responded without hesitation. "Of course."

Mulli nodded. "The ball is on your side."

Paul wondered what Mulli meant by that.

And wondered how MCF would fare against outside teams.

Paul gravitated to the competition. He felt himself come alive with a passion for physical excellence and mental toughness. *Train hard, win easy* became the coach's motto. Paul excelled at studying tactics, executing strategies, and learning positional play. *Be smart, be fit, be talented.*

They entered league play at the lowest level. They defeated teams and developed a rivalry with a school in a nearby town. They drove to that town for an away game, singing on the way there, excited for the upcoming match. When they arrived, the MCF players stepped out of their two vehicles. The opposing team noticed them and shouted *Chokora!* meaning *Street Children!*

The opposing team bullied one of the MCF boys. One of them slapped the MCF player.

The MCF team ignited into action.

A full-on battle erupted. Everyone on both sides threw a flurry of punches.

The boys felt justified in their behavior until they returned to MCF, where Mulli called them to stand in front of him. What seemed right only a short while earlier now felt altogether different. They wondered how Mulli would respond. How bad could it be?

"A fight? Is this what I heard from your coaches?" Mulli asked.

The quiet evening didn't help. With no daytime distractions, the boys had nowhere else to look except to meet Mulli's eyes.

Paul felt a wave of regret come over him. One of their own had been slapped. They had all been called street children. They had been insulted. They had the right to defend him, didn't they?

"What did Jesus teach us?" Mulli asked.

The team remained silent.

"Whoever shall hit you on the right cheek, turn to him and offer him the other."

That puzzled Paul. Meaning what? Were they supposed to let their player—their fellow brother no less—be manhandled while they stood there and watched?

"Your brother was insulted. He was slapped. That is humiliating. You felt angry and wanted to avenge him. But if you would have turned the other cheek, if you would have taken your brother and walked away, then the opposing team would have taken notice. They would have said—*What is this? Why does the MCF team not insult us back? Why are they not responding with harsh words?* You see, my boys? You missed the opportunity."

It now made sense to Paul. A little late. He wished he could take this knowledge back in time and redo things.

"I taught you boys how to bring peace to people. But you chose not to," Mulli said. "And so there will be no more games for the rest of the year. I have cancelled everything."

The next year, Mulli started the team again, reminding the boys of who they represented. The MCF team breezed through the county level. And they should have breezed through the higher levels. They were more talented. More organized. Better trained. But sometimes better teams don't win. Sometimes things do not go the way they are supposed to.

Sometimes money speaks louder than talent.

The MCF team lost out on advancing to a higher division because of corruption. Even at local soccer levels, officials could be bought. As disappointing as it was, Paul and the MCF team were not surprised. Corruption ran rampant in Kenya at so many levels.

That was the reality.

Now, how to respond?

The team gathered around Mulli.

"Remember, as followers of Christ we must treat our enemies well. Jesus said that we are to love our enemies. I know you are disappointed with the result of the games. But this is not the end. This is a test. In life, you will face many disappointments. Even me, at this place known as Mully Children's Family, I have had so many challenges. But we must trust the Lord our God, who will never let us down. Never even one time. No. He will never let us down."

Mulli invited the league officials to MCF. Paul watched as Mulli talked with them and walked them around the property wearing his leather cowboy hat. Paul saw no animosity in Mulli. Instead, Mulli smiled and answered their questions. Paul noticed a change in the league officials when they returned to their vehicles. They seemed gentler. Kinder.

The following year MCF excelled in the league and finished the regular season in first place.

TRANSFORMATIONS

"Be humble, boys. I have always taught you to be humble," Mulli said. "And now it is time to show everyone what can happen when street children become soccer players."

CHAPTER 5

Mulli called the players and coaches into the MCF church.

"You are being called upon to represent the entire family," Mulli said. "Everyone is looking at you. You have prepared this entire week. Now you have the semi-finals and the finals in one day. You must stay focused. Protect the name. Now go out in the name of the Lord, and remember that you are carrying His name, so you must behave accordingly."

Paul and the team travelled to Machakos and checked into their hotel. They assembled for evening devotions and prayed for God to give them strength and power.

It was all going so well until it came time to sleep. It should have come easily to Paul. It often did. He lay down. Closed his eyes.

But his mind would not shut off.

Over and over, he rehearsed how he would play. He prepared mentally how to respond to various attacks. Then he would remember he needed to sleep. But how could he stop thinking and let his mind be at rest?

He rolled onto his side. Then his back. Then the other side. He prayed. He thought back to life in Mombasa. Of life in his little hut. Of that day when he received a knock at his door and everything changed.

The first hint of light appeared in the darkness. It was time.

The team met for breakfast. Paul hardly ate. His nerves prevented him from taking anything in.

They arrived at the field. The coach called out the line-up for the semifinal.

Paul's name was not called.

It did not bother him. They were a team. He was happy for those who could play. The game started at ten a.m. MCF beat their opponents 2–0. They had lunch at noon and boarded the bus to travel to the finals match.

"Let's call Dad and let him know!" the coach said.

The team shouted in approval. The coach dialed and put his cell on speakerphone. The team pressed around to hear.

"Ooo-aye," Mulli said.

The team shouted, "Ooo-aye," in reply.

"We won the first match," the coach said. "We are going to the finals!"

"Amen, glory to Jesus," Mulli said as he laughed. "We have won the match."

That caught Paul off guard. *What?*

He wondered if he heard right.

Is Mulli talking about the semi-final match we just won, or is he talking about the outcome of the final match?

Paul wasn't sure.

Mulli can't actually see what is going to happen, can he? This is just optimism. Right? Isn't that what this is?

"I am waiting for all of you to come home after the game," Mulli said. "I have a special gift for you. Be well, boys. The ball is on your side."

The ball is on your side.

What did he mean by that? Is Mulli predicting the future?

The team returned to the pitch. The coach called them together for the line-up. Paul assumed the players who won in the morning would take the field for the afternoon game as well.

"Paul."

It surprised him to hear his name called.

You are putting me into this tough game? Why didn't you put me in the semi-final?

Paul stepped onto the field. Rain clouds gathered. The normally bright African sun disappeared behind a canopy of grey. The first drops fell. Then the tempo quickened. Suddenly, they stood in a deluge. Paul felt the relentless pounding of rain. Still, it could not drown out the noise of the fans who had come to cheer for the opposition.

And against them.

"You are Chokoras!" they screamed. "You will never go anywhere! You only eat children's food! You are all stupid!"

A wave of humiliation threatened to crash over Team MCF. Instead, they refused to dwell on the words. Refused to allow them into their hearts. Refused to accept them.

"You are all *Mayatema!*" the fans screamed, meaning the MCF boys were *without father and without mother.*

The team captain called them together for the pre–kick-off huddle. "You hear what they are saying?" he asked. "You hear the way they are abusing us with their insults? We are not going to fight back the old way. We are transformed. We are new in Christ. Let us take this as our stepping stone. The ball is on our side. God is with us!"

Paul and the rest of the team shouted in agreement.

"One, two, three," the captain said.

"MCF, God, forever!" the team screamed.

They lined up. Paul took his position in defence. His stomach turned. The rain suddenly stopped just in time for him to feel sweat forming on his forehead.

Blow the whistle. Blow the whistle. Let's get going.

The other team assembled. Paul watched the ball, feeling the nervous energy that comes with knowing that at any moment he would be catapulted into that unique realm of competition.

The ball is on your side.

Is a win a forgone conclusion? Or is it still a matter of us doing our best? Or ... or maybe it is both at the same time?

The referee blew the whistle for a moment of silence. Paul felt another shock of nervous energy rip through him. The teams waited as if frozen in time. With the second whistle the referee checked with the goalies and the linesmen. They gave the thumbs up.

The referee blew the whistle a third time.

The match started.

Paul jumped. Like a lion charging after prey.

Everything moved so much faster. Everything sounded louder. Paul felt his heart pounding in his throat.

The ball came to him.

Be careful! Last man back. Take care of the ball. Be relaxed. But not too relaxed. Come on! Move it!

Paul head-faked to the left and then passed the ball to the midfielder on the right. The opponent attempted to intercept the ball but missed completely, putting himself out of the play.

MCF broke out on an odd man rush. The midfielder made an incredible pass to the striker, who blasted it past the goalkeeper and into the net. Paul screamed. MCF screamed. They gathered together to celebrate.

MCF 1–0.

The players reset. The game restarted.

Don't get overconfident. It's one goal. Remember, you are most likely to concede right after scoring. Be sharp.

Paul read the plays. Intercepted. Passed. Played aggressive, but not too aggressive. He felt part of the game. Felt like he belonged at this level.

The passes were short. The play, fast. A few minutes later, MCF scored again. The opponents were shocked. The insults quieted. MCF was first on the ball. Faster. Smarter. Tougher.

Better.

At halftime, MCF was both amazed and yet not amazed at how well they played.

They drank water. Sat down. Stretched. Encouraged each other.

"Stay focused," the coach said. "The other team knows they are behind. They are desperate. But they don't know desperate the way you know desperate. They don't have the same reason to win as you do. You have a family back home that is pulling for you. Your family includes young children who have just come off the streets. They will look to you and see you as an example. You are not on this field for yourself. You have a bigger reason. You are on this field for them and for God."

"One, two, three," the coach said.

"MCF, God, forever!" the team screamed.

They took to the pitch. The referee blew the whistle. The game took off at a blistering pace. Paul expected MCF to command the game as much as they had in the first forty-five minutes.

But all those sayings about soccer being a game of two halves proved true. Whatever pendulum they were on swung hard the other way. They didn't recognize their opponents. They seemed altogether faster. Their passes were more accurate. Their shots harder. Their tactics smarter.

The fans screamed louder. *Chokora! Chokora! Chokora!*

Paul forced himself to adjust with each new attack. Pass attempts to strikers. Shots from distance. Crosses. He kept track of players around him, particularly the opposing strikers timing their runs through MCF defence.

Paul gave it his all. The final minutes felt more like a rugby match than soccer. Players banged into each other. Desperate shots. Desperate clearances.

And then, the final whistle.

MCF shouted and hugged each other.

The opposing fans stood in silence.

The officials handed them the trophy. "We said you would never make it. We never believed you could do it. But you are very strong."

Paul took his turn holding the trophy. It felt surreal. Was he really on this soccer pitch on the winning team? Or was this all just a dream, and he was back on that beach in Mombasa staring out at the endless ocean?

"Well done, Paul!" the coach said, bringing Paul back to reality.

"We did it," Paul said, handing off the trophy.

The team members each took their turn. Then they headed off.

Paul glanced back at the field.

He smiled.

They hurried onto the bus. The coach called Mulli and put him on speakerphone.

"Ooo-aye," Mulli said.

"Ooo-aye," the team shouted in reply.

"You are very excited, boys. Did you win?" Mulli asked as more a statement of fact than a question. He continued before they could respond. "Of course you won. Congratulations. Now relax and have a wonderful evening."

The team continued cheering.

But Mulli's words stuck with Paul. *Of course, you won.*

How did he know?

The MCF team passed the incredible fruit market at Kithimani. Persuasive merchants hurried out to the bus to offer pineapple, mangos, bananas, and many other fruits. They turned off the highway at Sofia and headed towards Ndalani. The players expected a normal quiet drive back. Instead, the intersection was packed with motorcycles. They heard honking and saw a crowd cheering for them. The motorcycles escorted them down the winding road through the Kenyan countryside. They passed humble huts and hard-working farmers making barely enough to feed their families—many of whom were helped by MCF medical, food, educational, and other programs.

They turned in at a white sign with black lettering that read:

MULLY CHILDREN'S
FAMILY
NDALANI BRANCH

The bus stopped at the church. The entire school cheered for the team as they entered the packed building. Paul hugged his many brothers and sisters.

The team came up on stage. As Paul looked out at the sea of siblings, he remembered how only a few short years ago, he had debated about whether to even enter the church at MCF Yatta. And now here he stood in front of all of them. He looked over at Mulli, who stood to address his children. Paul saw Mulli shed tears of joy.

"You are my boys," he said, "and I am very proud of you."

More cheering. Lots of jumping. When they settled, Mulli continued.

"I want each of you to look at these fine young men standing before you. Each of them was just as you were. You came from broken homes. You came from the streets. You had no place to call your home. These men are an example for you. People insulted them by calling them Chokora. But they did not shout back. God has gifted every single person. And at MCF we want everyone to know the love of Jesus and to develop the talents He has placed in each and every one of you."

They enjoyed much singing and celebrating. After the hugs and congratulations, Mulli and Paul found time in the quiet of the evening to talk under the mesmerizing stars.

"Congratulations, Paul," Mulli said. Then he laughed. "Paul who was once Saul. But Christ changed his life around. Completely."

"I thank God that you picked me," Paul said, thinking back to the MCF man who knocked on his door as a child.

"My son, I love your spirit and the heart that you have. You always make me proud. You encourage people around you. You are excellent and a great man of God. You are always welcome here."

"Thank you, Daddy."

"Remember, the ball is on your side."

"What does that mean? You keep saying that. It runs around in my mind," Paul said. Mulli burst out laughing as Paul continued. "*The ball is on your side*. I keep hearing this. What does it mean?"

In his trademark, unique manner, Mulli became quiet, serious, and gentle. "*The ball is on your side* means that God is for you. You are destined to win. But it does not happen just by watching the ball. You are designed and gifted to be active. With God, you can never fail."

They wished each other a good night. Paul watched Mulli head towards his humble accommodations on the MCF grounds. Paul smiled. He glanced up. The beautiful canopy of stars above made him feel life could go on forever.

PART 2
KEREN

CHAPTER 1

The bright African sun radiated off the children, illuminating their smiles and bright eyes.

They laughed as they played hide-and-go-seek in their Eldoret neighbourhood. They lived, as children should, near the edge of a world that was still free from the knowledge of good and evil. Unaware of how close they were to crossing that boundary.

Four-year-old Keren ran to her favourite hiding place behind her house. She glanced around the corner, watching her friend counting.

"Ready or not," her friend said, "here I come."

Keren pulled back out of sight. She felt her heart beat faster. Should she have picked the bushes in between the properties instead? Their small house made of mud walls and an iron sheet roof left little room for maneuvering if her friend approached.

Keren heard footsteps. The soft tapping against the dirt hinted at her friend closing in. Keren held her breath. Was she better off making a break for it around the other side of the house?

"I think you need to find a better hiding spot, Keren," her friend said, smiling as she put her hands on her hips, victorious.

Keren shrugged her shoulders. "Am I that easy to find?"

They started giggling. And their joy was about to develop into outright laughter, the way friends get when they have the freedom to express happiness in simply being together. Except a familiar sound interrupted them.

Keren heard her father shout at her mother. A sudden tremor ran through her as it always did when she heard him raise his voice. Her mother shouted back. This was nothing new. Her parents fought. A lot. That was normal, wasn't it? Because all parents fight like this.

Don't they?

Keren detected something different in her parents' tone this time. Something deeper.

Something angrier.

She heard a slapping sound. Then an incredible bang as a body rammed against the wall of the house.

Keren and her friend ran to the front. The shouting intensified. What was happening inside the house?

Keren saw the neighbours hurrying out of their homes. Their concerned faces justified her racing heart. Like waking from a dream, she felt herself crossing a line into a world she did not want to exist.

And then, just as fast as the shouting started, an uneasy calm settled on the house. Keren often equated quiet with peace. But this time she felt something different. A whisper of fear crept into her. She stood in silence. Oblivious to the burning rays of the sun piercing into her. Her eyes focused on the door, waiting for it to open.

It did not.

What's going on in there?

A neighbour, one of the men from across the way, stepped onto their property with a strange determination that signaled he was unafraid of what he might find. He touched the door. Pushed it open.

Whatever he saw inside concerned him. He stood there a split second, trying to absorb what he saw and move into action. It felt like an eternity to Keren. Normally, time was of no concern to her. But now it needed to speed up so she could find out what was wrong. Yet time would not comply with her request. Everything stopped and became like a living picture. Nothing moved.

Except her thoughts and racing heart.

The man called out instructions in a quiet, firm tone. He entered. Others followed. Keren stayed outside, absorbing what took place next in slices, as if someone put photos in front of her.

People carried her parents out. Placed them in the back of two vehicles. She heard the man say they had to be rushed to hospital immediately. The vehicles left.

What just happened?

The children resumed playing, hoping to return, and stay, in a world free from trouble and pain. Keren continued as best she could, bewildered and uninterested in the game.

The first hint of a setting sun brought further concern to Keren. *Where are Mom and Dad? Why aren't they back from the hospital yet? What is taking so long?*

The other children returned to their homes. Darkness fell quickly as it always does in Kenya. A slight dimming of the lights followed by pitch darkness.

Keren sat down in front of her house. Alone. Waiting.

She did not want to go in. Not without her parents. Instead, she kept watch. Hoping her vigilance might in some way help in the outcome of her situation.

Her tired eyes closed. She felt herself drifting off.

The sound of a policeman's voice woke her. She did not want to see uniformed officers. Even at her young age, seeing the police without her parents only heightened her fears.

"Keren," the officer said.

Keren looked up. The officer towered above her. He sat down beside her. She looked into his eyes searching for a reason for hope.

"I am sorry," he said. "Your parents have passed away."

What does that mean exactly? Passed away—as in, dead? And what did being dead mean? She didn't know anybody who had died. *Is that when someone leaves and doesn't come back? Why don't they come back? Why doesn't someone let them return?*

Despite her questions, the finality of her parents' parting gripped her with unbearable grief. It poured into her like poison and set like concrete. She felt herself pulled against her will into a different world. A world where things don't go the way you want them to. She tried to resist, but like a planet pulled on a course of orbit, she felt incapable of having any influence over the forces that now dictated her path.

The police took Keren to the station. She lay down on a mat.

"We are very sorry," the officer said, knowing his words were not enough to supply what Keren needed. "Do you have any relatives?"

Keren tried to answer. But the impact of the day's events proved too much for her. She shook her head.

"We will look for relatives for you to stay with," he said.

Keren tried to close her eyes.

Maybe if I sleep things will be different when I wake. That will work, won't it? I can go back to the way things were with Mom and Dad, right?

Exhaustion and shock overwhelmed her. She drifted off. Hoping things would be different in the morning.

Things were no different the next morning. The sting of not having her parents greeted her first thoughts when she woke. A female police commissioner took pity on her and brought her beans and rice for breakfast.

"Your mother was from Congo," the woman said in a gentle voice. "We will likely not be able to find relatives here in Kenya from your mother's side."

Keren nodded.

"But your father is Kamba. So, we hope to find someone for you today."

Keren looked into her eyes, hoping for someone to give her any semblance of stability in the earthquake that had obliterated her fragile world.

"A police station is no place for a child. You can stay with me today," she said. "There will be good news."

Keren moved in with the police commissioner. She waited for good news, but nothing came. Nothing came the next day either. Nor the next. By the fifth day she began to lose hope that there would be any relative who would be able to look after her. By the seventh day all hope disappeared.

"Keren, we are doing the very best that we can," the police commissioner told her at the breakfast table. "The police officers have worked very hard. They have searched throughout Eldoret and even beyond. Your father does not appear to have any relatives."

That surprised Keren. No relatives? How is that possible in African culture? Fear crept in. *What does this mean, exactly? Do I stay here now?*

"Do you remember ever having uncles or aunts coming to visit with you and your parents?"

Keren shook her head.

"Did you ever go out to visit anyone who was an uncle or aunt or even a grandmother?"

Keren shrugged her shoulders.

"We want you to have a good home. Keren. A good place to live. But I am not able to look after you long term."

Meaning what? What are you saying? I like it here with you. You are kind. You are smart. You are tough. Why can't you be my new mother?

"Have you finished your breakfast?" she asked.

"Yes. Thank you," Keren said.

"And did it taste good?" the police commissioner asked.

"Very good."

"I am glad, Keren. Are you ready to go?"

Go where? Where are we going? I have finished breakfast, so yes, I am ready to go with you. But no, I am not ready to be taken somewhere else.

Keren nodded. She placed her hands on the side of the chair, hoping that would help her to stay here.

"All right. Let's go."

Keren stood. "Where are you taking me?"

CHAPTER 2

The drive seemed longer than it was.

Keren looked out the window at the new office buildings of Eldoret, wondering where the police commissioner was taking her. Had they found a long-lost relative after all? Was she being taken to a home? Would she have a family again?

The car slowed. Keren looked ahead through the front windshield.

And quickly wished she hadn't.

She saw a fence surrounding a property. That made sense. She had lived in a gated community. But the buildings beyond the fence looked odd. Bulky. Massive.

Not like a home.

A large gate unlocked. The vehicle entered. Keren saw a concrete wall surrounding the complex. *Why is there such a large fence? How do you get out of here if you want to leave?*

Nothing looked friendly. Nothing *felt* friendly either.

The vehicle stopped. The police commissioner opened the door. Keren waited. Could she hope they were stopping here to pick someone up and would be on their way soon to leave this place?

The commissioner motioned for Keren to get out.

A representative from the facility approached. The man didn't look at Keren. Didn't acknowledge her. His dirty green dress shirt hung over his expanded belly. His stubble beard showed hints of grey. He spoke a few words to the police commissioner. Whatever deal they worked out seemed satisfactory to both of them. The police commissioner turned to Keren and looked at her with the kind of hollowness that made Keren suspicious this would be the last time she would see her.

The police commissioner returned to her car and drove away.

The man led Keren into the Juvenile Detention Centre.

The metal door creaked as he opened it. As she entered, Keren heard children shouting in the distance. The voices echoed against the concrete walls, amplifying the noise. Why was everything so dark in here? Were her eyes still adjusting from being outside?

Could somebody please tell me what this place is? Can someone tell me why I am here? Can I talk to someone? Can anybody tell me what is going on?

The concrete walls began to close in on her. Keren wanted to hurry back. Run out through the door and get away from this place.

What just happened? Last week, I had parents. This morning, I ate breakfast with that kind lady from the police station. Now I am here. I don't want this. I don't like how this feels. Why are so many children shouting?

He stopped at the administration office. Spoke with the secretary. They argued back and forth about documentation. Where was her birth certificate? Was there any form of identification?

Keren saw the man shrug his shoulders. He explained it was another street child from rotten parents who weren't capable of looking after their child.

The man led Keren down a cringey hallway. He opened a door. Keren saw a disorganized room filled with bunk beds spread all over the place like a confusing traffic jam. Mattresses had been strewn over the floor with blankets tossed here and there. It was as if someone had shouted *fire* and everyone had raced out of the place, leaving it a filthy mess. She noticed the concrete walls. The dirty, concrete floor.

Bars on the windows.

Keren felt her teeth begin to chatter. A sting of tears began to form behind her eyes. They ran down her cheeks and dripped on the floor. Despite the heat, she suddenly felt a chill.

"Are you crying?" the man demanded.

His angry tone shook Keren. She sensed she knew she had to stop crying. But how does a person do that exactly? Fear ran up from the cold concrete into her body, grabbing hold of her like a virus.

"Stop crying!" he threatened.

It was no use. She sobbed, unable to make sense of any of this.

The man slapped her in the face. Keren fell to the ground. The man walked away.

After a few steps, he turned, saw her on the ground, and spoke in a manner that was colder than the floor she was lying on. "Get up and follow me," he said. Keren hesitated. Still trying to absorb what had just happened. "I'm not going to say it again."

Keren struggled to her feet. She hurried to catch up. She passed other adult workers who had long since learned to tune out the desperate look in children's eyes. Besides, children get used to their surroundings. No point in indulging them in their unreasonable expectations of finding hope.

"Breakfast at six a.m. Lunch at one p.m. Supper at five thirty. Don't be late," he said, pointing to the eating area at the end of the hall.

A hand bell rang. Moments later, a stream of children poured into the eating area. They pushed past Keren as if she weren't there. Keren noticed their unkempt hair. Dirty clothes. Rough demeanour.

"If you don't want to eat, don't come crying to me." The man left.

Keren stood in the hallway.

Alone.

She pushed herself forward.

Children shouted in the eating area. The kitchen served *githeri*. Keren stood last in line. She picked up a plate and held it out for the cook, who scooped in a ladle of beans and maize. Keren sat down on a bench. Two older boys approached. Keren moved over to make room for them. Instead of sitting down, one of the boys grabbed her plate from her, and they walked away.

The kitchen door closed.

Her chores that afternoon consisted of washing the floor in the mess hall and taking out pails of garbage. All on an empty stomach. At suppertime, she received her food and stood beside the kitchen out of view of the others, hoping to avoid someone stealing her rations. She found it difficult to chew big kernels with her small teeth. She was last to finish eating. The rest of the children had run off to other chores or outside games.

She walked outside, stood by the door, hoping to catch the eye of someone—anyone—as they returned inside. Keren noticed the familiar hint of the dimming of the sun followed by a sudden darkness. The clanging of a bell signaled it was time for the children to return inside. She waited, hoping for a child to meet her gaze.

No one noticed her.

The emotional exhaustion of the day transferred to physical tiredness. She entered the dorm hardly able to stand. She found a bottom bunk and lay down on the soiled, lumpy mattress. But the moment she rested her head, she felt the mattress being yanked out from under her. She fell onto the ground and turned over to see what was happening.

The older girls grabbed all the mattresses, some from the bunks, some from around the room, and threw them flat on the ground and slept one per mattress. There weren't enough beds to go around, so Keren slept with three other girls on the slats of the bunkbed. She covered herself with a blanket.

Turning to the girl beside her, Keren whispered, "Where are the bathrooms?"

The girl pointed to a bucket in the corner. "We all use that one."

Keren didn't sleep that night. The next morning the children woke to the sound of the clanging bell. Keren didn't move. Her stomach turned rock hard. Her head pounded.

"Time for chores!" the guard shouted.

Keren forced open her eyelids. She couldn't focus.

Approaching footsteps.

"Did you hear me?" he said.

"I am sorry. I am not feeling well."

"Not feeling well?"

Keren shook her head. She felt tears beginning to form again and tried to push herself to stop.

"You think I am stupid?" the man asked. "You worthless children are all the same. You play games, pretending to be sick so you can get out of chores. You don't fool me. Not one bit."

Please. Please send a doctor or a nurse. I don't feel well. I need help.

"I am not falling for your tricks," he said.

I need someone to look after me. I need a hospital. I don't know what's wrong. I feel so sick. Everything hurts.

"I advise you to stand up and perform your work."

Keren struggled to her feet. *Is the ground moving? Why does it feel like everything is tipping to one side?* She saw the door in the distance. It felt a marathon away. She dropped to her knees, hitting the concrete floor. Was it possible to make it back to the bed? Probably not. She lay down on the concrete. Wrapped her arms around her stomach.

Why is it taking so long for the nurse to get here?

She alternated between lying on her side and on her back. A few moments in each position provided temporary relief. Sweat formed on her forehead. A chill ran down her back. The ceiling spun.

She lay there the entire day.

And the entire evening.

Two days later, she felt her fever break.

Not once did anyone check on her.

"You are going to the police station for a hearing on your case," the man said.

Keren joined a group of girls as they crammed into the back of a government Range Rover.

As they drove off down the bumpy road, a girl sitting beside Keren leaned towards the girl opposite her. "You ever think about running to the streets?"

Keren heard about life as a street child from conversations she overhead at Juvenile.

"How?" the other girl asked.

"We can escape. Look how many there are of us," the girl said. Her eyes looked a sickly yellow. Her tough expression revealed the reality of a battle-hardened heart.

"And if we get caught?"

"How much effort do you think they will put into chasing us?" the girl beside Keren asked. "These people hate us. They mistreat us. They want us out of there. They would be happy to see us go."

"I don't know how to do it."

"We make a break for it after our court case. We act all compliant and easy to maintain. Then, once we are outside, we run for our lives."

Keren thought it might make the perfect distraction. While the guards are busy chasing after the other girls, she could quietly slip away without anyone noticing. The street. Finally, freedom—freedom to come and go and do as she pleased. No more awful guards. No more sleeping on a concrete floor. Street life would be better.

Much better.

She found herself struggling inside her young mind to decide on a clear path of action.

Where would you live?

I have to get out of here first. That's the first problem. I can't stay here any longer.

Let's say you manage to escape. What then?

I would leave. I would go anywhere.

But anywhere has to be somewhere. You can't sleep outside. You don't have a home. You don't have relatives. Even if you manage to outrun that fat man, where would you go?

That will look after itself.

Really? Is that what has happened to you so far?

The court case came and went. Nothing changed. They began their walk back to their vehicle. The other girls wanted to make a break for it. They couldn't go back. No more. They waited for their opportunity to bolt. But the mean guard proved to be smart. He stuck close to them. No, he would not be able to catch all of them if even a few of them decided to run in different directions. But he would be able to catch some. And the resulting consequences would be more than any of them were willing to gamble on.

That evening Keren lay down on the bed. The slats dug into her back. She had learned to give up on trying to find a comfortable position.

I hate this place. I hate everything about it. I hate the adults. I hate the disgusting buildings. I hate the food. I hate the smell. I hate not being looked after. I hate not having any friends. I hate it. I hate it all.

Her tired mind became more and more confused.

Nobody loves me. There is not one person on this earth who cares what happens to me here. I am nothing. It doesn't matter to anyone that I am here.

She tried turning her thoughts off in the hope of going to sleep. Instead, she felt a battle raging that could not be silenced.

It's your fault.

What is?

That you are here. It's all your fault.

My fault? Why is it my fault? What did I do?

You are in Juvenile. You know why people are here.

No.

Of course, you do. Why are children brought to Juvenile?

I don't know.

But you do know, Keren. You know very well. You know why you are here.

Keren struggled to get her mind off these thoughts. But like trying to douse a fire with gasoline, the more she tried to get rid of them, the stronger they returned.

How could I possibly know?

Think, Keren. Think. Why are you here?

I ... I do know.

Correct Keren. You do know why you are in Juvenile. Say it. Say it, Keren.

A blistering hot wind ripped through her soul. *I am here because I am being punished.*

That's right. Juvenile is for children who are being punished.

But what did I do? I don't know what I did wrong. My parents died. No one was available to take me in. I was brought to this horrible place. No one here loves me. No one will tell me why this is happening. I hate everything.

But that's not the worst part, Keren.

Yes, it is.

But it isn't, Keren. Come now. You and I both know it. What is the worst part of this, Keren?

The concrete walls closed in so tight she found it difficult to breathe. Her mind began to fight the fear of where all of this was leading.

I know.

You know what, Keren?

I know the worst part.

Which is?

That I am going to be here forever. The thought chilled her.

That's right, Keren. This is all there will ever be. When you outgrow this place someday, you will be an uneducated, useless person. And if by some stroke of fortune, you do manage to get out earlier, there will be no one to help you. Either way, you'll end up a beggar on the street. Lots to look forward to. The future is bright.

Keren looked through the bars on the window and saw a star in the distance. Twinkling all by itself. She lay there. Scared. Confused. Unloved.

One day became exactly the same as the next day.

She stayed that way for a year.

And wondered if it was possible for something—anything—to change in her life.

CHAPTER 3

It was Christmas, but you'd never know it.

No decorations. No nativity scene. No songs about baby Jesus being born in Bethlehem.

The only hint of December 24 and 25 was the unexpected arrival of a group of smiling, energetic, clean children who entered Juvenile with such vibrancy that it suddenly reminded Keren of the existence of a world beyond these concrete walls.

The Juvenile children sat in their dirty clothes, with their unkempt hair, and looked with their desperate or angry eyes in wonder at the children who took to the front of the dining room. The chairs and benches had been arranged with the tables pushed to the side. A normally loud and agitated crowd at mealtime became filled with a sense of curiosity at the sight of these well-dressed children. Keren sat on a bench, her eyes fixed on the children in front of her. Who were they? And why did they look so different?

An older girl sat down beside Keren and pushed her further to the end. Normally, it would have bothered Keren. But she focused on the expressions of each of the children. Their faces were so bright. So energetic.

So happy.

And she wanted what they had.

The guests wore bright orange shirts. They smiled with deep, genuine joy that radiated into the room like when a curtain is pulled open to reveal incredible sunshine. Keren had never seen eyes with this kind of vibrancy. What was going on inside those beautiful shells that served as a window to their soul? Why were they so full of life? What was going on inside of them to make them have such hope?

Because they're not in here, Keren. Who wouldn't be happy to be somewhere else?

They have something I don't have.

They have freedom, Keren.

They have something more.

Parents. A decent place to sleep. A future. Take your pick, Keren. The list is endless.

But I see something in their eyes. They are full of life.

You're imagining things.

I'm not. Keren looked closer. *They have something I don't have. I want to be like them.*

The guests lined up, ready to sing.

An unassuming man walked to the front. Soft voice. Gentle demeanour. The moment he spoke a hush fell over the room.

"Ooo-aye," the man said, giving two thumbs up. The children in orange shirts at the front followed his lead and did the same. "We are very honoured to be here with all of you this Christmas. I wish each of you a very merry Christmas. Thank you for inviting us to be with you. We love you. And we hope you feel so welcome."

Keren felt a powerful tug in her heart. Her eyes locked onto the man. Her lips began to quiver. An uncontrollable and quiet stream of tears filled her eyes and ran down her face. Who was this man?

"Christmas is a wonderful time of year. This is when God sent His Son, Jesus, to be born in the city known as Bethlehem. Jesus came because He loves you. God made you for a purpose, and you are very precious to Him.

"My name is Charles Mulli," the man said. He turned to the large group gathered behind him. "And all of these are my children."

A gasp rushed through the room. Had he really said that? Are these *his* children? How was that possible to have so many?

"And there are even more," Mulli said, laughing. "Can you imagine? There are many more children back home."

Mulli shared his story. About being abandoned. Giving up hope. Then finding hope. Living a life of service to God and humankind.

"Even though Jesus is a mighty King, He was born in a little stable for animals. And do you know why? Because He is kind and He is humble. And this Christmas, He comes to you too to love you and to show that you are special to Him."

The MCF choir began to sing. The moment she heard them, Keren felt an unexplainable rush of power and peace come over her. The a cappella voices filled the room. The MCF singers clapped and danced. She watched their feet moving with the rhythm. Watched the way Mulli looked at his children with respect and love.

Mwanga wangu huu mdogo	This little light of mine
Nitaiacha iangaze	I'm gonna let it shine
Mwanga wangu huu mdogo	This little light of mine
Nitaiacha iangaze	I'm gonna let it shine

TRANSFORMATIONS

Mwanga wangu huu mdogo	This little light of mine
Nitaiacha iangaze	I'm gonna let it shine
Iangaze, iangaze, iangaze	Let it shine, let it shine, let it shine

An MCF boy and girl shared their testimony. They described desperate lives on the streets of Eldoret, not far from the Juvenile Detention Centre. They related Mulli's rescue of them physically to Christ's rescue of them spiritually. Keren felt drawn to their story. For the first time, she heard of God being a creator and a God of love. The children shared how God's Son, Jesus, came to earth and died for their sins. They told how, by repenting and trusting in Him alone, they received eternal life.

Keren wanted to hear more, wanted to hear each of their stories.

The scent of incredible food suddenly filled the room. Keren took in a comforting waft of cooked rice, beans, and a maize flour dish like porridge called *ugali*. It transported her back to when her mother cooked for her. She turned around, half-expecting to see her standing there.

The children shouted. They hurried out of their chairs, competing to get closer to the front of the line. Mulli prayed for the meal. Keren moved her head to see past all the bustling children to catch a glimpse of Mulli's face while he gave thanks. He looked so peaceful. So confident.

Like he really believed God was listening.

MCF served the children large ladles of food. Keren received her plate full.

She sat down quietly by herself and took the first bites. Finally, an excellent meal. Food she could enjoy. It transcended her expectations. While other children gobbled down their food and hurried to return for seconds, Keren felt a familiar tug of tears beginning to form. Yes, the food was great. MCF was great. All of it was great.

But it wasn't going to last. They would all be gone soon. And she would return to life at Juvenile.

She sensed the struggle of being alone, and what it meant to know how far removed she had become from real life. The MCF children were within talking distance. But in reality, they lived a world away. They lived in a place of hope. A place of opportunity.

A place of family.

And Keren had none of it.

It's nice, isn't it? Nice to see how far you have fallen. You had a good life once. Not anymore.

I want out of this place. I want to be where they are.

And yet, here you are. And there they are. You don't belong with them. You belong here.

Why can't I have a dad like that?

Because you had parents. They are gone. And this is what happens to children without parents. They end up in places like this. Cry all you want, but there is nothing you or anyone can do about it.

But things changed for those children.

It did. But they won the lottery. You did not.

I am going to be here forever.

You see? That's progress. You have come to accept your lot in life.

But it could be different, couldn't it? Those children talked about how their life was just as bad as mine.

Sure, life could be different. But not for you. They are different. They deserve a second chance at life. Not you. Eat up. You won't get food like that until—

Keren closed her eyes, squishing tears out.

She heard the commotion of children hurrying outside with the MCF team to play games. The racket turned to silence. She kept her eyes closed, hoping somehow her imagination could carry her out of this place. It was no use, of course. There was no point clinging to a hope that exceeded reality.

But unrealistic hope was all she had.

Keren sat in the quiet. No doubt someone from Juvenile would shout at her to stand up and get going. Someone would grab her plate from her hands and tell her to go outside. Someone would speak a harsh word to her.

"Ooo-aye." The soft voice reached into her. It touched her so deeply that it caused a whole new flood of tears.

Is he speaking to me?

Keren opened her eyes. The tears clouded her vision. She blinked. The image of the man who stood at the front of the stage earlier became clearer.

He was crouched down to be at her level.

She blinked again. He came into focus.

It *was* him. And he was taking to her.

She felt like turning around to see if there was someone else there. To make sure she wouldn't make the mistake of raising false hope. Was there someone behind her that he was talking to?

No. No, it was just them.

She focused on his eyes. Saw in them a depth of love that spoke to her heart. She studied him, felt enveloped by his gaze. What was it? What was it about him that compelled her to look at him?

She felt her fears disappear. She felt removed from this place. It was as if they had been transported someplace else. Someplace safe. She felt the compassion of his gaze.

And then it occurred to her. *He understands me.*

"What is your name?" he asked.

His words sounded like a gentle breeze, offering her a sense of calm in her otherwise tumultuous life.

She wanted to respond but couldn't. She sobbed.

It was the first time someone spoke to her in a way that was not interrogative. The first time someone crouched down so she could look at them eye to eye. In over one year, every conversation with an adult involved them talking down to her. But this gentle man came down to her level to speak directly with her.

And Keren felt the incredible impact of his love.

She wasn't able to piece this together.

Why is he here? Why is he talking to me? I don't have anything for him.

Mulli held out his hands, palms up, offering to pick her up.

She knew she was supposed to lean forward, or jump into his arms the way young children do when they are with someone they love. But it had been so long. When was the last time she had been held? The thought felt foreign to her. Like she was being asked to speak a language she once knew but could no longer recall.

She felt Mulli pick her up. She sensed relief. A warm wave of acceptance ran through her. In an instant she felt delivered from this place. Having her feet off the ground gave her sense of incredible relief. No concrete under her feet. She wiggled her toes.

Why is he doing this? Doesn't he realize that I stink? Why does he want to be around a smelly child? I am wearing dirty clothes. His clothes are simple and clean. But I am making his clean clothes dirty. What kind of person would pick me up like this? Why is he doing this?

Keren did not understand. But one thing she knew for certain: *I want to go wherever he goes.*

Mulli placed her back down. He went to speak with one of the workers.

Keren watched as Mulli asked questions. The worker responded. Mulli turned to look at Keren and then continued the conversation. When he finished, he returned. He looked so tall to young Keren. He crouched down again.

"Hello, Keren," Mulli said. "That is a great name. A woman in the Bible was named Keren. She was a beautiful daughter of Job. He suffered through many, many challenges. But in the end, God blessed Job. He had to be patient. But in God's time, he blessed Job with Keren, his youngest daughter. And I am convinced you will be a blessing to many."

In that moment, Keren felt like she was the only person in the world to him.

"I need to go to the court," Mulli said. "I am going to make a committal. This is an agreement to take responsibility for you. And when the court agrees, I will take you home and I will be your father, and you will be my daughter. How does that sound to you?"

That sounded good to Keren.

"I will come back for you," he said. "I will not leave you as an orphan. Just be patient. What do you think?"

Keren nodded. Mulli hugged her.

She watched him go. He was about to round the corner and disappear down the hallway when he turned back and waved at her. And then he left.

Keren stood in the room by herself. The place seemed different. The concrete walls didn't feel like they were closing in on her like before.

What was this feeling?

She took in a breath.

I wonder what happens now.

CHAPTER 4

This time felt different.

Whenever Keren heard her name called at Juvenile, it normally meant someone was angry with her. Her life consisted of either being ignored or being reprimanded for something she had not done.

"Keren!" a woman called out a second time.

But this time it meant something else.

Keren hurried towards the sound of the voice. She rounded the concrete corner. She saw one of the guards at the end of the hall. Beside her stood a humble man with a gentle smile. Younger than Mulli. Same kindness in his eyes. Keren walked towards him. He introduced himself.

"I am from Mully Children's Family," he said. "I think you have met Daddy Mulli."

Keren nodded.

This was it. This was really happening.

I'm out of here. I'm out of here. I am getting out of here!

"I have come to take you home," the man said.

You're not dreaming. This is real. This is a fulfilled promise.

"Daddy Mulli has obtained all the legal papers. I have presented them to Madam," he said, indicating to the woman. Keren did not look. She stayed locked in on the man with the gentle eyes.

"Are you ready to come home?"

Keren jumped up into the man's arms. He carried her out of Juvenile to the MCF vehicle.

Keren did not look back.

The drive through town felt freeing. For the first time in over a year she was leaving Juvenile without the dark cloud hanging over her head of having to go back. *What will MCF be like? How many other children are there? What do they do for fun? Do they have story time?*

She looked through the windshield. Up ahead, she saw a gate.

A black gate.

Why am I going to another gate? Is this another compound?

A tall man opened the gate. He waved at the man driving in the front, then smiled even brighter as he waved at Keren. The man looked so excited that it seemed to Keren that he must know her.

They stopped. The man opened the door for her. She stepped out.

Keren saw children laughing as they played a game of tag. In the distance, she saw a group of girls working on each other's hair. Boys played soccer. The children sounded different than what she was used to at Juvenile. Children laughed and giggled. It looked different, too. The buildings looked clean and well taken care of.

But more importantly, it *felt* different.

Keren relaxed. She let down her guard.

She absorbed her surroundings instead of trying to protect herself from them.

She felt free. Like she could run and play. A sudden rush of energy filled her.

An older girl wearing a yellow dress and an infectious smile hurried up to her.

"Welcome here," the girl said. Before Keren could respond the girl continued, "Mom is calling you. Let's go!"

The girl took Keren by the hand and led her past the large house through a gate into the backyard.

Keren saw a woman sitting on a bench finishing a talk with a young girl. The young girl nodded. The woman smiled and gave her a hug. The young girl left.

The woman turned to Keren. She smiled through her eyes. Something deep within her poured out and reached Keren. A powerful rush of love enveloped her.

"Hello," the woman said.

Keren felt she knew her. How was that possible? This was the first time they had met. She was sure of it. And yet, it seemed to Keren as if she were being reintroduced to her.

Keren stepped closer. Why did she look so familiar?

The woman laughed. "Come. Don't be shy. Do you know who I am?"

Keren walked up to her. The woman picked up Keren and put her on her lap.

"I am your mother," the woman said. "I am Mamma Esther."

Keren felt the instant connection between mother and child.

"I am very glad you are here, Keren. You are most welcome," Esther said, checking Keren's hair for lice. "God loves you, and we love you too."

She shaved Keren's head to match with all the other children as part of the MCF hygiene protocol. She gave Keren a bath and handed her two dresses, a green dress with black flowers, and a white dress with green and red flowers. Keren touched the green dress that hung down to the correct length. It was clean. She was clean.

"I want you to know that you can come to me at any time," Esther said.

Keren nodded. She believed her.

Esther gave instructions for the girl in the yellow dress and another older girl to take care of Keren. The girl offered Keren two bananas.

"I am sure you must be hungry. Do you like bananas?" Esther said, laughing.

Keren felt an unfamiliar surge of joy rise up within her. It released itself in a smile.

"I thought so," Esther said. "There will be lunch soon. But this will be a fun snack for you."

The older girls led Keren down a pathway showing her the outside of the iron sheet dormitories and classrooms. Keren bit into her banana. Finally, a place that understood children get hungry in between meals.

The lunch bell rang. The children gathered. A woman named Rose led them in a prayer. After the children received their food and sat down, Rose watched to make sure all the children ate. She sat down beside Keren and put her arm around her.

"Welcome to MCF," Rose said.

Keren felt absorbed into her embrace.

"How is your food? Have you had enough?"

"It is good," Keren said. She leaned into Rose.

Time could stand still now.

The children gathered for evening songs and devotions. Keren felt the power and volume of so many children singing. The man who picked up Keren earlier in the day from Juvenile, stood at the front to address the children.

"You are not an accident," he said. "You are here for a purpose."

Keren felt drawn to the man's words. She felt him speak directly to her.

"That purpose is to ask God to forgive your sins, to become God's child, and to allow Him to use you to do what He wants in your life."

It came as a new thought to Keren. *What kind of purpose? And how will I know it?*

They sang a song and prayed. The two older girls took Keren to a dormitory. As they walked, Keren's mind kept playing over the words she had heard. *You are here for a purpose.*

They opened the door. Bunk beds were organized in neat rows. Were those mattresses? And blankets?

"Here is your bed," the taller of the two girls said. "You have to share with me, but don't worry. I don't snore."

"Yes, you do," the shorter one said. She looked to Keren. "The one snoring never notices."

Keren giggled.

She changed into her bedtime clothes, a welcome relief from the day in, day out dress she was used to wearing at Juvenile.

Keren got into bed. It felt warm. It felt clean. It felt safe.

Her back felt comfortable. Her head rested against the pillow. She heard chatter from the other girls in the dormitory. The laughter. Then the quiet, as one-by-one the children faded into dreamland. She hadn't known peace like this before. And it came as a welcome new normal.

Keren whispered to the tall girl beside her. "Thank you for letting me stay in your bed."

"Of course," the girl replied, in a way that made it seem like it was no big deal.

But it *was* a big deal. It was a huge deal. All of it. Food. A bed. Clothes. A place where everyone loved her.

She closed her eyes. As she began to drift off, she heard those words in her mind: *You are here for a purpose.*

CHAPTER 5

The room became quiet. Mulli took the stage.

Evening devotionals became a focal point for Keren. She felt drawn in by Mulli's words as if being attracted by a magnet.

She sat with her brothers and sisters. Different tribes. Different backgrounds. One family.

"You are a family of brothers and sisters," Mulli said. "And I know many of you have had difficult backgrounds. Even me. I was left. Abandoned. At the age of six, I was beaten by my own father. I woke up, and my family had left for an unknown destination. I had to beg on the streets. Many of you know what that is like. I was not even able to go to school because I was so poor. And yet, God raised me up. But for what purpose? So that I could have all my money to myself? No. Look around. God raised me up so that I could be a servant of His."

The still African night offered Keren a sense of calm. At Juvenile, night-time was accompanied by anxiety. At MCF, it came with peace.

"Life is not just about getting an education or being safe from the streets. Jesus said, 'I have come that you might have life and that you might have it more abundantly.' But what is this abundant life? What does Jesus mean when He says this?"

Even with so many children present in the packed-out devotional, Keren had the unmistakable feeling Mulli was speaking to her.

"The Bible says, 'As many as received Him, to them He gave the right to become children of God, even to those who believe on His name.' God brought you into Mully Children's Family. But much more, He wants you to become part of His spiritual family."

Keren heard this many times at MCF. But tonight felt different. She sensed a pulling on her heart.

"This is why Jesus came to earth. To make it possible to restore you to God the Father. God created the entire world. He made Adam and Eve. Adam and Eve disobeyed God. Sin entered the world. The Bible says, 'For the wages of sin is death, but the free gift of God is eternal life in Christ Jesus our Lord.' What does this mean?"

She felt her heart pounding. She recalled being alone at Juvenile. She remembered how thrilled she was when Mulli came to rescue her from that place. And yet, here at MCF, she sensed something far stronger.

"Each of have sinned. Isaiah says, 'All we like sheep have gone astray. Each of us has turned to his own way. But the LORD has caused the iniquity of us all to fall on Him.' It is our sins that separate us from God. But Jesus died on the cross to forgive our sins. And He rose from the dead. If we will ask forgiveness of our sins and put our trust in Jesus Christ that He alone can save us, we will become part of God's family, and we will have eternal life."

It sounded so simple when he put it like that. More natural than breathing.

"'If you confess with your mouth that Jesus is Lord and believe in your heart that God raised Him from the dead, you will be saved.'"

Mulli led them in a prayer. Keren bowed her head.

"Dear God in Heaven, You have created everything, including me. You love me, and You have a purpose for my life. I have chosen my own way. I ask You to forgive my sins and every wrong thing I have ever done. I also forgive those who have done bad things to me. I thank You, Jesus, for dying on the cross for my sins and for rising from the dead. I put my trust in You. I ask You to make me Your child and help me to follow You."

Mulli's prayer was simple. No loud voice. No bright lights from heaven. Nothing apparently out of the ordinary.

Except for what happened inside Keren.

In the following years, Keren often accompanied Mulli on outreaches to streets, schools, and Juvenile Detention Centres. She saw his gentle interaction with children and how they gravitated to him.

Mulli invited her to listen at choir practices to learn the songs. Then, he integrated her into the choir far before she thought she was ready. Mulli soon encouraged her to sing solos. It all felt rushed, but it surprised her how Mulli seemed know how to advance her at the earliest possible opportunity.

Obey first, and the blessing to serve will follow.

Mulli owned land east of Nairobi that came to be known at MCF as Canaan. He often referred to it as the land flowing with milk and honey. Keren learned that when Mulli was in business, he bought property along the Thika River in the area of Ndalani. It was supposed to serve as his retirement home. But when

God called him to rescue children, he gave up everything. That included his retirement.

"Next year, you will be in grade five," Mulli said to Keren as they walked down the pathway to the dormitories. "Then, I will transfer you with everyone else in your class to Ndalani."

"Is it really that amazing?" Keren asked. "Is it really the Promised Land?"

"Oh yes."

"Really?"

"For sure. I would not lie."

"It seems ...." Keren wavered between being respectful and being honest. "It seems a little to be too good to be true."

"That is because you aren't looking with eyes of faith."

Next year came. Mulli, true to his promise, took the entire grade five class to resettle them in Ndalani—the Land of Promise. They children packed into buses. They rode to Nairobi, then took the highway through Thika and passed the village market of Kithimani. Shopkeepers hurried out, offering fresh bananas, mangos, pineapple, sugar cane, and many other fruits and vegetables.

The bus turned at Sophia and drove down the dusty road. The farms became smaller. The people poorer. Up ahead, Keren saw the white sign with black lettering: Mully Children's Family Ndalani Branch.

They turned onto the MCF property. Keren's eyes grew wide in anticipation. She imagined MCF Ndalani as someplace incredible, even better than when she first arrived at MCF Eldoret. She could envision the dormitories. The school. The playgrounds. The bright lights.

But everything was not as she imagined.

The bus came to a stop. Keren didn't want to get out.

Was this the right place?

She felt herself pulled by a vortex of kids begrudgingly trudging off the bus.

Keren felt the blistering sun. She coughed in the dry heat. She looked out at the humble iron sheet dormitories and schools.

Part of Keren wanted to either disappear or go back. The other part considered accepting that perhaps she had misunderstood what Ndalani was all about.

But had she?

Hadn't she been told that she would be entering Canaan? The famous Promised Land? If so, then what was this?

Keren looked over at Mulli. She wondered if it was wrong to challenge authority. Or maybe she wouldn't be challenging authority exactly. Maybe this would be more like asking for clarification. Not necessarily doubting like the way Zacharias doubted the angel about his wife getting pregnant at such an old age and lost his speech for a season. But more like Mary seeking clarification from the angel when she wondered how she would become the mother of Jesus.

Keren walked up to Mulli. He looked his usual vibrant self. So confident. So optimistic. What was he seeing that she could not?

She waited until the other children were out of earshot.

"*Baba ulitudanganya,*" Keren said, meaning, *Daddy you lied to us.*

Instead of taking offence, Mulli smiled.

"No, I did not lie," he said. "You just have not seen anything yet."

"I see what you see."

"And what do you see?"

"I see what everyone else sees."

"And that is?"

Keren pointed to the obvious. "I see nothing."

"Nothing at all?"

"I see iron sheet dormitories. I see dead trees. I see dry land. That's what I see."

"Me? I do not see that."

"Are we in the same place?"

"Perhaps."

"Are we looking at the same land? Because all I see is …."

Keren became confused. She exhaled. What was going on here? Where was this land of milk and honey? She looked back at Mulli.

"All you see is what is there," he said.

"I don't understand."

"You'll see."

"I'll see what?"

Mulli laughed. "You see this land?" he said, pointing to the property marker.

"Yes."

"That is as far as our property goes. But we will have much more. The land as far as you can see, it will all be ours. Oh yes. The neighbours will hear of what we are doing and will come to sell us their land at a fair price. And what about electricity?"

"Here? There isn't any electricity here."

"We will have kerosene lamps," Mulli started.

"That isn't exactly electricity."

"The nearest electricity is the highway and that is ten kilometres away."

"You see? It's too far."

"Is anything too hard for the Lord? You need to see with your eyes of faith, Keren. Like I do."

"I still don't understand."

"We will have electricity. And we will have beautiful schools made out of stone. We will have large dormitories. A wonderful kitchen. And a large church in the shape of a cross."

Mulli began walking and pointed to things that were there for him, but not for Keren or anyone else. He saw things that didn't exist.

Or did they?

What was he looking at?

Keren followed him. Confused at how her father could be convinced of things that weren't there.

This guy dreams. Oh, this guy really dreams.

Keren asked Mulli for a watch. She wanted an alarm to get up early to study. Mulli dismissed the idea with his catch phrase, "I will see," which meant neither yes nor no. He kept the idea inside that massive filing cabinet in his mind, retaining nearly everything his children talked to him about.

Mulli possessed a keen sense of specific wisdom for each of his children. He watched them. Prayed for them. Listened to how God was instructing him to encourage their individual giftings. Mulli noticed Keren's love for reading. When she reached grade seven, he gave her a copy of *The Chronicles of Narnia: The Lion, The Witch and the Wardrobe.* She devoured it in three days. Even Mulli was surprised how fast she read it. When she turned thirteen, Mulli gave her a study Bible, which she faithfully read to connect with God.

He bought her a John Grisham novel, wondering if perhaps this would help guide her interests. But her favourite book outside of the Bible that Mulli gave her proved to be the story of Ben Carson called *Gifted Hands*. She loved the idea of becoming a neurosurgeon. She loved the idea of a man who believed anything was possible.

She loved the idea of being used to heal people.

CHAPTER 6

Children came to MCF through different circumstances. And these circumstances sometimes affected how they would spend Christmas.

Street children were the most common rescue in the beginning of MCF. These children would turn to the streets in desperation as a means of escaping a troubled home life or finding food that was no longer available from their parents.

Later, MCF rescued children who came from other challenging situations such as *total orphans*, who had lost both parents and had no one else who could look after them.

They also rescued *partial orphans* where one parent had passed away, and the remaining parent did not have the ability to cope with raising the child.

Single parent children were born out of wedlock. The remaining parent (most often the mother) was typically not in a position to raise the child.

Abandoned children had parents who left them and there was no one else to help.

Neglected children had parents who did not have the means to raise them.

Child-mothers were girls who gave birth at an early age. Their situation made it impossible for them to look after their child and themselves, so MCF would rescue both of them.

Victims of post-election violence were children who had one or both parents killed, making the child a total or partial orphan.

Abused children involved cases where the child was not believed by authorities and, as such, needed rescuing by MCF.

The government placed children in Juvenile who did not have any means of adequate care. MCF rescued *Juvenile children* from situations where most of the time the child was not guilty of any crime.

Keren had the distinction of being both a total orphan and someone rescued from Juvenile.

Most MCF children who had a stable parent or relative in their life and would journey home for Christmas. But total orphans like Keren had no one but Mulli. All those with no place to go would spend Christmas together at MCF.

And Mulli made Christmas special.

He took them to Nairobi National Park to see the wonderful Kenyan animals. Ironically, in spite of all the giraffes, zebras, gazelles, and even lions that inhabited the park, Keren had a different favourite animal. In fact, hers was no animal at all. Her favourite creature was an insect.

A caterpillar.

It's been said people take a liking to a favourite creature because of a characteristic they admire. Keren admired the radical transformation process from caterpillar to butterfly. She took it as a reflection of what her own life would become. It didn't matter to her how long her transformation would take. Didn't matter if she thought nothing was happening for extended periods of time. Didn't even matter if she became discouraged when results didn't happen fast enough in school, or with her faith, or any other area. Deep down inside, she had a knowing. A conviction. A deep sense that one day MCF would make her ready to fly. She would become the woman she was designed to be. A butterfly, so to speak, that would be brilliant compared with where she had come from. Keren would take off into a whole new sphere.

Mulli gave Keren a new watch each Christmas. On Christmas Eve they would make *chapatti*—a flat pancake loved by Kenyan children. They sang Christmas carols. Reminisced about Eldoret and how everything started. Each Christmas at Ndalani marked a special time for Keren to connect with Mulli.

Year after year, they cherished time together. One Christmas evening, Keren walked outside. Mulli saw her. They greeted each other.

Keren glanced at the beautiful lights that graced MCF. Electricity had in fact come to MCF Ndalani. All the dormitories, schools, and other buildings featured lights instead of kerosene lamps. The iron sheet dormitories gave way to beautiful stone buildings with materials courtesy of donors with labour supplied by the MCF construction team. The landscape changed so much that it no longer resembled the place Keren first saw when she got off the bus way back in grade 5.

"Did you see all of this back then?" Keren asked.

Mulli chuckled.

"You did, didn't you?" Keren continued. "We only saw desert. But you saw electricity and buildings and everything. How did you see it?"

"Eyes of faith."

"Meaning what, exactly? Do you invent the future in your mind and then work to make it happen?"

"No. Not like that."

"Then what?"

"The Lord puts a vision into my heart. I don't give anything to Him. I am a vessel. I receive from God."

"And He shows you the future?"

"At times."

"This whole MCF Ndalani property? He gave you a vision to see all these buildings?"

"The buildings are a tool for the real treasures. God gave me a vision for you and all of you brothers and sisters—past, present, and future. I saw you in that Juvenile Detention Centre. I saw you crying all alone. But I saw more than that. I saw the promise of a woman who will go on to do great things."

"You saw all that?"

"Because Christ did."

"But how do you know I will do great things."

"Walking with Jesus *is* the great thing. Some people become famous. Some people achieve things in quiet. The key is not what we do. The key is following Jesus. When I go to the streets, when I go to a Juvenile Detention Centre; when I come to a semi-arid desert as this place was—I don't see what is there, I see what will be there."

"I wish I saw life with your eyes."

Breakfast consisted of nothing.

Mulli called the children together. They gathered as a large assembly. The children looked to Mulli for an answer.

"We have run out of food," Mulli said. "Practically speaking, we can look into the storehouse. And what will we see? We will see it empty. Gone. Completely. But we have eyes of faith. And by faith we declare there is food. However, to make this a reality, we need to pray, and we need to fast."

Keren thought fasting was obvious, given the circumstances.

"We do not know where the food will come from. But we know God will provide. Somehow, some way."

The children prayed.

Concentrating in school became difficult for Keren. She found it hard to focus when her stomach kept reminding her how empty it was. She felt tired. She operated at half capacity.

At lunchtime, they gathered to thank God for food that both was and was not there.

After no lunch, Keren recalled the words of her father. *Eyes of faith.* How did that work exactly? How was she supposed to see into the future? Wasn't it just wishful thinking? And just because she wanted there to be food, was that enough to somehow bring it into existence?

Or was faith deeper than that? Was it more about rejecting doubt and resting in the arms of Jesus?

She closed her eyes to see better.

She waited.

Waited.

A commotion. Children shouted with joy. A truck arrived. A large donation came through at the perfect time. Keren watched the children unload sack after sack after sack of food. The storehouse filled to overflowing. Sacks had to be stored in a neighbouring building.

At supper, they ate.

Keren caught a glimpse of Mulli as he walked by.

He was already on to other things.

"I think you should be a lawyer," Mulli said. "You are very good at debating."

Keren sat with her parents in the guest eating area. It had once served as the eating and the devotional area, where children sat on rickety wooden benches and listened as a speaker shared from the Bible. Above where Mulli sat there hung the only sign in the open-walled room. It read: *We walk by faith and not by sight.*

"I am not sure about law," Keren said.

"I agree," Esther said. "I think you would be more suited to journalism. You are a very good speaker. You can put words together. You are very smart."

"Thank you, Mamma," Keren said. "But I'm not sure I want to be a journalist either."

"All right," Mulli said. "What is on your heart?"

Her mind flashed back to Juvenile. She remembered being all alone in that concrete room. Remembered being sick with no one to look after her.

"Do you think our past experiences shape us for the future?" Keren asked.

"God can redeem anything. Good experiences and bad ones," Mulli said.

"I want to be a nurse," Keren said. "I want to be there for children who have no one."

Mulli and Esther waited in silence.

"You have made a wise choice," Mulli said. "You have my full support. But the ball is on your side."

Keren didn't understand. Picking up on her reaction, Mulli continued. "I can give you my support. But it is up to you to study and sit for the exams."

"I am ready."

Keren took the steps up to Mulli's office. She sat down in the chair opposite him. He thanked her for coming and for taking the time to meet with him.

"I want to share with you the story of Hannah and Samuel," he said.

Keren recalled the story of the mother in the Bible who was without a child and how she prayed and God answered her.

"At the end of the book of Judges, everything is falling apart. Israel is in a disastrous situation. People treat each other in horrible ways. Even the Levites, who are the religious people, aren't doing their job. But we need to connect Judges with First Samuel. If you don't connect the end of the book of Judges with the beginning of First Samuel, you won't understand what is happening."

Keren leaned closer. She knew the stories. But had never *connected* them.

"At the end of Judges there is chaos. Everyone does what they please. That is like today. There is so much chaos. And many children are victims of this chaos. There is much greed and much poverty as a result of the world we live in. I am like Hannah. And every child at MCF is like Samuel," Mulli said.

Keren didn't understand. She studied her dad's eyes for an answer.

"Hannah brought forth Samuel. Samuel would bring order to families because families would now depend on their relationship with God. This is where the motto of MCF comes from: *Saving one child's life at a time*. The Samuels are like MCF children being brought forth to help the country of Kenya and beyond. You, Keren, will be a Samuel in your generation."

The picture came together for her. She understood. And like so many things Mulli told her, this was both simple and profound.

"Whenever life gets difficult, turn to God. One curtain will close. But that is an opportunity to ask God: 'What do you have for me next?' And when the curtain opens, it will be a whole new opportunity."

"Thank you, Daddy. You always say the exact right thing that I need to hear." Keren felt herself begin to tear up. It reminded her of when she was a young girl and Mulli picked her up for the first time.

"You will be a good lecturer, Keren."

Lecturer? What? She hadn't even started university. How did he know she would be a lecturer?

"And you will be a chief nurse," Mulli said.

The correct term was actually *Director of Nursing*, not *Chief Nurse*. But she wasn't going to mince words.

She thanked her dad again.

She walked out of his office. Lecturer and Director of Nursing.

Somehow, he knew. Somehow, he saw into the future.

How does he do that?

University proved to be every bit as difficult as Keren imagined. She never gave up. She kept at it and graduated. She became a lecturer for nursing students and did so well that she was invited to apply for a position at a hospital. She met on the top floor of the executive offices for a company that managed hospitals in five counties.

The interview went well. When they offered Keren the job, they told her she would be the youngest executive in the hospital's history. They also informed her that her title would be different than what she expected. The typical term for her position was Director of Nursing.

But at this organization, they referred to it as Chief Nurse.

She stood on the balcony of her office complex overlooking beautiful Nairobi. She glanced at her watch. It was time to meet her dad.

She drove onto the MCF Ndalani property. Many years ago, she had arrived here in grade five to see a desert. But now, it had been transformed into an oasis. Trees everywhere. Beautiful buildings. And most of all, children who grew up in a safe, thriving environment in the fear of the Lord.

Mulli invited her to sit down at his outdoor office.

"I want to share something with you," Keren said.

Mulli nodded.

She'd had this all planned out on the way here. What to say. How to say it. But now that it was time to deliver, she found it took everything in her to convey her message. She paused. Looked into her father's eyes. So compassionate. So deep.

"You are exemplary," Keren whispered.

She was a lecturer. A top executive. She was accustomed to meetings. She should be able to crank out this talk with ease.

But this proved different. Father and daughter. Both of them knowing where they had come from.

"You are rare," she continued.

She blinked to push away tears so she could refocus on Mulli. He was looking at her in a way she had not seen before.

"You are so humble. So meek," she said. "You are a lion, and you are a lamb. You are a fierce protector of your children, and you are so gentle and approachable."

She gazed deeper into his eyes. And then it occurred to her. So many times he had impacted her. So many times he had impacted his children and many others. But now she could see she was having an impact on *him*.

She wiped the tears from her eyes. "Even now, with over twenty-five thousand children that you have rescued, if I call you from another line so that you don't see it's me calling, the moment you hear my voice, you know right away that it's me."

"Of course."

"Easy for you to say. I would have lost track way earlier," Keren said, taking a drink of water.

She looked into him. Saw how her words reached him, validating all his efforts. And for once, she was glad she could do something for him.

"Street children and presidents both feel comfortable approaching you," she said.

"Thank you, Keren," Mulli said.

"Thank you," Keren replied. "So …."

"So …?"

"I know I have my own job and place to live and all …."

"And …?" Mulli asked, grinning.

Keren smiled. She looked away a moment and then returned.

"Christmas is coming up," she said. "Am I going to get a new watch again?"

PART 3
MOSES WAFULA

CHAPTER 1

What other option did he have?

Seven-year-old Moses Wafula trembled.

What do I do? Where do I go?

His three siblings stuck close to him, just as bewildered as Moses as they struggled to make sense of what to do. They stood on the farm of their extended family's meager property. Their uncles shouted at them. Insulted them. So little food to go around. So many mouths to feed from their tiny farm.

Moses's father had abandoned them. And the rank poverty in the Kenyan province of Nyanza had driven his mother to leave them with relatives, while she moved far away to Nairobi in the hopes of finding work. Mother came home once a year. She sent back money when and if she could.

That left Moses and his siblings at the mercy of the extended family to provide for them.

But family lines ended at the threat of starvation.

"You are pathetic, Moses!" one uncle shouted, his face growing stern in rage. Spit flew from his mouth as he screamed. Whatever compassion he might have possessed at some point had dried up along with the shrivelling crops.

"Where is your father?" the uncle shouted. "He is nowhere. Nowhere! He left you. And now we have to feed you? We don't even have enough food for *our* children!"

What to do? It wasn't like Moses could start his own farm or run to his nonexistent father for help. His mother could not provide. And he lived way out in the country in an area so poor there weren't even streets for him to run to. He wanted to disappear. He hated feeling guilty when he ate their food. Was he really stealing food from his cousins? Was it really his fault his father had left?

His uncle swore at him. Moses stepped back. He knew what was coming next. But he did not move away fast enough. His uncle whipped out his hand and struck Moses across the face. The force of the blow spun young Moses around, sending him to the ground. His cheek hit the dirt. His body landed with a thud.

This was nothing new. He knew how to deal with this.

Don't get angry. Don't fight back. You need food. Don't give him a reason to withhold giving you something to eat.

Moses struggled to his feet. He sat down with his siblings, away from the others. They shared a small plate of beans. They huddled together under a tree. Its branches offered temporary relief from the scorching sun.

Suddenly, a shadow came over them. A shock of fear ran through him and his siblings. It told Moses someone stood behind him. He glanced down and saw the man's feet. His uncle had returned. A shiver ran down his spine.

He could run. But how far could he get?

Was he better off looking his angry uncle in the eye? Or was it better to be subservient and look down to avoid another beating?

"This is our lucky day," his uncle said. "Finally, a solution that works for all of us."

Moses looked up into his uncle's uninterested eyes.

"Your mother sent money for you. She wants you to travel to live with her in Nairobi. Get up. I'm taking you to the bus stop. None of you are staying here a minute longer."

It surprised Moses how boarding a bus could suddenly give him a powerful and optimistic outlook on life. Stepping off the ground and onto the bus meant he was now out of his uncle's reach. It was like a backpack filled with rocks had fallen off his back. Moses felt an incredible burden removed from his heart and mind. Only then did he realize the unbearable weight of guilt and shame that had been thrust upon him all this time. With each step up to the bus, he and his siblings felt the memory of their uncle disappear and the memory of their mother grow stronger.

The promise of seeing her again after all these many months built a thrill within Moses. He thought about her every day. He imagined what it would be like to see her glowing smile when she made her annual trip back to Nyanza. Yet now, he would be reunited with her, permanently. The way it should be.

The bus pulled away. Moses looked out the window. But the uncle had already left. No wave goodbye from him. No tears of departure. Just as well. The extended clan had not fulfilled the meaning of the name *family*. Moses turned his gaze out the front window. In his mind, he recalled all the things people had said about the great capital city.

The tales of Nairobi created large realities in Moses' imagination. People who traveled to Nairobi rarely came back to Nyanza. But those who did journey back, brought stories of buildings so tall that you could not imagine people could construct structures so great. They spoke of electricity that created bright lights, making it possible to walk at night without a flashlight. Nairobi featured paved roads, cars, and beautiful houses.

Nairobi offered everything Nyanza didn't.

For those from Kenya's rural areas, Nairobi became the land of opportunity.

Moses blinked at the first hint of sunshine. The sun's rays looked different for him this morning, offering a sudden burst of hope that changed his perspective. The dull surroundings of what was once his home were gone. Things now looked brighter the way things do for people when they can leave the past behind.

The 420-kilometre journey to Nairobi took twelve hours, but for Moses it felt like only a moment. Every turn in the road brough him closer to his mother, closer to a new life. The sun began to set, giving way to growing lights in the distance. Moses's eyes grew wide in amazement.

The stories *were* true.

He gazed up at the towering buildings as the bus drove into the city centre. He'd imagined them, but their reality exceeded all the creations of his mind's eye. The paved highways with multiple lanes filled with cars finally painted the correct picture of transportation in a modern city.

And it proved to be more than Moses could have hoped for.

The bus arrived at the massive Nairobi bus station. Dozens of buses and passenger vans called *matatus* crowded the area as far as he could see. How anyone could find their way out of here seemed a mystery to Moses. How would they ever find Mother?

They stepped off the bus.

And there she stood.

The tractor-beam bond of mother to child pulled the children towards her. She hugged them tight, reminding Moses what it felt like each year when she visited.

"I love you," she said.

Moses longed to hear those words again. Finally, the world had been set right again.

"Did you have a good trip?" Mother asked.

Moses nodded.

She led them to a matatu. Normally, matatus carried twelve people. But oftentimes, they crammed twice that many or even more inside (and even outside) the vehicle. Moses and the others squished into seats. Moses looked out the window feeling the comfort of his mother beside him.

The matatu struggled to get into gear. When the driver finally managed to find the right position the matatu sputtered and jerked into motion. He honked to warn people ahead to get out of the way.

They turned off the property and drove into the Nairobi night. They passed beautiful buildings. Moses saw reflective glass panels for the first time, amazed that an entire building could act like a mirror. They turned at a traffic light and headed down another road, this one much darker.

Moses looked back. The lights he had become so used to had suddenly disappeared. He looked through the window and saw a group of shabbily dressed boys, each with a rag pressed against their noses.

"Mom, what are they doing?" Moses asked.

"Don't worry. We will be home soon."

Moses noticed the houses on one side of the road stood beautiful, wide and tall, protected by a large concrete fence with barbed wire and crushed glass at the top. But on the other side, the shabby huts looked awful. It was like some giant had compressed together a city of junk and crammed it into a tiny fraction of what it once was, and then sprayed everything with a massive can of eyesore brown rust paint.

Don't turn that way. Don't turn that way. Please don't turn that way.

The matatu slowed down. Which way would it turn? What were the odds of going up to the rich area versus down to the poor area? If the sinking feeling in Moses's chest was any indication, the lottery was not in his favour.

He felt it before the matatu turned.

Sure enough, it pulled down into the depressing, dilapidated housing area.

"What is this place?" Moses whispered. Fear gripped his heart. He pressed his feet against the floor in an involuntary attempt at trying to hit the brakes.

His mother hesitated. Others nearby on the bus heard his question but did not respond. There was no easy way to introduce a convict to prison. No easy way to introduce a terminal patient to the palliative care ward.

And there was no easy way to introduce a child to the unforgivable realities of slum life in Kibera.

The matatu stopped. Moses did not want to get off.

Was this better than Nyanza? Mother was here. That was the bonus. But if perception is reality, this place scared him. And what made matters worse for him was that he knew he had not even set foot in the slum yet.

How much worse could it get?

Moses followed his mother out, forming a chain of hand-holding with his siblings. He had not even made contact with the ground when he sensed this would be a terrible experience.

Stay positive. Stay positive.

An unbearable pungent odor overwhelmed his senses. He held his breath. What was that awful stench? It filtered into his eyes. He blinked and saw the open sewer running nearby. He turned away, hoping it would somehow clear the putrid smell from his nostrils.

His feet touched the ground. One small step for a boy. One giant leap backwards for his future.

Suddenly, the noises of the slum came to life. He heard people screaming louder than any of his uncles ever had. He grabbed his mother's arm and pulled his siblings closer in. A man with unkempt hair and a crazed look in his eyes ran up to the matatu, shrilling at the top of his lungs. The driver motioned him away.

Mother led them down the dirty road. They passed through the crowd. Moses had never seen such a throng of people before. Did they all live here? Where did they come from?

They turned down a narrow alleyway. Dwellings made of mud or dung walls and rusted roofs filled his field of vision in every direction. The pathway dropped and then turned without warning. The stench grew fiercer. He passed one hut and heard a woman screaming followed by the sound of a man shouting and slamming the door. A young child cried.

Moses gripped his mother's hand tighter.

This never-ending walk into the slum felt like days. The duration of every step felt magnified a thousand times by the pounding of his heart.

They made a sequence of turns that left Moses lost for directions. How could anyone find their way in this maze during the day, let alone at night? The tight alleyways become even more narrow. The shouting and screaming from one area were replaced by those in another.

Finally, she stopped. She produced a key that opened a lock. She opened the scrappy metal that acted as a door.

They entered their home.

Mud walls. Iron sheet walls. Mud floor. A beaten-up couch on one side of the hut sat lopsided. A sheet hung partway down to act as a wall. A few blankets lay on the ground to act as beds.

"I don't have much to eat," Mother said. Her tone reflected both her sadness in not being able to provide for her children and her worry that it might never get better. "But we are together, right?" She said the last part more as a way of hoping for affirmation from her children that she had made the right choice in bringing them down here.

Had she?

Was it better to be rejected by family in Nyanza, or to be here with motherly love and be subjected to the vile slum life?

A wave of exhaustion drained Moses.

"I love you, Mom," Moses said.

"I love you, too," she replied.

A loud set of angry voices erupted outside their door. It shook Moses. Could a person get in? Were they safe in here? Did people break into other people's houses in slums?

He lay down and listened to the sound of angry people all around him. He had not prayed much as a child. There was a semblance of religious life back in Nyanza, but nothing with any personal connection to the Almighty. Their religious activities consisted of the occasional service and a lifestyle that was functionally distant from any supreme being operating in the here and now.

But Moses had run out of options. Nyanza was bad. Nairobi was supposed to be the answer. And maybe it was the answer for people fortunate enough to live in those fancy buildings and homes. For those living on *that* side of the wall. But if the introduction to Kibera was any indication, this place was going to be a full-on disaster.

Moses clasped his little hands together. He had one wish. One desire in his heart. If just this one plea received an answer, it would be all he would ever desire.

"Dear God, I beg you to get me out of this place. Let me live anywhere in the world except in Kibera."

CHAPTER 2

S omeone had to make a change.

Defining success in a slum is different than in other places. Secure and stable environments attribute success to people who have achieved educational, financial, marital, business, or humanitarian accomplishments. But slum rules work differently. At its most basic level, a person who survives in a slum is considered successful. Anything more is a bonus.

Moses tried to distinguish himself by not only surviving in Kibera, but also by studying. In grade 8, he prepared for national exams. Passing the Kenyan Certificate of Primary Education would enable him to go on to grades 9 to 12. If he could graduate grade 12 with good marks, he might—*might*—be able to proceed on to his dream studies of political science, get a good job, and get his mother out of this place.

Since arriving at Kibera some ten years earlier, Moses saw how nothing changed. Poor people stayed poor. Wealthy people who owned much of the slum became wealthier. Children started out in poverty and attended school with the hope that life could be different. But often, they came to realize that eventually the majority of people in slums, for different reasons, didn't rise above their apparent assigned lot in life.

They wanted out. Everyone did. Like Moses, they wanted a way out of Kibera. And the way out was getting a good job. Not a job like his mother selling *githeri* on the side of the road. But a real job. Nursing, teaching, construction management, banking. Something above being a casual labourer. That required education. And not just any education. A real education where you could prove on a national grade 12 exam that you could set yourself apart from the thousands upon thousands of other students competing against you. Then a person could go to university. And Moses decided that becoming a politician would give him the ability to effect real change in Kibera.

Politics is power. And politics is people. In an effort to become a politician, Moses realized he needed to become known to people. Unknown politicians aren't politicians for long. He either needed to be the son of a famous politician, which wasn't an option, or he had to make a name for himself.

He had to become recognizable.

Moses Wafula needed to become a household name.

And he found the perfect opportunity.

The recent election results were hotly contested. The result was incredible violence. People took to the streets to fight and demonstrate. Every male was expected to be outside taking part in correcting the course of their country. To stay at home, to hide inside, was to be a coward.

Moses chose the route of taking part in a demonstration. It would signal to others that when his country needed a voice for change, he marched with others in a peaceful path forward.

He joined a large crowd demonstrating in Kibera slum. Watching others in the march, he tried to gauge the political climate. What specifically made people angry? Were they all angry for the same reason? Or were there multiple reasons, and people came together because they reached the same conclusion of dissatisfaction, albeit via various channels? Did the election in general cause them to become angry, or was it how the results were tabulated in specific? Were they caught up in the emotion of marching because their side told them to, or did they take time to carefully think through their position?

He spoke with different people. Introduced himself. Learned their perspectives. Some began chanting one slogan. Others chanted another. The crowd swelled. It took on a life of its own. Everyone became louder. More forceful. Exactly where was all this leading?

They marched through Kibera pulling in more and more people, like a devastating flood that starts with a small stream and becomes more forceful. Moses looked around. The size of the crowd amazed him. He couldn't see the end of it. He felt the power of the crowd. People would remember this. And he could say that he had been part of it.

Though he quickly wished it were not so.

Police shot tear gas into the crowd. The canisters broke open. Stinging chemicals irritated Moses's eyes. Water cannons slammed into the crowd. People raised their arms in a futile attempt to shield themselves from the powerful blasts.

Still, people continued to protest. Moses looked at the uniforms. Were those real police officers? Their uniforms didn't look correct. Were they actual police or just people dressed to look that way?

The crowd would not be deterred. In spite of the water and tear gas, they only grew in their determination. Their screaming intensified. He wiped tears from his eyes in the incredible heat. He felt the crowd's unmanageable anger.

Suddenly a shot rang out. The piercing sound of a gun blast cut through the air. People screamed. In an instant, everything fell apart.

Pandemonium broke loose. Everyone began running. But no one knew which direction was safe. Some ran this way. Others that way. Moses's heart pounded.

Which way?! Which way do I run?

TRANSFORMATIONS

Someone fell beside him. Moses turned to the person lying there and assumed they would stand up and continue running. But a shock ripped through Moses when he noticed a bullet hole in the man's head. What? What was happening? Didn't police use rubber bullets to disperse crowds? Wasn't that part of the standard deterrent package? Tear gas, water cannons, and rubber bullets?

Moses pulled back. Fear gripped him. He had to get out of here. But which way? He picked a direction and sprinted.

And hoped he picked correctly.

These are real bullets killing real people.

More shots rang out.

People ran hysterically. Shouting. Crying.

The crowd dispersed into every alleyway, down every narrow street, and into any home they could find to escape the onslaught of damage.

Dear God, please make this end.

Moses ran until he was out of breath, his adrenaline pushing him further than he would otherwise have been able to go. He stopped behind a hut. Took in heavy breaths. Sweat poured off him.

Did that really just happen? Did I just see people die in Kibera?

The commotion subsided. An uneasy calm filled the air. It felt that at any moment everything would erupt into chaos again. He waited, hoping for his nerves to settle. They did not. He stood there shaking, like electricity was ripping through him.

He forced himself to keep moving in spite of his mind telling him to stay put. He walked down the narrow alleys wondering if he would suddenly meet a gunman. He reached the main street where they had marched.

And saw bodies lying everywhere.

None of it seemed real. His mind struggled between seeing things the way they should be and the way they were.

Moses had no strength to stand. He sat down on the curb. Was that safe? He wasn't sure. So many lives lost. And for what?

He struggled to his feet and walked home. He wondered how things would ever change. Wondered how he would ever get out of this place. It had been a decade. Ten whole years and still he was in this place.

And he sensed the first inklings of fear beginning to creep into his mind that the Kibera slum might be his final stop.

Moses wrote the exams for his grade 8 class. A teacher approached him as he was about to leave school. The teacher's tall figure towered over Moses. He sat down in the wooden desk beside him. He had the kind of inquisitive attitude that put people at ease despite his height.

"What do you want, Moses?"

"What do I want? I want what every kid in Kibera wants. I want out."

"And then what?"

"Study political science. Get a job and become someone in power who can help these people."

"And you're the one to do it?"

"Of course."

"Those are fine goals," the teacher said, sounding like Moses would need heavy outside intervention to make them a reality.

"I pray to God that I will be able to continue my studies."

"I attended a special school for my studies," the teacher said. "It's a home, actually."

"What kind of home?"

"Mully Children's Family." The teacher explained MCF to Moses. "Some of the students from our school will have the opportunity to study at MCF."

"What about me? What chance do I have?"

"I can't say anything for certain. I don't want to mislead you in any way."

"But there's a chance? That's what you're telling me?"

The teacher took in a breath. "Moses, promise me you will not get your hopes up too high. I don't know what will happen."

"It is a good school?"

"It's not a school."

"What?"

"It's a family," the teacher said. "A rather large family."

"They accept outsiders?"

"They *only* accept outsiders."

"I might be able to continue studying with them?"

"You would also have a father again."

The thought pierced him. Moses assumed his main purpose was to find a way, any way, to reach his goal of graduating high school, then study political science and enter the field of public life. But the part about having a father reached deep into him and revealed to him that he had been searching for something without knowing it.

The notion of having a father had been so foreign to his mind. His dad was gone. And he wasn't coming back. Not for him. Not for any of them. Yes, of course he needed a dad. That much was obvious. But why hope for things that are never coming true?

Or could they?

The possibility of having a father uncovered a long-forgotten wish in his heart. Bigger than political science, if that were even possible.

"Bring your documentation with you tomorrow," the teacher said.

Moses nodded.

The teacher stood and walked to the door. He stopped. "Remember, no promises, okay? I will do what I can."

The teacher left. The door closed.

Moses glanced out the window at the rust-brown slum. People packed the street, each person struggling from one meal to the next.

Maybe. Maybe I'm getting out.

CHAPTER 3

"You're going to MCF," the teacher said.

Moses stood in the sunshine just outside the school. The words sounded both amazing and impossible at the same time.

"Really?"

The teacher smiled and felt the joy teachers feel when one of their students will get a chance to excel.

And just like that, Moses was out of Kibera.

When Moses arrived at MCF Yatta, he heard other rescued children talking about their *Daddy*. He assumed they were referring with affection each to their own birth father. But as he listened, he discovered every child called the same person *Daddy*. A sudden thought struck Moses. Something stirred deep in his heart. He sensed a longing being reborn that he had long thought had been laid to rest.

Moses had never called anyone *Daddy* before.

Did that matter? Of course it did. Something had gripped him. Every child needed a father. He knew that all along. Being here revealed a desire he did not know he possessed. And as he joined the other children heading to the evening devotional, he discovered he wasn't walking there so much as he was being pulled by a force he could not explain. Neither was he able to understand why the thought of having a father lay so heavy upon him.

Big deal. A father. A mother. No father. No mother. What difference does it make?

If it doesn't make any difference, why do I have such a desire for a father?

Because you are in a new place. And you are out of sorts. You are looking for an anchor until you fit in. You are a strong young man. Don't give in to this belief that having a father is such a big deal.

Every child here seems to think it is a big deal.

People place way too much emphasis on having a father. Especially those without one.

Many children here were fatherless before they came here. They met God and they met a father on earth, and now they have real hope. I can see it in them. They are secure. They are vibrant. They are ....

They are what?

They are …. Moses looked at the children around him.
They are what, Moses?
They are not like me.
You don't need a father, Moses.

Moses entered the large chapel filled with children. He looked for the white man who ran this whole place. His eyes scanned the floor, but he could not see anyone who could fit the description of *Daddy.*

A young man came to the front to lead singing. Music started. Everyone stood and clapped. They moved from side to side, swaying with the rhythm. Moses felt the whole place come alive.

Maisha yale ya kwanza	My past life
Yalikua mabaya	It was bad
Hayangenipeleka	It would not lead me
Mbele ya Mungu wangu	Before my God
Ooh namshukru Mungu Baba	Ooh I thank God my Father
Naimba Halelyuya	Singing Hallelujah
Sasa nimeokoka	Now I have been delivered
Kama ndege mtegoni	Like a bird from a snare
Mtego umevunjika	The snare is broken
Nami nimeokoka huo	I am saved
Haungenipeleka	My past life would not take me
Mbele ya Mungu wangu	Before my God

Moses felt peace and joy rush through him. He found it odd that he could be in this place for the first time, and yet it felt like home. What was it? Was it that he was at MCF? Was it that he was in a church? Was it both? He closed his eyes and absorbed the sense of family and of being where he was meant to be.

The singing stopped. The children sat down. Moses saw a quiet, unassuming man stand and approach the platform. He looked shorter than Moses assumed he would be. No fancy suit. No fancy clothes. No big presence in the way he walked. Humble. Gentle. Black.

Where was the white guy?

Was this Daddy? *His* daddy? Couldn't be. He didn't look at all the way Moses envisioned.

He looked so unassuming.

The children clapped and cheered with such vigour that it echoed off the walls.

"Ooo-aye," the man said. He spoke with such gentle power that it reached the entire auditorium. Everyone replied with a loud *Ooo-aye*.

"I welcome each and every one of you here," the man said. "I especially want to welcome our ten new family members from Kibera. You have just arrived today after a long journey. I will meet each of you soon, and I am very much looking forward to seeing you in person. Me, I am your daddy. I am Daddy Mulli."

There were other children in the chapel, of course. Many. Hundreds in fact. Yet when Mulli introduced himself as his personal father, Moses felt he and Mulli were the only ones in the room.

"We are all a family. The biggest family in the world. Family is essential. Having a father and a mother is critical for every child. That's why you have Mamma Esther and I as your parents. I know some of you grew up with only one parent. And others of you grew up with neither a father nor a mother. But God brought you into this family. And why? Why did God bring you here? The reason God brought you to MCF is not just about you. It is also about how God wants to use you through Jesus Christ to bring hope for the hopeless. To share His love with people in slums, in your families, or wherever you will work in the future. We are a family so that we can extend this hope of faith in Jesus Christ to others and invite them to become part of God's family."

Moses felt he had always been here. Kibera felt a lifetime ago. And now that he had seen Charles Mulli, it felt impossible to remember life before knowing him.

Everything felt altogether different.

Three years later, Moses stood by himself at midday looking out at one of the massive reservoirs at MCF Yatta. The water captured his attention the way water does with its strength and calmness. As he studied it, he found himself strangely transported to a different location. He still felt his feet on the ground at MCF Yatta, but he was in *two* places at the same time.

Moses found himself preaching in a church. He felt the wood pulpit in front of him. Felt the concrete beneath his feet. He looked out at the congregation. But instead of seeing a sea of people, he saw many individuals. He saw each person. Saw the desperation in their eyes. The fear in their faces. The poverty in the clothes they wore.

The vision made no sense. Why was he here? And anyway, where was *here* exactly? And why was he preaching? His future plans didn't include preaching. He came to MCF with the express purpose of studying political science and becoming a politician. That's why he took part in the demonstrations in the slum. That's why he was studying hard at MCF to get into university.

So why didn't he see a vision of himself at a political rally?

Why was he inside a church?

And why was he of all people the one preaching?

Mulli called the grade 9 to 12 children together for an evening devotional inside the large chapel.

"You are all doing very well," Mulli said. "And I want to encourage you to continue to study hard. To read your Bibles. To pray to God. He is your heavenly Father who loves you. And He has a calling on each of your lives."

Moses felt an unmistakable direct connection with Mulli each time he spoke.

"The Bible says: 'You did not choose me, but I chose you.' God created the world and God created you. He created you with a purpose on this earth. But sometimes like Jonah we will want to run from that calling because it does not seem to fit what we want to do."

Moses felt a nervous rush of energy rip through him. He thought back to his vision.

"I want to encourage you to follow God's plan," Mulli said. "This is a very short life down here. And for all of you who have repented of your sins and who have put your faith in Jesus Christ alone, we will have eternity with Him in heaven. So why not live for how God wants you to live while you are on the earth?"

Moses felt an incredible combination of joy and fear at the same time. He sensed a struggle within him.

You know why you were rescued. You know your purpose. You know your calling. You are meant to become a great politician.

Maybe I was rescued not just from the slum, but also from what I wanted to become.

So now being a politician is a bad thing?

No. Politics is fine. But maybe ....

Maybe what?

Maybe being a politician isn't for me.

Isn't for you? Was it for you when you were ducking bullets in that demonstration? Who do you think kept you alive? God spared you so you could become a politician and prevent riots like that from ever happening.

But I had a vision.

Visions don't belong in our time. Visions and miracles and all that stuff were for people living in Bible times.

But I know what I saw.

You know what you think *you saw. There's a difference. All kinds of people claim they have seen visions. But can you really prove a vision is from God?*

"I want every one of you who senses a calling from God to be a pastor to come to the front."

Without hesitation, Moses stood. And the moment he got up, his fear evaporated.

Moses came to the front with two others.

"Don't ever be discouraged, my young brothers. Remember, do not ever compare yourselves with other occupations. Oftentimes, pastors do not earn a lot of money. It is a difficult calling. Remember how Moses in the Bible was called by God to lead so many people. The needs of the people can feel overwhelming. But where God calls you, He will also sustain you. 'They who wait for the LORD shall renew their strength; they shall mount up with wings like eagles.' And you will have many opportunities to share the gospel of Jesus Christ."

Mulli dismissed the children with their evening prayer, which they all prayed together.

"Now may the grace of the Lord Jesus, the love of God and the fellowship of the Holy Spirit be with us all. Amen."

Moses returned to his dormitory. He lay down in his bed, amazed at how his perspective on his life had changed in these short years at MCF. He thought of the demonstration. He thought of being rescued at MCF. He thought of his vision. He thought of Mulli's words this evening.

And he thought about where he would study, where he would pastor ....

And where God would lead him next.

CHAPTER 4

It was after he graduated from MCF that the challenges in his life grew intense.

Moses studied hard *to show himself approved*. He loved the Lord, loved the Bible, and loved people. He focused on his studies with such determination that he didn't give much thought to what it would be like to study at Bible college. He assumed it would be a smooth transition from Bible-based MCF to a Bible-based Bible college. But as grade 12 graduation drew near, he found an ever-increasing struggle within him was threatening to pull him away from the gospel.

At first, the thoughts entering his mind were a mere annoyance, much like the way a mosquito buzzes around your ear. But as time passed, the attacking thoughts became more persistent. And he found himself in a constant struggle to stay the course.

You came here with the express purpose of wanting to study political science. But now you are allowing yourself to drift from your course.

Is that what this is about? My course? I thought this was about following God's course for my life.

Mulli is right. You should think about what your father says. Money will be a struggle for you.

I would rather live humbly and do what I have been called to do, than to change my calling for the brief pleasures of life.

Very wise. Moses in the Bible did the same. No one likes to be poor. Did you like to be poor in the slum?

No.

I don't blame you. Not one bit.

Moses wondered where this line of reasoning was leading. He felt the sting of temptation. It typically started with stating a fact. That way, the tempter could get him to agree with something undeniable. But a twisting of the facts always followed. And he prayed to have clear understanding to fight off the attack.

You want to have a family, don't you?

Sure.

How will you provide for them? Being a pastor is demanding on your time. It's full-time. And I don't just mean Monday to Friday during normal working hours. People come to you with their problems at all hours. You won't have time for a second job. So how will you provide for your wife and children on a meager pastor's salary?

God will provide.

Easy to say. Hard to live by. But there is a way to make this work.

Moses felt a sting in the last line. Soothing words that came with a distinct bite of venom.

I don't need to make this work.

Of course you do. You want a family. You want to preach. That requires money.

It requires faith.

Tell that to your family when they have nothing to eat.

We have been out of food at MCF. We have prayed and God has provided.

From time to time. But not every day. There are many donors who make MCF possible. Sales from the farm produce helps. Will you have a farm? No. Will you have donors? No. But you will have church attenders. And what do church attenders do?

They come to hear the Word of God. To be in fellowship with Him and others. To be instruments of God to share the gospel.

Sure, of course. That is what they think they are getting. But what are they really there for?

That's why they are part of a church. To be part of the body of Christ.

Sounds nice. Really it does. But everyone knows what church attenders do, Moses.

I'm not following.

Church attenders tithe.

There it was. Out in the open. A fog crept in on Moses' mind. He shook his head to rid himself of it. But it only grew stronger. A quiet, heavy mist sought to infiltrate his soul.

They tithe out of obedience and out of joy.

For your benefit, Moses. They are commanded to. And here is where things can change for you and your family. All you have to do is tell people that the more they tithe, the more they will get.

That is full-on false.

Is it?

Prosperity preachers are false teachers.

Are they? Does the Bible not say that it is God who gives you the power to get wealth?

Prosperity gospel preachers are false teachers because they mix a truth with a lie.

That's being a little harsh, isn't it? Didn't Daddy Mulli prosper in business? Hasn't he prospered with all this land since starting MCF?

None of which he owns. It isn't for himself. And he doesn't preach a prosperity gospel.

Yet the Bible says: "Give and it will be given to you. Good measure. Pressed down. Shaken together. And running over." Am I right? ... Moses? Am I right?

When the motivation is to receive, the purpose of giving is lost.

Yet people want to hear that they can be wealthy.

What people want is not always what they need.

People want to be lifted out of their troubles.

But you can't take advantage of people in their struggle. They have to be told to work hard. To be content with what they have. A man can receive nothing unless it has been given to him from above.

And giving money is the way to receive.

It is not. The cross is the way to receive eternal life from God. Out of that flows a life willing to serve God where people give out of joy.

But if you focus on giving, you will get a reward.

But focusing on money distracts people from focusing on the kingdom of God. The key is to point people to a deeper relationship with God.

Yet the promise of wealth will draw people to you. Many people will come. You will gather big crowds. Do you remember the vision you had? Preaching to all those people. How else will you attract people?

Moses thought back to his vision. He saw the many faces of individuals in the crowd. Each person with their own story. Each with their own challenges. Each with a unique look of desperation in their eyes.

I don't need to attract people. If they are attracted to me, then I will have failed as a pastor. But if they are attracted to Christ because of my life, then I will consider my work to have been a blessing.

But you have to get them in the door, Moses. You have to make your vision come to life.

Did Peter cause the fish to miraculously come to his boat?

Preaching about money will draw people to you. It's been proven all over the world.

Prosperity preaching is attractive because people are going through so many challenges. They need money, and it is easy for them to listen to prosperity preachers because they think money is the real answer to all their problems.

Money solves problems. It buys food.

But money does not cure people's sin problem. Some want to hear that obtaining more money is their deepest need. They don't want to hear about how to cure their true deepest need which is having a saviour cleanse them of their sins, restore them to God and enable them to live a victorious life regardless of their circumstances.

Easy to say here. Let me know how that goes for you when you preach to an empty church.

People need to know that Jesus loves them and that He is willing to take them home to heaven if they will repent and put their trust in Him alone.

A wave of exhaustion came over Moses. He felt the tiredness that comes with fighting a spiritual battle.

Have it your way, Moses. The prosperity gospel is here to stay. And people won't know the difference between you and a prosperity church. You will be cast in the same lot and get swept away in the tide. You're better off just going along with it and reaping the benefits.

People will know the difference in whatever church I am in. I'll take my cue from Moses. From Jesus. I'll preach the word faithfully. Like the way Daddy Mulli taught me. God in His wisdom will lead people. Some will prosper more than others. I'll leave the prosperity to God. He has used many wealthy people to do great things for His kingdom. But not at the expense of twisting the gospel.

You're going to be a poor preacher.

Better poor and faithful than rich and unfaithful.

Fine. Fine, Moses. Sounds great. Brave words. You think you're strong? Go and tell your mother your news.

Another sting ripped through Moses. This one worse than the others. How would Mother react to this? In her slum. In her poverty. She had great hopes that her boy would lift her out of Kibera. As a good son, he would get a good career and get her out of that mess.

Wouldn't he?

CHAPTER 5

Moses's journey to the Kibera slum to visit his mother proved more difficult than he expected.

Normally, the matatu ride gave him much expectancy at seeing her again. The joy of reconnecting. Of sharing. Of her being able to see that she could be proud of him.

But this time felt different. Would she understand? Of course she would. Being a pastor is a noble calling. She knew that. She would support her son. This was obvious. So, what was bothering him so much?

He stepped off the overcrowded van and walked into the overcrowded slum. The stench of the open sewers filled his senses, reminding him of the desperate life he once led here. He negotiated the narrow alleyways between huts made of mud and dung walls. The rust brown roofs hadn't changed. A group of children hurried by him on their way home. A husband and wife screamed at each other behind closed doors in a hut nearby. A young girl stood outside her door with sullen eyes that she could not lift to make contact with Moses. He turned a corner and saw another girl, standing, waiting, doing what she was told to do by her mother to help bring in money. It felt as if the entire slum cried out to Moses for help.

Finally, he reached her door. He knocked. She opened. Her eyes lit up with the special kind of joy a mother feels in seeing her child. They hugged. She laughed. He sat down in their one-room hut. A sheet hung down to divide her bedroom from the cramped living room. An old couch. A wooden table between them. She asked about MCF and his health; then she pressed him on why there wasn't a significant other in his life. She asked about university now that he successfully completed grade 12.

He nodded. Paused.

She asked for more details. He looked into her bright but exhausted eyes. Existing in the slum had pulled so much life out of her. The never-ending mental strain. The desperate surroundings. A human being can only take so much for so long. And she was way past that point.

How to say it?

She knew the money wouldn't be rolling in just yet. It takes time to go through university. Four years of studying. But then he would find a job. A great job. It wouldn't be a big salary at first. But there would something. And every year it would grow. She could hang on for four years. Life in slums becomes more manageable when there is hope. When there is a light in the distance that is coming closer. When there is a son sitting in front of you with the ability to bring in the money. Just hang on a little more. Just a little more.

"I am planning on studying to become a pastor."

The walls of her tiny hut closed in on her. The odor smelled stronger. The visions she had clung to all these years of finally one day—this day in fact—hearing the news that she would be pulled out of this slum, came crashing down around her.

He had told her that he was coming to visit after graduation. She knew this would be the moment. The moment he would announce his plans to study and in four short years obtain a job that could lift her out of all of this. Those four years would have felt like a moment.

But now, every moment felt like a lifetime.

The joy in her eyes disappeared and was replaced with a deep sense of betrayal.

"A pastor?" she asked, hoping that saying it out loud would somehow cause him to shake his head and clarify that he had said something else. Anything else.

He nodded again, feeling her broken heart.

A sense of desperation came over her. All these years. All these awful years. She had managed to make it this far on hope. On conviction. On the belief that her ticket out of here was going to come by way of her boy. Instead, he came to hand her a life sentence.

"Why would you do a job that will not earn you any money?"

Any was the operative word. Of course, it would pay. But it would not pay enough to have anything left over for her. His salary was as good as nothing.

"People need a God-fearing pastor," he said.

"And I need a son who will provide for me."

"God has provided all these years."

"You call living in Kibera *provision*?" she asked. "I can't afford anything. I can't get ahead. I can barely feed myself. You are my hope, Moses."

"I know it is not easy."

"Do you? I wonder if you would be saying the same thing if you were living here these past years. You made it out of here. How easy to tell someone like me to stay."

"I'm only doing what God has placed on my heart. This is what He wants me to do."

"To leave your mother in a slum?"

"To serve God. That has to come first."

A wave of grief came over her. This was really happening. She had no other hope. Too poor to start a business. Too much competition with other women to be able to demand a better wage. Too old to beg for schooling. It felt as if her feet had become concrete, anchoring her to the floor of this inescapable doom.

"This is the career you are being called to?"

"It isn't a career, mother. It is a calling."

What was left to say?

She sat there, feeling foolish for allowing herself to cling to a false hope all these years.

Moses waited, wondering how the silence would end. Finally, his mother looked at him.

"I am not in favour of this."

The journey back to MCF Ndalani was much harder than the ride there. The ride down carried the possibility that things could turn out all right. The ride back reminded him of the cost of following Christ.

Moses served at MCF the next year and a half. He worked in the kitchen department preparing and serving meals day in and day out to hundreds of children. Later, he served in the spiritual department, where he counselled children and taught a course called Christian and Religious Education. He studied three years at Bible school, majoring in Bible, theology, chaplaincy, and counselling. After graduation, he returned to MCF to serve an additional year in the spiritual department.

One evening, after finishing a counseling session with a child recovering from life in the slum, Moses walked down the pathway between the primary and secondary school. On the way, he met Charles Mulli. They exchanged greetings. Mulli's presence offered Moses a familiar sense of peace, optimism, and wonder.

"I am glad to see you again, my brother," Mulli said.

"And you, too, Daddy."

"You notice, I did not call you *son*. You are my son, of course. You know that. But you see, now you are growing in the ministry. and now you are my brother. Is that okay?"

Moses laughed. He admired Mulli's uncanny ability to make you feel like a child.

"Yes, that is fine," Moses said.

"It is like a promotion," Mulli said with a laugh. "You are graduating. How does that feel?"

Moses burst out laughing. "It is an honor."

A choir began practicing in the distance. They felt a stillness in the MCF evening air.

"You are going to embark on a great journey, Moses. The calling of a pastor is noble, and it is demanding. I know you will trust the Lord and do a fine work."

"Thank you."

"I want you to remain positive and to trust God no matter the challenges. Never lose heart. Never say that it is over or that it cannot be done. No. All things are possible to him who believes. Always resist the temptation of despair. Be honest to God with your heart, and remain firm in your faith."

"You are an excellent example of that attitude."

Mulli accepted the comment with a humble bow of his head. "Our Lord is the best example," he said in a soft voice. "And we can look to Him at all times."

"I will."

"Always look at how to *solve* a problem. Never run away. Problems take prayer, and they take thinking. The key advantage problem solvers have is that they do not give up. They wait on the Lord and think through many alternatives until peace arrives."

"Thank you, Daddy."

"You are welcome, my brother."

Moses laughed on instinct. It reminded him of the verse, *Whoever believes in Me, as the Scripture has said, out of his heart will flow rivers of living water.*

"And be a great man of faith, Moses."

Moses nodded as Mulli continued on his way. Mulli's comment played over in his mind. *Be a great man of faith.*

They would prove to be wise words.

Because Moses was going to need them.

The decision to *be* a pastor proved not as difficult as deciding *where* to pastor. With each passing week, Moses felt an ongoing struggle about where to land. He walked down the pathway to the soccer field. The sun began its rapid descent. He felt a struggle within him. He sensed where he needed to go. Where he *must* go. But how difficult it felt to stay the true course when it would be so easy for him to drift into another path. Especially to drift into another path where everyone would think it was the right way. No one would ever assume he was disobeying God.

Except for God and him.

The boys finished their practice. They laughed as they walked off the pitch. Moses smiled then felt the weight of the decision that lay before him.

You did it. You finished your program. You have gained experience here at MCF. You are now a pastor. Well done!

God helped me.

Now comes the big decision. Where are you going to pastor?

I am wondering the same thing.

Wondering about what? The choice is obvious.

Obvious?

Isn't it?

I'm not sure.

Not sure?! After all you've been through? You're going to Nairobi. You'll find a big church. They will love you there.

I don't think so.

Of course they will. You are wonderful person. The people of Nairobi will take to you.

I am not sure about going to Nairobi.

Why not? The churches pay well. You can raise a family. You can finally honour your mother. Help her out of poverty. After all she did for you. You can finally pay her back. Think of how happy she will be. She was mistaken about pastors being poor.

I am thinking about Charles Mulli. About his example.

He sacrificed a lot for you. Now you can make him proud. A pastor of a church!

He had everything. But he gave it all away.

In order for you to have a better life.

What does it mean to have a better life?

To have a career. To be secure. To be able to serve God without worry.

He sacrificed everything. Christ sacrificed everything. That's why ....

That's why what?

That's why I am going ....

To a large, established church.

Is that the answer?

Is a solid church not the answer?

It certainly can be. Yet I don't sense that is where I should go.

Feelings. Feelings. Feelings. Can you really trust them?

This isn't a feeling. It's a conviction.

A conviction to not be a pastor in a big church in a city where you can lead people to Christ and provide for a family and your mother?

It defies ....

If defies what?

It defies what is expected.

No. It defies what you deserve and what your mother deserves.

Sometimes Christ asks us to do things that are hard.

Does He? I thought He took your sins on the cross so you could be free?

Yes, free to follow Him. Enter by the narrow gate, for wide is the gate and easy is the path that leads to destruction, and many are those who follow it. But narrow is the path and difficult is the way that leads to life, and only a few are those who find it.

So a large church is destruction? I think you might need to check your theology.

There is nothing wrong with a large church. But it is wrong for a pastor to go to a large church in a large city if in fact he was called to go somewhere else.

And now you are prophet? Called by God somewhere? Did you get this in another vision? Did you see it written in the stars somehow?

It's not easy. Part of me wants to run like Jonah. But I refuse to back down. That's why I am going ....

To?

I am going ....

Going where, Moses? This is your chance. You can really have it all.

Moses closed his eyes. It was time to make the decision. Time to be a man of faith.

I am going back to Kibera. Back to the slum.

CHAPTER 6

A re you crazy?
I don't think so.

Kibera? The slum is not a place to which you return. It's a place you leave.

But I can help people.

By getting a job outside the slum.

I can help people in the slum because I've been there. I understand life in Kibera.

This is your chance to get out of Kibera for good.

No. This is my chance to stay in Kibera.

This makes no sense.

Maybe it's not supposed to.

Your mother needs your help.

That stung. Poor Mother. She needed someone to lift her out of poverty. And he could give it to her. So simple. Just take a position in a large church.

Moses looked out at the soccer field. The sun had set, ushering in the typical quick African transition from daylight to pitch darkness.

The people of Kibera need me, too.

Do those people have the right to make you turn your back on your mother? That's not very grateful of you, Moses. She did everything for you. Might be nice to at least do something for her in return.

Doing the right thing is not always easy.

You're not the right person to pastor in a slum.

I don't have to judge myself. I only have to follow Christ.

You've been elevated from the slum. Mulli wants you out of that place.

I reached where I am today because Mulli followed God's call. Mulli had a difficult background. And that helped him understand how to help people. He rescues children like me so God can work through them to impact others for Christ. Who among us gets to decide where God will place us? Who am I that I should dictate to God where I should serve Him?

Are you honoring Mulli by going to a slum and rejecting his help to get you out of there in the first place?

Mulli wants me wherever God wants me. And that's Kibera. And that's my final decision.

Re-entering Kibera felt strange for Moses. It seemed as if he were voluntarily going back to prison. *This is not about me, it's about Christ and serving people.* Which was true. Still, it did not ease the burden of the reality. He pushed thoughts out of his mind of what it might have been like to be welcomed instead by taking a pastor posting in Nairobi. Big church. Big crowds.

Big budgets.

He stepped off the matatu. The unmistakable stench of the slum filled his nose. It didn't bother him. He had not forgotten his roots. The dilapidated mud and dung walls looked the same. The scrap metal roofs still looked as if the entire slum had been engulfed in a sea of rust brown. Haze from the smoke filled his field of vision. All of it looked the same. Especially the desperate expression on the faces of people, revealing the hopelessness in their hearts.

He had seen all this before.

But this time it *felt* different.

This time Moses was not a victim of the slum. He wasn't part of the tidal wave of people desperate for a way to get out. This time Moses was a servant of the slum, showing them the way to be saved.

He joined a large church in the slum. Three hundred or so attendees on a Sunday morning. He spent his evenings ministering to people. During the day, people worked at whatever jobs they could find, often having to walk long distances to their place of employment. Girls would often journey outside town to work for wealthy families who could have easily paid them triple their wages, but chose instead to take advantage of the ocean of desperate people willing to do most anything to survive. Others found ways to plug into the intricate economies of the slum, where profit margins proved to be razor-thin in an ever-changing market. What worked today might not work tomorrow.

The financial stress on families tore many of them apart. Fathers abandoned their responsibilities. Mothers struggled under the weight of depression, their minds drowning in an impossible current of accepting their sealed fate in this unforgiving slum, while hoping for some brighter future for their at-risk children.

Moses listened to their stories, absorbed their pain to ease their burden. He preached on Sunday mornings. Lived on a meager salary. So hard to rely on money from parishioners who themselves did not have anything to eat.

The people loved him. He bonded with the congregation and with many others in the community. They respected him for choosing to be among them. He preached and lived the true gospel according to the Bible.

One Sunday morning after church, Moses finished a conversation with the last person in the service. He listened with the dedicated attentiveness of a pastor. They prayed together; afterwords, the man thanked Moses for his friendship and then walked down a narrow path, grateful for the opportunity to share his burden.

Moses pulled out his keys to lock up when a young woman approached him. He recognized her as a daughter in a family from his congregation. He began to smile but stopped when he noticed tears in her eyes.

"Ayira, are you all right?"

She nodded in a way that was neither convincing to herself nor to Moses. Her demeanor indicated she wanted to deflect any hint of trouble from reaching others who might be watching. She knew there were no secrets in slums.

Her soft brown eyes yielded access to a soul filled with sadness. Her light skin, which usually offered a radiance reminding others of the brightness of the sun, now seemed to bear the marks of strain exuding from deep within.

"Can we talk?" she asked in a quiet voice that had abandoned her normal cheerful self and had been replaced with a cry so desperate that Moses had to strain to pick up her words. He nodded.

Opened the door.

They sat down at the front of the church. It felt both safe and odd to be in such a large, empty space in the midst of a slum marked by unimaginable crowds.

Ayira touched the sides of her face, resting her fingers on her high cheekbones. Her slight frame leaned forward, crushed by the weight of whatever was consuming her.

Moses waited with the patience men of God have when they wait in long silence to show they can be trusted with someone's deepest concerns.

She tried to find the right words. How to begin? It had taken so much courage to finally make her way to the church to talk to Pastor Moses. She admired him. Felt so loved by him and his wife.

Which made this all the harder.

She brushed her plaited hair back, hoping somehow to stop the accusing thoughts from consuming her mind.

You are a member of this church. A member. How dare you?

She closed her eyes as if doing so could close out the voices. But still they persisted.

You think he will care? He won't care. Not about you. He will dismiss you. No, he won't.

*No? Go ahead. Start. You will say those words, and he will bounce you out
of the church for good. You think the slums are tough? At least for now you still
have a place to call home. But let me know how it goes this evening when you
will have neither home nor church.*

The words felt louder than if someone were beside her screaming them
into her ears.

"I'm in trouble," she whispered.

Of course she was. Everyone in a slum is in trouble. But when someone in
a slum says they are in trouble, it means they are in *real* trouble.

"What kind of trouble are you in?"

She stared ahead as tears streamed down her exhausted face. She thought
back to being a little girl where an afternoon nap cleared up whatever was
ailing her. If only that could work now.

Ayira tried to gather more courage, but strength eluded her. She felt raw.
Empty. Exposed. How had it come to this? The longer she waited, the worse
she felt. Still, she kept hoping for a sudden rush of confidence that never came.

"God loves you, and you are His child, Ayira," Moses said.

She nodded. She knew that. But God felt so distant. Which made sense to
her. He wasn't the one who had moved.

She wiped tears from her eyes. Then wondered. To look at him or to avoid
eye contact? She couldn't bear to face him. She closed her eyes and covered
them with her hands.

"I'm pregnant," she whispered. Her soft words echoed in the quiet church.

Moses gave her a tissue. She thanked him.

Moses tried to remember her age. Somewhere in the high teens. Old
enough to get involved. But not old enough to be married yet.

"I am condemned," she said.

"I do not condemn you."

"You might be the only one."

"Have you shared with your parents?"

"No," she said.

"Why?"

"You know why. The outcome would not be good."

Moses knew the parents. Dysfunctional. Lots of fighting and
misunderstandings, common in all bad marriages but especially magnified
under the slum pressures of poverty, insecurity, and fear. The parents felt
overwhelmed by their circumstances and did not take the responsibility of
raising their daughter. No matter. The attention Ayira did not receive at home
was gladly fulfilled by a man in the slum who showed her too much affection.
He was now gone. But she remained. Worse off now than before.

"What is your plan?" Moses asked.

"My plan is to terminate the pregnancy."

"Abortion?"

"Yes."

A sting ripped through Moses. He thought of the thousands of children at Mully Children's Family. Thought of how many of them had mothers who had also been in this same situation.

His Bible college training came back to him. He prayed a short prayer in his mind. Then challenged her thinking.

"Do you know the risks?" he asked.

"Of the procedure?"

"You might lose your life as well. People have died having abortions. Especially in slums."

She scrunched her eyebrows trying hard to distinguish between a desperate desire to be freed from her condition and a need to accept truth.

"It's the only way forward," she whispered.

"That's what Nanjala thought, too."

It was Ayira's turn to feel a shock run down her spine. That was spooky. Had Nanjala talked to a pastor as well? Had she been told of the dangers of abortion? In her final moments on this earth, had she wished for a chance to undo things while dying at the hands of an abortion practitioner?

The thought chilled Ayira. And shook her from what she had thought was a clear path forward.

Moses evaluated the best path forward. He thought back to his studies. He needed to present to her both the medical and scriptural arguments. The challenge with only using the Bible was that she might not be on the same level spiritually as him. If he kept quoting Bible verses to her, she might not understand, and he might lose her.

She might also be angry with God for allowing this to happen, or too ashamed of what she has done to sense any connection to the word of God.

"How am I going to take care of this baby?"

"That's the right question. I will help you. And we will trust God to provide."

"Why can't I terminate?" She looked up at Moses, her eyes filled with the hope of undoing this situation. She struggled between what was and the way she wished things could be.

"God created us. And God is in charge. He does not allow us to take life."

"He makes it impossible."

"There is a way. And if you trust Him—"

"This is the end of me. I will never get out of Kibera."

"It may seem that way now. But God is working even when we can't feel Him."

She buried her face in her hands, unable to keep her head up. "Everyone is going to reject me."

She had a point. There would be no place to hide in a slum. "It is true that people will look on you as a sinner."

"The very worst of sinners," she said.

"God's love is unconditional."

"Then why do I still feel so guilty?"

"Because you have sinned."

"I know that."

"But you don't seem to know that if you repent, God will forgive you."

She sat up. A shaft of light pierced the air between them.

"He doesn't want me. Not anymore," she said.

"But He does. The Bible says, 'For God did not send His Son into the world to condemn the world, but that the world might be saved through Him,'" Moses said.

She closed her eyes and spoke in a tone that was honest and matter-of-fact. "I am sorry, God. Please forgive me."

That was it. Nothing fancy. Nothing earth-shattering. At least nothing that she could see with her eyes.

"My wife and I are in this together with you," Moses said. "And most importantly, God is with you. 'The LORD is my shepherd.' We need a shepherd at all times. When we are close and when we have drifted. And He will make something good out of this."

"Thank you."

"Can we call your parents? They need to know."

She closed her eyes as if doing so could protect her from the thought of seeing them shout insults at her. All she could do was nod.

Moses called them and asked for a meeting without giving details. The father declined. He was not a member of the church and did not want to trust Moses. The mother agreed to come.

A few minutes later, they heard a knock at the door.

CHAPTER 7

The familiar sound of the church door opening felt different this time for Ayira.

A pulse of anxiety gripped her. Like when a doctor's office door opens and someone is waiting for test results. A tidal wave of fear poured into Ayira. *I let Mom and Dad down. I let God down. I've let everyone down.* There was no escaping anymore. There would be no going back. Ayira felt the weight of reality.

Somehow when Mother comes into the room, everything becomes very clear. Her mother's face bore the stress that comes to women who have had to claw their way through the anxiety, fear, and desperation of the slum. Yes, as a young girl, she too had visions of making it out of here. And yes, she too eventually reached that point of realizing that was not going to happen for her. Still, she clung to the last glimmer of hope parents cherish when they forsake their own lives and live for the prospect that things might be different for their children.

But if her desperate and despairing eyes were any indication, the reality of failing at that last hope had become all too clear to her. Meetings at church were rarely a good thing. And a meeting where a pastor calls a mother to sit down with him and her daughter, who is of age, rarely brings tidings of great joy.

She sat down and struggled between wanting to cling to that last ray of optimism that maybe this would all turn out okay, and giving in to the crushing, unforgiving burden of life that only a slum could offer.

Ayira could not bring herself to make eye contact. She had failed. Failed miserably. She knew she represented her mother's hope, and now would have to deliver the news that the cycle of poverty would continue the way it had for generations of people in Kibera.

Ayira's mother greeted Moses. She glanced at her daughter. How many options were there about what had gone wrong here? Deep down she already knew. Mothers can tell. And now it meant decades of not only her having to wait to die in a slum, but to see that her efforts at pushing her daughter out of this mess had been totally in vain.

She had taken time to fix her hair as best she could. Put on her one nice shirt. Wore an ankle-length blue skirt. She had been slender once. But stress wreaks havoc on a body. And the years had been relentless.

"Thank you for coming, Hawi," Moses said.

She nodded, then looked to her daughter. So sullen. So fearful.

"Are you pregnant?" Hawi asked with the kind of direct candor that revealed she had neither the energy nor the time to spend on speculation.

Ayira's eyes filled with tears.

Hawi exhaled. "Rape?" she asked with enough compassion to convey that if the answer was yes it would change how she felt about Ayira.

Ayira paused. Was it forced? Either way, the situation left her with an unplanned pregnancy. Wasn't that enough to draw her mother's compassion?

"How could you do this?" Hawi shouted.

Ayira shuddered. Could the neighbours hear? Any raised voices meant problems. And the rumours would spread almost as fast as disease. *Can we please just keep this between us three? At least for now? Please, no yelling. I don't know how to make sense of this mess I am in.*

"I understand you are upset," Moses said.

She was. But she struggled to understand with whom she was upset. Was she mad at herself for not doing a better job of raising her daughter? Or had she done a good job, and it was Ayira who had gone off the rails? Or was she angry with God, who hadn't done His job of protecting Ayira? And did she feel guilty about questioning the Almighty?

"We are not here to mislead anyone," Moses said. "I will give the best path forward that will honour God. This needs to be our guiding principle. We are not here for ourselves. We are here for the honour and glory of God. We could have terminated the baby. But one way to honour God is to honour the servants of God. I am a servant of God, and I am telling you the Bible does not accept abortion. Termination is not an option. We are not in the place of God. We do not get to decide who lives and dies."

"You are from Kibera," Hawi said. "You are one of us. You know what bringing this child into the world will mean."

"Every child is born with their own blessings into this world."

Abortion was wrong. Both Hawi and Ayira knew this. At least that was their belief before this happened. Now suddenly things seemed grey. As though a subtle mist had drifted into their conscience and with such incredible ease began to shift them away from what they thought was an immovable conviction.

"It *is* an option," Hawi whispered, and then wondered who or what had said that.

Clouds rolled in to cover the sun. It felt strange for it to look and feel as dark as midnight at this time of the afternoon.

Moses considered how to proceed.

"There are consequences to abortion," he said. "You might lose your life. You may not be able to have children in the future. You will live with self-condemnation."

Hawi looked to her daughter, who still could not meet her gaze.

A memory came to Moses. "A woman came to me once and said she heard children crying. I didn't know what she meant. She explained that in her dreams and even during the day she heard voices. When I dug deeper, she admitted she'd had an abortion."

"These are scare tactics," Hawi shot back.

"They are reality. Few get to explain the heartache they experience from abortion."

Ayira buried her face in her hands. Ever since discovering she was pregnant, she had hoped for a different reality. She wasn't showing. Not yet. It isn't real until others can tell, right? Until then, she could pretend, couldn't she?

"But we already don't have enough to eat," Ayira said. She lifted her head. She looked into Moses's eyes and saw someone with whom she could be honest. "We have one meal a day. That's on a good day. How much worse will it be when I have a child? My child will be born into a poor family. It will be doomed. And being pregnant at my age will guarantee I will stay locked in this poverty."

"Do you believe God is a good Shepherd?" he asked.

"Do you believe there is always a path forward out of mistakes?" Hawi asked.

"Do you believe Almighty God is capable of making good things out of difficult situations?"

A glimmer of light crept into Hawi's and Ayira's mind. Ayira saw a possibility of a positive ending. But how to get there?

"This isn't what I wanted," Ayira said, feeling the burden of a crushed future coming down on her.

"Your pregnancy does not end things," Moses said. "It changes things. But it does not end things."

"But I could get back to what I had. I could get back on the path I was on just a few weeks ago," Ayira said.

"You could," Moses said. "But do you seek His glory or your own?"

"I want out of this slum," Ayira said. "And this child is the weight that will keep me here."

"You don't know that. You need to continue to be exposed to caring people and positive influence. My wife and I will help you. This way you can believe that a life beyond the slum can exist. We will encourage you to work hard in school. To fight for a job. This way you can break out of here."

Ayira shook her head. "There is no world beyond the slum. Not for people like me."

"I got out. So can you. We love you. Christ loves you. There are real dangers to abortion. Physical. Mental. Emotional. Especially spiritual. It is sin before God. And our God makes anything good that we have made bad. So don't give up on God. He parted the Red Sea. He can make a way for you."

They sat in silence. The mist began to evaporate.

Ayira whispered. "Do you actually believe this?"

"I do," Moses said. "I know many, many single mothers at Mully Children's Family who gave birth and went on to finish their schooling and had their family. I would not sell you an empty promise. I would not call you to walk a difficult road without being willing to walk alongside you on that road."

Ayira chose to have her baby. She had her son stay with Moses and his wife for a week. They helped Ayira and her baby boy to settle in and stayed in regular contact with them. Ayira continued with her studies.

After an evening of visiting with Hawi, Ayira, and her son, Moses returned to the church. He sat down at the front where he had sat when Ayira and her mother came to meet with him. So many people had sat in those same chairs. So much unending need.

As he felt the cool of evening, the windows allowing a breeze through the building, Moses felt the sense of purpose that comes with helping those in poverty. An overwhelming sense of gratitude poured out from him. He thanked God for raising him in Kibera, rescuing him from Kibera, and returning him to Kibera so that he could help the people of Kibera hear the gospel.

He thought back to Daddy Mulli's encouragement to become a pastor.

Moses walked out of the church.

He headed down the twisting alley to reach another family in need of help.

PART 4
RUTH

CHAPTER 1

Four-year-old Ruth gazed up at the dazzling display of stars. The shimmering lights flooded the night sky, captivating her imagination and inviting her to wonder about what existed beyond. She lay beside her mother and edged closer to her for warmth. Their tent stood empty only a few feet away. It would have offered them shelter from the chilly night in the northern Kenyan desert. But they chose to sleep outside. They had to.

This way they could hear if their enemies were sneaking up on them.

How many stars are there exactly? And how did they get there? And are there more stars out there than what we can see? They are so beautiful—

Ruth's thoughts were interrupted by a twig cracking in the distance. An eerie calm crept into her. She waited. Listened. Wondered. She didn't hear anything, but she *felt* it. Felt something—or someone—approaching.

She touched her mother's shoulder. Her mother grabbed her hand in a nervous gesture, trying without success to put her daughter at ease.

The pulse in Ruth's throat pounded so hard she felt it throb in her ears.

Will we be all right tonight? Is it safe to go to sleep?

She exhaled and only then realized how tense her shoulders had become. She focused on the stars. This time, she found it a challenge to return to her innocent world of wonder. Instead, her mind tried desperately to win the impossible game of forgetting fear.

Suddenly, the sound of a rifle shot ripped through the night. An electric shock raced through Ruth's body with such force it was as if the bullet had hit her. She froze in a cocoon of fear.

Her mother was more experienced with violence and kicked into action. She picked up Ruth. The boys woke from the commotion. She gave instructions. "Get the cattle! Let's go!"

The nomadic region of Turkana offered two items of value. Cattle and AK-47s. And not always in that order. It might have been faster for Ruth's family to leave their cattle behind and race off on foot. But without cattle, they would have nothing to bargain with and would then drop to the bottom of the world poverty scale.

Another burst of shots rang out. Screams filled the air. Ruth struggled to look through the darkness, trying to find her brothers. She heard them whispering to each other as they rounded up the cattle and hurried to catch up.

Ruth, her mother, and her two brothers ran down from their meager settlement towards a path. Her mother wrapped Ruth in a traditional scarf that held Ruth on her back.

"Run boys!" she shouted.

The entire village erupted in chaos. Multiple AK-47s exchanged gunfire. Parents shouted for their missing children. Babies cried. No electricity meant everyone was guided by the faint light of the stars for direction.

They reached the path. Which way to go? Left or right?

Gunfire seemed to be coming from everywhere. Would they be running away from the shooting? Or directly into it?

A sudden burst of gunshots nearby forced Ruth's mother to take them in the opposite direction.

"This way, boys," she whispered. She glanced back to see them struggling with the cattle.

Ruth clutched her mother's shoulders. Tears streamed down her cheeks. She tucked her head down, hoping to avoid contact with the outside world.

She bumped up and down the uneven path. The shooting and screaming intensified. People shouted instructions one moment, then were silent the next.

Ruth heard her mother's heavy breathing as she ran down the path. Forcing herself to continue, Ruth's mother missed a step in the darkness and twisted her ankle. She grunted with the pain, hobbled, and then pushed herself to get back into running form.

A loud shout rang out nearby, sending a shiver through Ruth. A man shouted, and another shot rang out.

Unable to continue, and out of breath, Ruth's mother stopped and crouched down. She pulled the boys towards her, using the cattle as shields.

The sickening racket of erratic gunfire embedded itself so deep into their souls that all they could do was sit there immobilized, shaking with uncontrollable fear.

Then, Ruth's mother wiped sweat from her forehead. "Katilo," she said. "We have to make it to Katilo."

That sounded hopeful. The village of Katilo was not that far away. But would it be far enough?

She regained control of her breathing, but not her emotions. She stuttered as she forced out her words in a barely audible whisper. "And then we have to continue on to Lokichar. To our relatives."

Not good. Not good at all. All the way to Lokichar? They were to continue running exposed in this desert all the way to Lokichar?

The boys nodded. They didn't have any other option. This was their mother. Their job was to obey. And where else would they be able to go?

The only other possibility was to stay here and wait for the attackers to reach them.

Ruth's mother found courage to lift her head back into the line of fire. She stood.

"Let's go."

Ruth bumped up and down as her mother hurried down the path. Ruth's mind played tricks on her. One moment she saw nothing but darkness. The next moment, her imagination created militia ready to shoot them. The sparse village of Katilo suddenly appeared from the darkness. Shabby huts. Sparse farms.

Mother looked for anyone who might be able to help. Finding no one, she continued on to Lokichar.

Ruth listened. Were the gunshots becoming quieter, or was it just her mind delivering on what they hoped to be true?

She looked on either side of her but was unable to see if anyone was approaching. Exhaustion from the unbearable trauma began to take over her body. She tried to keep vigilant. Tried to do her part for the family's exodus.

The shooting faded into the distance. Soon, all they heard was the shuffling of their feet.

The earliest hint of sunrise allowed them to see the town of Lokichar in the distance. Humble settlements. Small huts. Ruth peered over her mother's shoulder. It didn't look familiar. When was the last time she had been here? And would they be staying here?

Ruth rested her head against her mother's back. She looked at her two brothers. The older on the one side, the younger brother on the other. She looked back and forth to reassure her young mind that they were in fact still there.

They reached their relative's settlement. A dilapidated tent. A few underfed cows. Their presence startled an uncle who woke. His thin frame looked almost ghostlike. His eyes filled with red as evidence of his exhaustion.

"What are you doing here?" he asked, exuding all the fear a desperate man has when he may be forced to share what little he has with still more people.

"We were attacked," Mother said.

She fell to her knees, drained of strength. Taking Ruth off her back she put her on her feet beside her. Ruth hugged her mother.

"You can't stay here."

"Water," Ruth's mother said.

"Did you hear me?"

"For my children first."

"I don't think you understand."

She turned to her boys who had performed so valiantly under such pressure. "Get yourselves water. And bring some to me and your sister."

Ruth saw her mother lie down. Her eyes rolled back and closed.

Ruth nudged her. "Mother?"

"I'm all right," she said, not knowing for sure whether she was or wasn't.

The boys brought a jug of water they found near the hut.

"That comes from the river," the uncle said, implying how hard it was to bring water all that way and that it shouldn't be wasted on them.

Ruth's mother gave water to Ruth first. Ruth felt the warm liquid reach into her dry mouth and run down her throat.

The rest of the family woke. No greeting. No sense of welcome. All they offered was the look in their eyes, which revealed disappointment at their presence and the wish that these additional mouths to feed would soon be on their way.

Ruth's uncle sat down beside her mother. "There is nothing here," he said. "We ...." He paused as if trying to convince himself of what he was about to say. "We can't even feed ourselves. It's not that I don't want to help ...."

Ruth looked into her uncle's eyes. He could not return the favour.

Her mother took a drink of water from a plastic cup. "I ... I just don't know what to do," she said.

"If you stay here it is going to mean trouble. Everyone here is scared. Everyone is desperate," he said. "I don't want to make a terrible situation that much worse. You have to leave."

Leave? Leave where? Ruth couldn't think of any other place to go, except ....

"All right," Ruth's mother said. "I understand. Tell them all I understand. I will figure something out."

He approached the others, assuring them that their family visitors would soon be on their way. Blood counts. But not always that much.

Ruth studied him, wondering why her uncle could not do something to help.

The sun rose and brought the familiar scorching heat to the desert land. By the cool of the afternoon, Ruth's mother called her kids to get ready to go.

"But where, Mother?" Ruth asked. "Where are we going?"

"We're going back home," she said. "What other place do we have?"

CHAPTER 2

Ruth, her mother, and her brothers made the unpredictable return to their village near Katilo. They journeyed at night. The unbearable daytime temperatures made it impossible to travel under the unforgiving sun. Ruth's mother decided to send the brothers to join their other siblings in the Kipsongo slum located in Kitale. She agonized over the decision. Turkana offered no father, no food, no future. How desperate she had become to see the slum as a possible step up for her boys.

Ruth watched them leave down the path, wondering if she would ever see them again. She felt torn. Part of her wanted to stay with Mother. The other wanted them all to go to the slum together. Maybe that would be best. Maybe finally giving up on Turkana once and for all would be the only answer.

Ruth returned to her duty of fetching water for the cattle. Three times a week she dragged a five-litre jerrycan one hour down a beaten path to the river. Then she would push the heavy container all the way back, taking two more hours to return home.

When she saw her mother, she sensed a familiar feeling that everything was going to be all right. Ruth gave her the jerrycan.

"You have done well, Ruth," she said, looking into her young daughter's desperate eyes and wondering if hers looked as desperate. She wanted to give Ruth more. Wanted there to be something different, something better for her. But generations had come and gone in Turkana without any change. She weighed whether there was any point in believing things could be different, or if she should simply resolve herself to admitting this was as good as life would ever get.

"There's a surprise coming tonight," her mother said.

"What kind?"

A message reached the village that a film was going to be shown. The villagers gathered together under the late afternoon sun. The blistering heat of the day had smoldered out, ushering in bearable temperatures. A curious crowd gathered. Ruth sat beside her mother wondering what a film was and why people had to be together to see it.

Out of the corner of her eye, she caught an image that both shocked and amazed her. In that instant, she wasn't sure whether to be in awe or to grab her mother's arm for reassurance. She turned her gaze to focus on what she saw. Her eyes widened. Her mouth dropped open.

White people.

Who knew there was such a thing? Wasn't the whole earth filled with people who had the same skin colour as her? How did their skin get so pale? Were they really sick or did they always look this way?

They smiled as they approached the Turkana people. Ruth noticed life in their eyes that she had not seen before. A vibrancy. A hope so real it seemed *unreal.* Two members of the team set up a screen. Others set up a generator and a projector. She watched them interact with other villagers through a translator. *Why did these people come here of all places? Don't they know how dangerous this place can be?*

The sun set in classic Kenyan style, where the light changed to darkness in a matter of minutes. A projector started. An image shone onto the screen.

Ruth grabbed her mother's arm. "Mother, look," she said.

Ruth's mother smiled. "It's a movie."

"This is amazing," Ruth said, pointing to the screen. "Look, there are people."

"And you know what they say about movies?"

"No, Mother. What?"

"That you need to be quiet while watching them."

"All right," Ruth said as they both giggled.

Soon, her attention was drawn to a man named Jesus. She listened to His words, which had been translated into her language. She wondered if the people who had come with the film were also from the Jewish tribe because they looked similar to the disciples acting on screen.

She saw Jesus work miracles and wondered what it must have been like to live during a time when such things happened. She saw Him arrested and beaten and nailed to a cross. She closed her eyes, remembering the attacks on her village. When she reopened them, she saw Jesus suffering, and it occurred to her that He would understand how she had felt when they had been attacked.

After the scene of Jesus dying on the cross, Ruth felt a sense of despair. A tragic end to a story. She had come to love Him. Had come to admire Him. The Son of God. All He did was help people, and yet a group of people hated Him for it.

She took in a breath, trying to process her thoughts.

Then all of a sudden, Jesus was alive again.

Wait. Did that just happen? Did Jesus come back to life? How did He do that? Is this a real story or is it a pretend story?

"Mom," she said, breaking the rule of no talking. "Did that really happen?"

Ruth lay down under the starry sky. Without being able to necessarily explain why, she *knew* God existed. She knew in that part deep down inside that knows when it knows. And she felt convinced God loved her.

And wondered if maybe He was the One who made all those incredible stars.

She fell asleep, which, given the insecure nature of Turkana, proved to be an amazing feat in and of itself. She drifted off and journeyed to the world of dreams. She noticed people. White people. Many of them. She conversed with them without an interpreter. How was that possible? How was she able to speak English? Was this just a unique way dreams work when they override certain functions critical to life on this side?

As she talked with many of them, she found herself feeling comfortable with them. She loved being around them. White people everywhere. In fact, she could not find a Black person among them besides her.

When she woke, she found the dream mysterious. She considered it to be just that—a dream that would soon be forgotten, discarded as the leftover fragments her imagination built from seeing people with a different colour skin the night before.

But the dream did not leave her.

The arguing never stopped.

When Ruth's father finally returned, her expectations of life together with him sank faster than the Kenyan sunset. The moment he returned, she forgot about asking all the questions about where he had been and why he had left. He was back. Her dad was home. That's all that mattered.

Wasn't it?

But he proved to be a father in name only. She hoped to hear encouraging words from him. Hoped he would spend time with her. Instead, she felt as if she had evaporated into the sand. She wondered if he even noticed she was there. A sick and hurtful sense of neglect crept into her body. He would pass right by her without any comment, as if she were no more interesting to him than the merciless desert.

Ruth stood under the shade of a tree. She watched her father and mother and struggled to understand how her father could not find the energy to keep her company under the tree, and yet could find unlimited energy to argue with her mother. Lots of fighting. Arguing about the lack of food. Arguing about her not working hard enough. Arguing in endless cycles that ended neither in understanding nor forgiveness.

Ruth wanted her father beside her. It didn't matter if he did not have words of wisdom. Didn't matter if he wasn't funny. Didn't matter if he didn't know what to say. His presence alone could have accomplished a lot. And as Ruth waited under the tree, she sensed a vacancy in her heart left by her father, who did not find her valuable enough to spend even a short time with her.

Her mother approached. "We're going," she said. She carried a large bag of millet on her head and held a jug of water.

"Where?" Ruth asked as she walked with her mother. "Will we need more water?"

"We need more of everything," she said, leading them down a familiar path.

"The sun is about to set, Mother. Shouldn't we be heading home to Father?"

"We're safer walking alone in the dark than we are with him," she whispered.

Ruth followed her mother. And hoped her words would prove true.

When they reached Lokichar, her mother looked for transportation.

"Mother, where are we going?"

Her mother spoke with a man standing beside a beaten-up passenger van. He shook his head.

"Mother?" Ruth asked again. But her mother moved on to another man. This one gave her an unsettling feeling with the way his eyes ran up and down their figures. They talked briefly; then Ruth's mother shook her head and turned away.

She led Ruth across the road and found a younger man with a small build and an eager smile, wrapping a canvas over the back of his truck. As she spoke with the man, her shoulders drooped. Out of options, she handed the man her sack of millet. He motioned to the back of the truck. They stepped on and sat on wooden benches. The truck took off.

"We're leaving your father for good," Ruth's mother said. "We're going to Kitale. We're going to look for your siblings."

CHAPTER 3

Strictly speaking, Kitale is the name of an entire town. And like most towns, it included residential areas, business districts, schools, and parks ... but unlike all other towns, Kitale also offered a slum. And when the poor journeyed to Kitale, they typically weren't visiting the nice parts. They were traveling to the slum commonly known as Kipsongo.

The truck stopped. They stepped off. A rush of unbearable stench ripped into Ruth. It was unlike anything she had encountered before. The desert might be boring. And it might be unforgiving. But having nothing in the desert also meant there was little that could cause such a putrid odor. Could you get sick by taking in this awful air? She breathed in slow bursts through her mouth, hoping to avoid the smell.

The size of Kipsongo alarmed her. She looked out at the massive array of dilapidated dwellings. *How many people live here? Does everyone know everyone else? Why do they live so close together? Why is everything so dirty? Where are all the cattle? Where are the trees?*

Her mother approached people. Asked questions. She led Ruth through the unending twists and turns of the slum. Finally, she found the rest of her children.

Ruth assumed that when she met her three sisters and her two brothers that it would be a fantastic reunion. That being together again would exceed the joy she felt in Turkana viewing the dazzling stars. But when she found her siblings, she noticed how their lifeless eyes resembled stones. They looked beaten. Helpless. Exhausted.

Defeated.

And Ruth suddenly felt powerless to push back against the threatening slum walls that closed in on her.

How was this possible exactly? How could a slum be *worse* than Turkana?

Mother built a temporary shelter for them. Ruth wondered where her siblings had been sleeping all this time.

Her sisters explained that they worked as housemaids where the benefits consisted of low wages, long hours, and endless abuse. The boys survived on the street. They stole. Slept under verandahs. Ate out of garbage bins. Moved in and out of gangs for protection. All of them grateful each evening that they survived to live another day in paradise.

"We'll sleep here tonight," Ruth's mother said. But Ruth knew better. They all did. The plastic sheet propped up by scrap wood was not going to be a temporary shelter.

It would be their new home.

The sun set. A feeling of uneasiness drifted over them. During daylight hours, Ruth lived with the assumption she could see trouble approaching. But at night, the cover of darkness brought with it the insecurity that anything imaginable could erupt from the shadows.

She edged her way closer to her mother, just like she had when lying down under the Turkana sky. There were no stars tonight. None that she could see through the plastic sheet above her.

"One day at a time, Ruth," Mother said. It was early evening, but exhaustion had consumed her.

"Is there anyone we can talk to?" Ruth asked. "Anyone who will listen? Anyone who can help us?"

Ruth heard shouting in the streets. The cramped housing all around them made everyone's private life public. Secrets disappeared in a slum.

As Ruth closed her eyes, she thought back to Turkana. Thought back to the Jesus film. Thought about how He spent time with people and how much good He did for everyone.

"God?" she asked, not knowing for sure whether there was someone on the other end of the call. "Can You help me?"

The next morning, Ruth discovered she was poor.

One of the few advantages of living in the desert was that everyone everywhere displayed the same lack of material possessions. Poor is relative to what a person knows. And when everyone has nothing, everyone has the same. In this way, it is not immediately apparent to young eyes the true nature of their condition. If there is nothing to be compared to, there is no reason to feel inferior.

Slum life, however, does not have that luxury. In Turkana, Ruth's young eyes saw only endless desert filled with nothing. In Kitale, there were wealthier parts of the city within eyesight of the Kipsongo slum. And when Ruth awoke and saw how life could be, she was greeted with the life-sucking reality that she was at the bottom of the bottom.

She saw houses. Good houses with windows, doors, and roofs. And the people who lived in them? Wow. They walked in and out of their homes dressed in clothing so spectacular that her filthy rags made her feel awful and embarrassed. Cars drove by. Many of them. For the first time, Ruth sensed an *us* and a *them*.

Sure, she could cross the street. Sure, she could try knocking on the door of a house and make believe that it was possible to be in *that world*. But that place across the street was not *her world*. She didn't have access. Not real access. Didn't have the right to be there. She would be pushed away. She did not belong there. She belonged here. Money created a separation that was understood everywhere in the world, especially to a young girl coming to grips with the reality of the *haves* and *have-nots*. Lack of money would keep her right in the place where she stood.

Walls were unnecessary.

Her side featured bad roads, open sewers, pathetic housing.

And danger.

But so what? What difference did Ruth's problems make if she had no one to complain to?

This isn't fair, she thought.

And in the deep crevices in her mind, she felt a response.

Fair according to whom? You?

I don't want to live like this.

Tough.

Life can be better.

You want what they have? The ones across the street? Sorry. This is your lot in life. Accept it.

I don't want to accept it.

Then please feel free to complain. No problem. We have a complaint department. They will make a record of your complaint. And they will correct everything. Just one moment ....

That's not what I mean. I want to have someone to talk to.

I'm trying to get that complaint department for you. No one seems to be answering. Let me try again ....

I want someone to know that what I think matters.

Just be patient, the complaint department will be right with you. As soon, of course, as it gets invented.

I have no voice to defend myself.

I feel sorry for you.

Because I have no one to help me?

No, Ruth. I feel sorry for you because you still think someone cares.

Poverty forced Ruth's mind to grow quickly.

Her need to survive pushed her to look for opportunities to eat and earn money any way she could. The key was to start with anything. Try something. If it didn't work, try something else. She discovered she had to keep going. If begging didn't work, stop asking for things and do something else. Try buying and selling something. Don't quit. Don't ever give up. Staying alive proved very much to be a battle inside her mind.

Can we do some math?

Stop it. I have to focus.

How many of you street girls are there?

Many.

Exactly. And if there are many of you, and very few jobs, that means most of you won't get a job.

I can't speak for others. I can only speak—

Can you? Do you have any skills that anyone here needs? It's supply and demand. Too many street children in supply, and such little demand for you.

I can't allow myself to think that way.

To accept reality?

To give in to it.

After days of succeeding at nothing, an idea came to her. Perhaps she was going about finding a job the wrong way.

Think. Think. Think, Ruth!

She stood in the street at midday. The sweltering sun scorched down on her. She felt sweat dripping off her face. She studied people selling fruit. How often had she asked for a job? Just to get paid a little bit of money. Anything. Even the smallest ….

Wait.

For what? A miracle? That might take a very long time.

I have an idea.

Make money appear out of nowhere?

She approached a vendor at the market.

Great idea. Wow. Haven't you been turned down enough? Go! Go, Ruth! This should be fun.

"Ma'am," she said to a mother working behind a cart of fruit. Her two young children played on the ground beside her. If the woman heard her, she gave no indication that she cared.

How is it going, Ruth? What? No response. I can't understand why not.

"Please. I can help you. I can go and get customers for you."

The woman acknowledged her with a look of disgust and fear. Ruth recognized this expression in many people. Street children are dirty kids. Smelly kids. All of them are thieves of some type. Some of them are dangerous. Ruth felt an unbearable rush of humiliation run over her.

TRANSFORMATIONS

How is this feeling, Ruth?

I can't just stand here and die. I have to keep going. I have to try.

Ruth watched a customer give the woman money. That's what she needed. She needed money. She needed ....

"You can pay me in fruit," Ruth said.

The woman stopped. She looked back at her. This time they made eye contact. And for the briefest of moments, Ruth felt a connection with a human being besides her family.

"Fine. You bring me customers and I will pay you in fruit."

Ruth's hunger pushed her to set her quiet nature aside to contact passersby. She worked early mornings until late in the evening. *Sir, here is good fruit for you. Ma'am, come this way and buy your fruit.*

And it worked. New customers came to the shop. And Ruth came home bringing what little fruit she earned to share with her mother.

By the time Ruth reached six years old, both she and her mother independently reached the conclusion that the Kipsongo life was about as worthless as that in Turkana. Both places were poor in their own unique way. At least Turkana offered a glimmer of hope that perhaps moving to the city could help. Back there, they could hang on to the hope that if they made the move, perhaps things could be better. But now that they were here, now that they had really given it their best shot and failed, they were out of further options. There was no other place to look forward to.

No place that could offer them hope.

This desperation caused the imaginary walls of the slum to completely hem them in.

They never had time to talk. No money for schooling for Ruth. Her mother found a new hobby: drinking illicit brew of *busa* and *changa'a*. Mother became drunk to let herself deal with the challenges of life without having to feel how much life hurt.

The alcohol did wonders for her when she was drunk. But when she was sober, she realized she had fallen even lower than before. None of this was helping. Of course, it wouldn't. But she had started the inevitable spiral down, down, down. And within weeks she became a different person. Shouting. Cursing. Blaming.

The crushing weight of slum life left her with little reason for hope and no means of help.

In the chill of the evening, Ruth left their upgraded yet still meager hut made of scrap metal to go nowhere and do nothing. She walked barefoot in the dirty streets, her feet as calloused as her heart.

I'm poor and I'm nothing. This is never going to change.

She looked up at the stars. They never did look quite as bright here as they did back in Turkana.

I shouldn't be living. This all feels so very wrong. I don't have any purpose. Nothing is working.

She thought back to the Jesus film. *He did all those miracles for others. What about me? Can Jesus do a miracle for me?*

She remembered the scenes of the crowds around him. *All those people talked with Him. He seemed so friendly. Why can't I talk to God, too?*

She heard voices approaching. Time to head in for the night.

Ruth entered their hut. Mother was either asleep or passed out. Ruth lay down.

I want to disappear. I don't want to suffer anymore. I have no future. I have no voice.

But unbeknownst to her, as she drifted off, life was about to take a curious turn.

CHAPTER 4

Nothing travels quite so fast in a slum as news.

Ruth observed how poverty connected people. Their need for one another created interdependency. And these networks proved invaluable for the transfer of information.

The other street children referred to him as Mzee Mulli, *Mzee* being a term of honour used to describe someone older. The whole idea of Mzee Mulli seemed too fantastic to be true. Ruth should have scoffed at the idea of a man who gave up his wealthy lifestyle to help poor children. Would someone actually do that?

Sure, she *wanted* someone like that to exist. But what about that place called *reality*? Was it reasonable to believe someone like Mzee Mulli could exist in the real world?

Even though slum people lived in poverty, Ruth believed they possessed a wealth of human perception. Living so close to the edge of existence forced people to avoid the luxury of naivete. People couldn't afford to be gullible. So when Ruth heard her friend speaking about Mzee Mulli, something deep inside her perceived him to be real.

"He rescues children. And they become successful," her friend Mary said as they walked down a typically crowded street on an untypical day.

"How do you mean, successful?" Ruth asked. She eyed the fruit market stand, knowing she needed to get back to work.

"Some learn a trade. Others go to Uni. People leave MCF with real skills," Mary said. Her friendly attitude never suffered, even in slum life.

Ruth admired the transformation from nothing to something. Without being able to explain it, she sensed a connection with a man she had not met. She wondered if change could happen for her.

"I need to see that man," Ruth said.

"He's been to Kitale before."

"Kipsongo?"

"Yes, of course Kipsongo," Mary said. Her short frame bounced in between the potholes on the street as if she were playing a game.

"Is he coming back?"

"Yes."

"When?"

"Tomorrow."

They hurried to the open area where rumours indicated Mulli would arrive. With each step, Ruth felt increasing confidence that if she could only meet him, it would be enough to be chosen by him. Her whole lineage, as far back as she knew on both sides, lived the same life of poverty. Maybe this would be it.

Maybe she would be the first out.

If I can be better, if I can get out, I can help my siblings and mother.

Ruth and Mary waited in what might be referred to as a slum park. Garbage lay strewn all over. Broken benches served as seats. Ruth noticed a blue pickup truck arriving. A white bus followed behind. It came to a stop near them. Children from the slum crowded around.

She watched the bus for any sign of the man known as Mulli.

"Mulli! Mulli!" children shouted. She turned her attention. It surprised her when she saw children crowding around a smiling, quiet, humble man stepping out of the blue pickup. Although she was seeing him for the first time, Ruth had the strangest sense that she knew him.

He brought milk, juice, and bread. The children grabbed the clean food with their dirty hands and devoured it. Youth from Mully Children's Family helped to give out food. Ruth received hers and took a bite. Oh, that tasted good. Not from a garbage can. Not leftovers from who-knows-where. She observed the MCF people. Kind. Sharp dressed. Clean. Speaking with courage and compassion.

They mirrored what she hoped to become.

Mulli organized his children into a choir. Ruth felt power and love in their singing. Crisp, clean high notes. Booming low notes. They all looked so … alive.

A youth from the choir stepped forward. The vibrancy of her beautiful orange and yellow dress matched that of her expression. She spoke in a soft voice that reached those assembled.

"I was once in the street using drugs," she said.

As if. I wouldn't believe a word of it. No offence, but she doesn't look anything like you.

"I had no hope in life," she continued.

I hate to bring math into this again. But look around. Can you even count the number of kids? This man is a lottery ticket. And they've all shown up hoping Santa is going to take them up in his sleigh.

He's the man for me.

Is he?

He is.

It's not for you to say. It's a question of probability. So many children. So few get chosen.

"When I met Daddy Mulli and Mamma Esther, I felt fatherly and motherly love."

The words *Daddy* and *Mamma* reached into Ruth, touching the part of her heart that craved those words to become true for her. Yes, her mother loved her and tried hard. But not once in her life had she experienced both parents talking with her or showing her any kind of love in solidarity. And now, with Mother riding the alcohol train to Doomsville, she wondered if she even had one parent.

"I received all my basic needs. I never have to worry about where to get food. I was introduced to God, who changed me entirely. And now, I am living in a good environment. Daddy is very good to me. He is a man of his word. And he is a man of incredible love."

Ruth admired the girl's words about Mulli, thinking that nothing speaks so much of someone as what someone else says about them.

Mulli finished the program by giving thanks to God. He and his team distributed still more food to over two hundred children, who received it with desperate hands. As Ruth stood in line, she watched the bread and the drinks being passed out to the mass of children. It reminded her of the scene in the Jesus film where Christ prayed and the five loaves and two fish offered by a young boy were multiplied miraculously to feed the crowd. She watched Mulli. Studied him. Felt captivated by him. There *was* something different about him.

Ruth accepted her food from Mulli. She was about to ask to go with him, but the crowd of children pressed in against her, anxious for their meal. Ruth sat down with others. But as soon as she started eating, she heard a commotion. She looked up.

Mulli started choosing children.

Pick me! Pick me! Pick me!

Ruth's eyes grew wide. She focused on Mulli. She felt hope flood her soul.

He's coming for me!

He drew closer.

This is it! I'm getting out of here!

He came right near her.

And then he passed by.

Mulli gathered the children he had chosen and placed them in the back of his blue pickup.

Such is life. You win some, you lose some. Oh well. Back to the slum for you.

This isn't fair.

It's not about being fair, Ruth. It's about not having enough place for you. I don't mean to downgrade you, but seriously, why would he pick you?

Is it because I am dirty?

Probably.

Or is it because I am bad.

More likely.

I want to go with him.

So does everyone. But some have to stay. Time to grow up. We can't all get what we want. You received food. That's something, isn't it? Maybe it's time to be thankful.

A rush of emotion ripped through Ruth. From deep within her erupted uncontrollable crying.

And her cries reached Mulli's ears.

Mulli returned.

He crouched down.

"Little child, don't cry. I will come for you another day."

Sure he will. Another day means never. It means—you're not wanted.

No. I believe him. He will come for me. But when? When will that be? Will I even live to see that day? I am in the slum. There are no guarantees in life, much less in this pit.

Mulli was about to turn. And he would have left, had it not been for the older street children.

Three of the boys approached Mulli. Their sickly, yellow eyes served as evidence of their oppression. They gave off a strong scent of glue.

"You have to take her," one of the boys said. He was fourteen. But his diet of rotten food and drugs stunted his growth and made him look closer to ten. "She's small," he said. "And young."

Mulli understood the code. Young girls don't last long. And when they become of age, the slums are even worse. Often unimaginable.

Ruth wrapped her arms around Mulli's leg.

This is it. I have to be taken now.

Always such drama. He told you he would come back. Let go of him and stop embarrassing yourself.

I am vulnerable and without hope. Pick me! Pick me!

Mulli bent down.

Ruth looked through a flood of tears. They distorted the image of man in front of her.

"Hello," Mulli said.

Suddenly, like that storm Jesus calmed in the movie, a hush came over her. The desperation inside her vanished, replaced with a sense of calm. She blinked. Mulli came into view.

She had nothing to offer. Nothing with which she could make herself worth rescuing. She looked at him with eyes desperate and incapable of self-rescue. At his mercy.

Mulli touched her shoulder. And for the briefest moment, Ruth saw in Mulli's eyes what appeared to be a reflection of herself. He gave such a slight nod that only Ruth could see it. They looked into one another, each recognizing something in the other.

"All right," he whispered. "Let's go."

Mulli picked her up. A smile broke out from Ruth's heart.

I'm going!

She hugged him. Up ahead she saw the blue truck. Saw the other children cramming into the back. She sat down at the edge of the bench. Mulli started the engine. As it took off, she looked back at the boys who had stood up for her. They could have used that opportunity to bargain for their own release from captivity. But they had stood in the gap for her. She watched as they disappeared.

The truck bounced up and down. The children laughed. She heard them giggling and found herself doing the same. It felt both new and wonderful.

Is this what joy feels like?

The truck took a turn. The kids laughed as the momentum caused them to press into each other. It slowed down. Ruth gazed ahead. She saw a black, metal gate. Behind it stood a massive house—far bigger even than the ones she saw from the slum. A young man with a smile and joy that exuded through his eyes opened the gate. The truck drove through.

"Hello children!" the man said.

The truck stopped. Mulli stepped out. He came around to the back.

"Welcome to Mully Children's Family."

CHAPTER 5

Mulli led Ruth and the other newly rescued children to the backyard. As Ruth rounded the corner, she saw a woman's eyes light up. The woman opened her arms and laughed as she approached. She hugged each child with the kind of warm embrace that implied both strength and gentleness.

"Welcome to each of you!" she said.

Ruth sensed the woman's joy as she wrapped her arms around her. It caused Ruth to wonder: *Doesn't it bother her that none of us have bathed? That we come directly from the streets? Does she know how dirty we are?*

"This is your new home," she said. "And I am Mamma Esther. Your new mother."

Ruth gazed at her with admiration and sensed that unique mother-child connection that comes with belonging.

"God loves you. Your father and I love you. Whenever you need something, you can ask your dad or me. We are your parents. And we are here to take care of you."

Ruth believed her.

Esther smiled and laughed with a peaceful honesty that reached into Ruth, convincing her that her old life was gone and that a new journey had begun.

Esther led the girls to their dormitory. Ruth experienced a warm shower for the first time ever. She changed into clean clothes. Smelled their freshness. *Wow. Incredible how good* normal *can be*. Ruth felt her problems wash away. She felt calm. Good. In such a short time, she adjusted to a world of love and optimism.

Ruth and the new children ate a special flat pancake called *chapati* along with potatoes and meat. Each bite tasted amazing and safe. Ruth ate more in one day than in the previous week. She had eaten meat before, but it normally came from leftovers found in garbage cans. This time, food had been cooked fresh for her. She loved it.

And she could eat as much as she wanted.

She giggled with the other children. How interesting to sit down with strangers who moments later felt like family. When she finished eating, she sensed the comfort that came with being able to relax. The constant anxiety of having to search for food was over.

Her dorm captain led Ruth towards her dormitory for the night. She glanced up at the stars as she walked down the path. They looked brighter now, like when she was a little girl, unaware of what life could give and take. She gazed in wonder at everything around her. Mulli's backyard had been transformed into a network of schools, washing facilities and dormitories. Boys on one side of the yard. Girls on the other. She felt herself thinking about what life could be like down the road. With her thoughts released from the all-consuming shackles of having to search for food, shelter, and safety, Ruth discovered the freedom of a clear mind.

She could think. She could imagine. She could explore places she had never been.

Ruth was shown her bunk bed. The other girls had already fallen asleep. Ruth lay down. A wave of peace poured over her. She drifted off without any fear. No fear of who might barge in. No fear of what tomorrow might bring. No worry of having to scrounge the garbage bins for food.

She let go of the defence mechanisms she needed for survival in the slum.

Ruth felt the pillow under her head. The warm blanket around her.

And the comfort of loving people who had nothing to gain from her arrival.

For a shy person, Ruth found it surprisingly easy to enjoy the company of her new brothers and sisters. Her family felt natural. She learned well in school. Felt at home with MCF life. And she loved guests.

Many visitors came from all over, including outside Africa. Ruth enjoyed meeting a young man with blue eyes. When he left, she recalled her dream. White people gathered all around her. And she wondered if there was more to be understood.

Ruth felt especially loved by a woman with red hair who gave her big hugs and conveyed deep acceptance. It impacted young Ruth to think how people on the other side of the world would come all this way to love them. And she found it all the more interesting how people on that side spoke of loving the same Jesus as Daddy Mulli.

Ruth hurried outside after the last class of the day with the other children. She caught up with a group who took turns skipping. They sang songs as they clapped. When Ruth finished her turn, she sat down under a tree, trying to catch her breath.

"You are doing very well," Mulli said.

Ruth looked up. The world always felt right around Daddy Mulli.

"Thank you, Daddy."

"Would you like to join me?" he said, pointing to a nearby outdoor table.

She nodded and sat down opposite him. She felt the warmth of the sun. The sound of children laughing. The affectionate compassion of her father's presence.

Esther brought them each a glass of water.

"Thank you, Mamma," Ruth said.

"And me, too," Mulli said, turning to Esther. "Me, I am very grateful. Wow. A nice glass of water on a hot day like today. I have a good wife. The very best. In the whole world. Oh yes. I know."

Mulli laughed. Esther smiled as she returned to the kitchen.

"And how are you, Ruth?" Mulli asked.

"I am fine, Daddy."

He took a drink of his water.

"How is your water, Ruth? Is it too cold?"

She took a sip. "It is good."

"Very good. And the sun, you are out of the shade? Not too hot?"

"Not too hot," she said.

"Great," Mulli said. "I want to encourage you, Ruth. God makes each of us in a unique way. You see how many leaves there are in the tree above us? There are many."

Ruth gazed up at the tree. It seemed there were as many leaves on the tree as stars in the sky at night.

"No two leaves are the same. God took time to plan you and create you. And you may think to yourself—'I am a quiet person. I am not someone to speak. Not someone to talk. I am shy. I will just stay in the background.'"

How did he know that? She had not shared this with anyone. Yet somehow, he had access to her hidden thoughts and fears.

She nodded, wondering how he discerned what was going on inside her mind.

"Expressing yourself is a God-given gift. We give testimony not about ourselves, but about God who made us. He will enable you to share from your heart. And you have a beautiful heart."

"Thank you."

"I think you like to sing."

Ruth smiled. She nodded.

"And I think you like to dance as well."

An even bigger smile.

"You are already singing in a choir. But one day you will be sharing your story with other people."

That seemed a step too far. Singing in a choir and dancing in a group offered the comfort of being with others. But talking to a crowd by herself? That seemed out of reach.

"Jesus was only twelve years old when He sat with wise men. A young boy in the Bible offered his lunch, which Jesus used to feed five thousand men, plus women and children. Jesus also said, 'Let the little children come to me.' God is also at work in you. He has many plans He wants to fulfill in you. But you need to respond to Him."

She nodded, though she was not entirely sure exactly what Daddy was referring to.

But you need to respond to Him.

What did Daddy Mulli mean by that?

The friendly young man who greeted children at the black entrance gate rose to become in charge of the entire MCF Eldoret branch. Mr. Tom led evening devotionals for the children. And whenever he spoke, the children listened with complete amazement.

Ruth gathered with other children under the canopy of the night sky. Mr. Tom held his Bible out and stood in front the crowd of children. His soft voice had the uncanny ability to carry clean to the last row.

"Jesus was born in Bethlehem to Mary and Joseph. He was born with a mission to save us. Jesus was born to die for your sins and for mine."

Ruth thought back to the Jesus film she saw in Turkana. She recalled the scene of Jesus being born. Of Jesus being beaten.

"God loves you. He wants to be your heavenly Father. But we are separated from God by our sins."

Despite the incredible change Ruth experienced in her circumstances from living in the slum to living here at MCF, she felt something missing. All the pieces seemed to be here. But they pointed at something greater. Something Daddy, Mamma, Mr. Tom, and others possessed. Something she wanted.

"What is sin?" Mr. Tom asked. "God created the world in six days. The first people He created were Adam and Eve. Male and female He created them. All of us on earth are descendants of Adam and Eve. They sinned by disobeying God. Since then, sin entered into each one of us. We are born separated from God.

"The Bible tells us that each of us have sinned. Every bad thing we have done, every bad thought we have had. Sometimes people say what they do or think is not that bad." Mr. Tom lifted up his Bible. "But God's Word is settled in heaven. It does not change. And it tells us what is true and what is false. And that has not changed since it was written."

Ruth imagined herself reading the Bible herself one day. She imagined learning English and Swahili well enough that she could read her Bible every day the way she saw Daddy Mulli reading it.

"Jesus is the Son of God, and He *is* God. And Jesus died on the cross for your sins."

The image of Jesus hanging on the cross made sense to Ruth now. He was suffering for her. For everyone.

"The Bible says none of us has done enough good to reach God. But Jesus's death and resurrection makes it possible for us to come to God. We cannot do this on our own. Jesus is the only One who can bring us into a relationship with God so that we can have everlasting life. By confessing your sin, by putting your trust only in Jesus, by believing that God raised Him from the dead, you can be born again and have eternal life. And you can speak with God."

That shocked Ruth. Speak with God? She considered it an honour whenever she could meet with Daddy Mulli. To talk with him. Listen to him. But Almighty God? Could a girl from the slum really talk to Him?

Moreover, would God actually listen?

Would He do that?

Would He *want* to?

The devotion ended with a song, and Mr. Tom dismissed them for the night.

But for Ruth, the evening was far from over.

Ruth walked back with the others, glancing up occasionally at the spectacle of stars. The more she looked, the more she saw. They entered her dormitory. The other girls giggled and talked the way Ruth did on other nights. The lights turned off. Everything became quiet.

She lay in the stillness of the night. Thinking. Wondering.

God, if You really love me that much—if You love me so much to create me, to have Jesus die for me—then why shouldn't I love You back? Is this life about me? Or is it actually about You?

She thought about the many challenges she experienced in Turkana and in the slum of Kipsongo. She thought back to when she clung to Mulli's leg, begging him to take her. And now, she found herself in Jesus's presence, hoping for Him to take her.

I want to love You back, Jesus. I always wanted a family down here on earth. And You gave that to me. I am part of the biggest family in the world. But I want to be part of Your family. To be Your child. I was not able to get myself out of a slum. And I am not able to get myself saved.

A voice interrupted her prayer.

Here we go again. More drama. You are doing just fine. Focus on your education.

It's not enough. What is education and success without using it to serve God?

You want to serve God? Work harder at doing what is right. You can't come to God until you have your life together. Fair is fair. He died for you. You clean yourself up. Then come to God.

But Jesus said, "Let the little children come to Me." He did not put a requirement on them to come a certain way.

You must be obedient first. And once you are good, you can come to God.

Was I cleaned up before Daddy Mulli came to get me? Were the disciples whom Jesus chose all cleaned up before He called them?

Ruth rolled over on her bed to lie face down. She folded her hands. That other voice disappeared. Everything became still.

God, You made the stars. You made me. You love me. I am a sinner. I ask You to forgive me because of Jesus's death on the cross. I put my trust in You only for my whole life. I ask You to make me Your child. Help me to serve You and follow You.

That was it. The heavens didn't open. Not that she could see. Ruth rolled back over on her side. She closed her eyes. Began to drift off.

And wondered what her new life would bring.

CHAPTER 6

Ruth transferred to MCF Ndalani. The large property gave her freedom to explore. To meet new siblings.

"What's your name?" Ruth asked, sitting under a tree during recess next to a quiet girl with a smile so big it made Ruth feel good inside.

"My name is Hannah," the girl replied.

"And what kinds of giftings do you have?"

"I love to sing."

"Really? Me too. What kinds of songs?"

"Anything about God. About His love for me. What about you?"

"I love sports. All kinds of activity," Ruth said. As she shared about her life, she sensed Hannah's compassion and admired Hannah's ability to listen with her heart.

In such a short moment, they bonded the way best friends do.

"Have you thought of karate?" Hannah asked.

Mulli walked with Ruth from the schoolhouse down the crowded path towards the dining area. Children greeted him with an enthusiastic *Hi, Daddy* as they hurried past. They sat down at table under the shade of the trees.

"You are doing very well in school," Mulli said. "I spoke with your teachers, and they say you are excelling. I want to congratulate you on a job well done. You are also singing so well. And you have been gifted in sports."

"That is why I wanted to talk to you," Ruth said. "I am wondering if I could take part in the MCF karate program."

"Of course," Mulli said. He replied so quickly it made Ruth wonder if he had read her mind. "I support you in pursuing karate. I will speak with Frederick and let him know to expect you in his karate class."

"Thank you, Daddy," Ruth said, her smile growing almost as wide as Hannah's.

"Karate is for self-defence. Not for aggression. You never prove anything by attacking anyone. But you know the world we live in. It can be dangerous.

And I think it is very good for you to learn. Remember that karate, like anything else, takes focus and determination. Nothing in life comes easy. When you train, you must train with absolute attention. If you are attentive in one thing in life, it will impact other areas of your life. But if you are lazy in one area of your life, it will bring down the other areas."

"I will train hard."

And she did. Early in the morning. After school. On weekends. Ruth committed herself to learn how to punch, kick, and defend. Frederick had taught dancing and singing in Eldoret and added karate to his skills at Ndalani.

"Train hard, win easy," Frederick said from the front of the class to his karate students. "How you train is how you will fight. If you are not prepared here, you will not rise to the occasion on the mat or in a street fight. If you dedicate yourself here—if you fight as if your life or the life of someone in trouble depended on it—you will be ready when called into battle."

Ruth balanced on the front of her feet. She formed her hands into fists. Her eyes focused ahead on an imaginary opponent. Frederick called out a kick, shouted, and the students followed with that kick and gave a loud shout.

"Whenever you are tired, keep going. The results will be good if you do not quit."

MCF appointed Ruth to the karate team that would fight in tournaments. Competitors initially thought rescued street children would pose no threat. But they discovered that former street children had an incredible drive to survive. Their history in the slum did not afford them the luxury of *wanting* to win. They *had* to win in life. And this mentality catapulted MCF to the top rankings.

Ruth performed so well that she was selected to try out for the Kenyan National Team.

"It is a great honour," Mulli said as they sat down in the dining area.

Mamma Esther brought them a cup of tea. "We are very proud of you," she said.

Their words reached into her the way they always did. Ruth felt like crying. Hearing affirming words from her parents meant more to her than any medal. She thought back to Turkana. To her father who was not around when they were attacked. And when he was home, he didn't even offer Ruth the courtesy of talking with her. Yet here at MCF, with the stars shimmering above, she felt a much-needed stamp of approval on her life. Such simple words, spoken by her parents, gave her unlimited courage.

"Do your very best. Don't hold back. Be strong. Have confidence. God has given you strength to do karate," Mulli said. "He is in control of everything in your life."

Ruth arrived at the tournament. She looked out at the massive gym. Girls practising. This was it. This was nationals. Six girls would compete in her weight category for two spots on the Kenyan team. She would fight each person once. The two with the most points at the end of the tournament would earn the right to represent Kenya.

Ruth studied the other girls shadow-fighting in preparation for their matches. She wondered how tough they were.

Wondered if she was tougher.

She changed into her uniform. Ran through her training exercises. Ready to go.

She heard her name called. Adjusting her uniform, she took her place on the mat. She studied the eyes of her opponent and noticed fear. It surprised Ruth. She felt no anxiety herself. Why would she? This wasn't Turkana. There were no AK-47 bullets flying around her head. There was no one threatening her life. This was a controlled fight. With protective equipment. There was a referee.

What was there to be scared of?

The referee shouted for them to begin. Her opponent started with a terrible mistake by backing up. A sure sign of apprehension. Ruth shuffled her feet to switch her stance. She faked with a punch. Her opponent backed up yet again. Ruth drove a fast kick to her sternum. It caught her opponent off guard. Ruth won her first point.

With the bravery and strength of a lion, Ruth went on to win all three matches in the first day of competition.

She faced three more opponents the second day. She beat the first two girls and tied her last match. Her last opponent won on overall tournament points. Ruth finished second, guaranteeing her a spot on the Kenyan National Karate Team.

She sat in the passenger seat as her coach drove her and the team back to MCF. She thought back to being in the slum. To grabbing onto Mulli's leg, begging him to rescue her. From the slum to the highest level in her country.

Wait until Daddy finds out.

The thrill of representing Kenya proved to be more than Ruth could imagine. She stood with her Kenyan team at the East Africa Karate tournament. She touched the black, red, green, and white Kenyan flag on her uniform. Red represented the fight for independence. Black signified the people. Green for the beautiful landscape. White for peace. And the Maasai shield stood for defence. A deep sense of honour and pride filled her heart. She said a short prayer, dedicating the matches to God. Then, the rescued street child who once fought for her life by eating out of garbage cans stepped onto the mat to fight for her country.

As she expected, competition proved tougher at this level. Opponents moved faster. Kicked harder. And attacked liked their lives depended on it. If they had any fear, they certainly knew how to control it. But Ruth was equal to the task. Even as a mild-mannered, quiet person, she drew incredible strength from a reservoir of training. As the tournament progressed, the matches grew intense. She felt the impacts of their strikes. Felt the initial hints of getting tired. The words of her coach echoed in her mind. *Whenever you are tired, keep going. The results will be good if you don't quit.*

She found herself fighting against her opponents in the tournament, and against the one in her mind.

You did good. Look how far you have come. But this is enough.

I have to keep going.

For what purpose? You've made it from the streets all the way here. Impressive. You can't go further. You've met your match. So don't bother trying.

I am required to do my best.

Against these girls? This is real competition. You can't make it further. No one will blame you if you don't do well.

Ruth shook her head. *I will do my best right to the end.*

And risk getting hurt? You've seen these girls. They're rough.

They are nothing like the people of Turkana.

Their kicks will damage you. You don't want to give all this effort and risk getting humiliated.

I was humiliated living in the streets. No more. God has prepared me for this.

She forced her mind to concentrate. She pushed out the negative thoughts. And went on to win bronze for Kenya.

The Kenyan Olympic Committee selected Ruth to be a training partner for those participating at the Tokyo Olympics. But due to a visa issue, she was not able to compete. She felt no anxiety or anger. She had not built her identity on whether she would succeed at such a high level. Instead, she joined Mulli by the Thika River.

"You have done very well, Ruth." Mulli motioned to a chair. Ruth sat down and looked with eyes of admiration into her father. "You have many gifts and abilities God has given you to prepare you for the road ahead," he said. "I would like to speak with you about your future.

"Do you remember when I first met you?" Mulli asked.

She did. Powerful moments stay etched in a person's mind. In an instant, Ruth felt transported back into the slum. Desperate. Fearful. Without hope.

"I remember how much I wanted you would pick me," she said.

"But I began to leave."

"And I began to cry."

"I came back for you."

"You did."

"But it was not about me. It was not even about the street boys who stood up for you and strongly encouraged me to come for you. It was all about God's plan for us to meet at that time. I became your father. You cried out of desperation. And I trust you know you can always come to me as your earthly father. But more importantly, that you can always cry out to your heavenly Father."

"I am convinced He will hear me."

Birds chirped in the trees, offering a symphony of African natural music.

"Always remember where you came from. Your story shapes you. Your past is not an accident."

Without realizing, Ruth leaned in closer. Drawn in by Mulli's ability to speak into her.

"My happiness is seeing you progress and become a successful person. That starts with understanding God has His hand on your life. As you look into your life, into your heart, what has God placed there? What is important to you?"

Ruth thought of Turkana. Thought of the raids. Thought of the slum. Her struggles in the streets. The unbearable poverty. Ongoing suffering without any voice. Without anyone to help her. Until God brought Mulli.

"Human rights," she said.

"And when you say *human rights*, what do you mean?"

"The right to be heard. The right for children to have food, safety, love, and the opportunity to pursue their talents. And to enjoy them, no matter their tribe, colour, or race.

"And why do human rights matter? Where do human rights come from?"

"From God."

Mulli pressed his lips together as a sign that he agreed. He paused with his trademark patience to ensure that his child had finished everything she wanted to say. They waited in the comfort of silence, neither feeling the pressure to fill the space in their conversation. When Mulli was sure both of them had the chance to absorb each other's points, he continued.

"When God created all things, He created the human being. The Trinity took their time to make sure everything stood in the correct order. We are special to God. He is the one who gives us life. Life is more valuable when people take care of it. We need to provide protection of human rights. You understand what it means *not* to have those rights. And this gives you compassion for people—the same way I have compassion for children who don't have love. The pains of our past make us uniquely fitted to help those who are where we once were."

"I understand, Daddy," Ruth responded. His words stirred within her the thought of the apparent paradox of how a loving God allows tragedy and yet, in His providence, offers the opportunity for people to choose to trust Him to make something out of past experiences.

"The love of Jesus is for all of us," Mulli went on. "He died on the cross for everyone. And in His love, we need to help our fellow human being. Not just those who are of the same tribe or mindset as us. We are here to serve humankind. If we lose this love for others, the result is that children are left orphaned, and women are hurt. But as we serve others in the name of Christ, people will be drawn to Him. And we will fulfill our purpose on this earth."

CHAPTER 7

A friend from overseas sponsored Ruth to complete her degree in Kenya in international relations and security studies with a minor in business administration. She marvelled at their generosity. She wanted to continue studying by pursuing her master's in human rights. It would make her that much more competitive in an overly competitive Kenyan job market.

In the slum, she knew only begging. But after seeing God work so many times at MCF, she learned she could pray.

I know, God, that You have a good plan for me. You can convince a university to accept me. And You can make the funding possible.

In spite of the many victories she had seen, she sensed a stubborn resistance attacking her faith.

You expect too much. Why would God give you funding for your master's when that money could be better used to give someone else the chance for their bachelor's degree?

It is on my heart to learn more.

At the expense of someone else not having their chance? That hardly seems fair. Does God not want you to share?

If this dream were not from God, would I be pursuing it?

And you know for certain it is from God?

Ruth quieted her heart before God. The account in the Bible of the people of Israel coming up against the Red Sea came to mind. She recalled how God sent Moses to deliver Israel out of Egypt to the Promised Land. But on their journey, they became stranded. The impossible Red Sea stood in front of them. The unrelenting Egyptian army closed in behind them. The Israelites regretted their decision and accused Moses of bringing them out of Egypt only to have them die in the desert. But God opened a way for them. And Ruth recalled the many times God made a way for her. Out of the slum. Into MCF. To join the Kenyan national karate team. To complete her bachelor's degree. Would He not continue to lead and guide her? Still, being able to study for her master's seemed far off.

A medical team visited MCF. Ironically, the team included a member who had met Ruth at MCF Eldoret some twenty years earlier. Another member of the team was drawn in as Ruth shared her testimony and her desire to further her studies.

That evening, Ruth listened to Swahili gospel music at her home at MCF. She received a phone call.

"Hello, Daddy," Ruth said.

"Can you come to my office in the next five minutes?"

"Of course."

Ruth ran from her home. She was used to running. She ran fifty minutes each morning from MCF Ndalani to Kisiki and back. So many thoughts raced through her mind that the five-minute run to Mulli's outdoor office near the flagpoles seemed longer than it was.

When she arrived, she was neither out of breath nor had a racing pulse.

"We really need to thank God," Mulli said.

"Why?" Ruth asked.

"Because God has answered your prayers. There is a visitor who heard your story about needing fees for your postgrad. This visitor has agreed to pay all your expenses."

A sudden rush of amazement came over Ruth. Her hand flew to cover her mouth. Tears streamed down her face.

Mulli smiled. He folded his hands and rested his elbows on the table. "You will become a great person," he said, as if looking past her and into the future. "You will make a difference in the country. Not just in Turkana, but in Kenya and around the world."

Ruth wondered what he saw.

Wondered what would become of her life.

Wondered about her incredible responsibility to use her gifts to serve others.

PART 5
MUCHOKI

CHAPTER 1

The forest town of Timboroa lies along the equator, marking the highest habitable point in the Kenyan highlands. The lush bamboo trees stretch out far into the horizon, giving the false impression people living here fare as well as the surrounding greenery. Poverty at this elevation is as common as leaves. People struggle at every level, and many eventually run out of options trying to deal with the scarcity of food. They are forced to evaluate trading the advantages of cleaner air and relative security against a move to the slum in Eldoret, with all its danger, for a better chance at survival.

It proves to be an unwelcome decision.

On the one side, a family can stay at the higher altitude where they will be safe but will likely starve. On the other side, they can increase their odds of finding food in a slum but take on the added risk of physical and emotional harm by disease or violence.

Hunger becomes the deciding factor. And families often take their chances in the slum.

Such was the case for five-year-old Muchoki.

Painful nights going to bed without food dragged on for days. His small frame grew thinner. Anxiety consumed his parents, filling their desperate eyes with bewilderment and fear. It seeped out of them like the morning mist and infected their four children. Fear reached into Muchoki and filled his mind, stressing him with worry about how long his family would last. They came to the realization that there would be no improvement here. The best they could hope for was to hang on as long as they could. But was this living? Was it better to accept this reality or to take a risk for something better?

His father and mother gambled on moving to Langas slum in Eldoret, hoping that perhaps they might beat the unlikely odds of victory and have their number come up.

The first sight of Langas slum sent a shock through young Muchoki. So many people. The crowds bustling in all directions, exceeded anything he had ever imagined. Muchoki squeezed his mother's hand tighter as they entered the slum. They negotiated the narrow, dusty road under the unforgiving African sun.

The hardened, strained expressions on people's faces revealed lives filled with stress. Muchoki felt their concern. Felt their fear. Descending from the thinner, lighter air of the highlands caused him to enter a world where the weight of problems became that much more unbearable.

He wondered why his family had bothered to make this move.

They settled into a house of sorts. A rusted corrugated metal roof. Mud and dung walls. Mud floor. Cramped. His father told them to never walk alone. And gave strict instructions not to leave the house after dark.

No exceptions.

His father walked out the door. The family stayed in silence, feeling the strange new reality of not being free to walk about as they had before. Their one-room accommodation felt increasingly warm. Muchoki wondered: *Is this any better? Can this become any better?*

His father returned with supper. They ate a meager meal of beans and rice. It was something. It was a start.

But a start of what?

The sun set, ushering in an unpredictable darkness. Even though Muchoki had often gone to bed hungry in the highlands, he never worried about his safety when he laid down his head. Never wondered if something might happen to him while he slept.

But he did now. Many things ran unchecked through his mind. His mother told him his fears resulted from his overactive imagination. But this time felt different.

This time, his fears felt justified.

Muchoki had the unshakeable feeling that his fears in a place like this had more power to become reality—that what was playing over in his mind could come to life.

It was only his first night in the slum.

But already he wanted out.

There was a knowing.

No questions needed to be asked. No one needed clarification about what was happening. Most of all, no one pretended about what was really going on.

Slums have a crushing way of forcing people to deal with reality.

And when people—newcomers especially—came face-to-face with the unforgiving reality of the near-unchangeable future of slum life, it caused some to rise above their desperation and continue fighting.

But others abandoned everything and everyone.

People like Muchoki's father.

One day, he was simply gone. No one in the family saw him again. He vanished the way people do when they can't, or won't, cope with their responsibility. It left Muchoki with an unbearable sense of abandonment. Attacking thoughts bombarded him.

You're not lovable. If you were, your father would have stayed. Notice the other kids? Many of them have fathers. Why is that?

Mochoki's young mind lacked the defence strategies to deal with the onslaught of emotions tormenting his heart.

Maybe he'll come back. Maybe he went to look for work. Maybe ....

But deep down, it was there. A knowing. Deep down, he knew without anyone having to tell him. His dad was gone.

You got that right. Gone. He would have stuck around for better kids. Right? Really, this is your fault.

Panic gripped him.

I have to get out of here.

Sure thing. First bus to your mansion leaves in fifteen minutes. Get on that bus, and your problems will be over.

A wave of humiliation came over Muchoki. He and his siblings took to the streets to beg for food. Day after day, mile after mile, they hoped for the leftovers from restaurants, searched through garbage cans, or knocked on people's doors.

He earned money collecting nylon bags or metal for resale. Other times, he resorted to outright stealing. Grab and run. He was a good thief. Though not perfect. Whenever he was caught, the beatings would eclipse any benefit stealing had brought.

His mother didn't make things any easier. The pressure would have been bad enough had it been just her alone in a slum. But a delinquent husband pushed her to the very edge of the cliff of sanity. And the shame of not being able to care for her children pushed her over. She resorted to the oldest profession to do what little she could to help. But the accompanying guilt of her actions caused her to cry out for relief. And that relief came by way of spending all she had on changa'a to drink away her problems.

Muchoki noticed the faint glow of life in his mother's eyes dim as she went from a struggling yet vibrant person to a dull, vacant stare. It served as evidence she lived in an emotional prison, caught in a hopeless cycle of addiction.

She couldn't afford the rent. No big surprise. She moved around a lot with the kids. Muchoki and his siblings came home every night after exhausting days trying to survive. Unprovoked beatings from his mother became the norm.

One evening, her abused and drunken mind reached an intolerable level. Muchoki avoided eye contact as he entered. He had no food to offer her. No money. Nothing but sickly eyes that shouted a guilty verdict to his mother's incapacity to provide. Maybe that's what set her off. So hard to tell. The reason didn't matter. She smashed her hand against his little face with such force that it spun him around, sending him crashing to the floor. His siblings objected. That was admirable. But proved useless. The one room hut turned into scene of furious rage.

Muchoki tried to stand and come to his siblings' aid. But his mother beat them all with such intensity that it was only when she was overcome by exhaustion that the violence finally stopped.

Muchoki heard nothing. Were his siblings still alive? He coughed up blood. He felt himself drifting off.

And wondered if he would be around the next morning.

Muchoki opened his eyes. Everything looked a blurry mess. His head pounded. A high-pitched ringing sound filled his ears. Each breath made his bruised body ache.

He sat up, and the room swirled. He closed his eyes. Waited. When he opened them again, he could make out his siblings. They all made it through. The older three talked. Staying here was pointless. So was going to the street.

But the street offered the *possibility* of something better.

They decided to take their chances and go to the street for good. They wouldn't be able to care for their little sister. Too young. Too many risks. Without any other options, they left her in the untrustworthy care of their passed-out mother. Muchoki was the last to leave. He looked back at his little sister.

How had it come to this?

The trio searched for food in garbage bins and asked for leftover food from restaurants. Muchoki begged the best out of them all. His lovable face drew pity out of people.

They battled the Kenyan sun by day and searched for refuge from the frigid temperatures at night. The cold reached into his bones. No matter how many clothes or blankets he stole, Muchoki went to sleep shivering each night, hoping it would not be his last.

TRANSFORMATIONS

One method for coping with the cold was to numb himself to it. He stole bottles of glue or dug around in garbage cans near shops. Sniffing glue caused his mind to journey to happier places. He felt lighter. Indestructible. The glue shut down those irritating nerves that told his body he was freezing. Like turning off critical alarms, the glue turned off the bad indicators of life. It might not have been real. But it was real to him. And he could finally live without pain.

The first night, sniffing glue worked like a miracle. No shaking. No shivering. No tense muscles to fight off the lack of heat. It functioned as a perfect sleeping medication, causing him to drift off. The risk of catching malaria still scared him, but it seemed he had the cold problem solved.

Night after night he breathed in glue. It took more and more to keep the high. As the days moved into months, he discovered he could not live without it. Neither day nor night. He made glue his best friend. A guaranteed, temporary escape. A place where the voices would finally be quiet.

Until it wore off.

And then the voices returned with even more force.

Pathetic. Scouring the slums for food? This is your life, Muchoki.

I can make it. I can get enough food.

You are getting food because you are young and people feel sorry for you. But with every passing month you are getting older. Your act is wearing off. You'll never make it.

Maybe you're right.

Maybe? Of course, I'm right. Your father leaves you. Your mom is in such rough shape that you leave her. You're a glue sniffer. Which is kind of like alcoholism for children.

I need more glue.

He searched for his bottle.

Oh, that's good. Resort to your drug to avoid hurting. How is that working for you?

He took in a deep breath of glue. His mind felt that familiar spin.

Well done, Muchoki. You're really something.

Another deep breath. He exhaled. A few more and those voices would stop.

That's better.

No, it isn't. You're sinking down into quicksand, and you know it. You're a drug addict. A thief. A complete loser. Who wants you, Muchoki?

Go away.

I'm not going anywhere.

You will. Soon the glue will dull me out completely.

Until tomorrow.

At least I can escape for a moment.

I asked you a question.

Come back tomorrow. We're all closed up for the night.

Who wants a kid like you? You're the bottom of the world.

We open early in the morning. Be happy to help you then, sir.

Is there anybody in this world who is lower than you?

We have a sale on tomorrow. Special sale. Everything for free.

No one is lower than you. You are at the bottom of the world. How does it feel to be no one?

To be at the bottom?

No Muchoki. How does it feel to be at the bottom and to know that no one will ever want trash like you?

It doesn't hurt.

It's reality, Muchoki. Reality doesn't care how you feel.

He lay down his head.

I'm never going to amount to anything.

That's right.

I'm worthless.

That right. Who wants a worthless kid? No one, Muchoki.

He felt himself slip into sleep. A brief respite from the world around. Dreams still existed. They were real, weren't they? Real enough. Real enough for a kid in Langas to escape.

Everything will be fine. Just fine. Just fine.

CHAPTER 2

Invisible to the crowd.

Muchoki walked the slums as though he were a ghost. He moved through the masses unnoticed. Two worlds existed. One for those who could offer something of value. And a world for people like him.

Sometimes these worlds came together. Like when he stole from someone and got beaten. Or when he slept at an unwelcome place and got chased away. Then people would see him, struggling at the bottom.

But mostly, people stuck to their own worlds.

Muchoki befriended other street children. They could see each other from far away. They shared information on places where they could sleep. Where to obtain food. How to avoid dangers.

"Be careful," a girl about his age said. Her hair had turned rust brown to match the decayed roofs in the slum. They studied a fruit stand, wondering when to make their move.

Muchoki glanced at her eyes. The whites had been replaced with a sickly yellow. "What have you heard?"

"It's not good," she said.

The older man behind the fruit stand turned his back. They edged closer. "Police?"

She shook her head. "Worse."

The owner turned back to a customer.

"Gangs?"

She broke her gaze away from the fruit stand to look at him. Her eyes shifted in and out of focus. It seemed to Muchoki that she struggled to maintain her balance. For a split second she left her dizzying high. Her pupils stopped wandering and drilled into him. It spooked him how she could change like that.

"There are rumours."

"About?"

"Children being abducted."

Her eyes shifted back to being in and out of focus. Strange how she could come and go like that. Suddenly, without any warning, and as if responding to years of training in the art of theft, she saw her opening and made a mad dash for the fruit stand. She sprinted with incredible speed. Grabbing two bananas, she darted past the outstretched arms of the owner and disappeared into the masses, the way street children do when they return to their unseen world.

The owner would have shouted at Muchoki if he cared to notice him standing there. Muchoki should have left. But he couldn't move. People walked around him as if on autopilot, their subconscious directing them away from danger. Muchoki wanted to go. But he stayed locked in position as if he had become a picture. Unable to break free.

The girl's words about children being abducted chilled him right to the core.

The weight of the bags grew heavier.

Little Muchoki picked up another nylon bag from the filthy ground and added it to his sack. A few more and he would have enough to redeem. He struggled up a pedestrian bridge and glanced over at the grimy river. It served more as a sewage canal than a source of any remote vitality. Garbage littered the banks. Nothing left of value. He had picked through it. A filthy stench filled his nostrils. He would have reacted had he not still had enough glue in his system to reject the pungent odor.

"What are you doing in the streets?" a woman's voice behind him asked.

Muchoki continued walking. He knew better than to think someone was talking to him.

"You, young boy with the bags."

She *was* talking to him.

He stopped. Saw no other kids with bags. He turned.

In front of him stood a woman with the kindest eyes that had ever looked into him. It seemed to him in that moment that she knew everything about him. As if she had already met him and learned his whole story. As if she understood him. Had they met? Impossible. If not, why did it feel like they knew each other? He felt a wave of warmth fill his body. Was it the glue? Was it the sun? No. Somehow this felt altogether different. Altogether deeper.

She approached him.

He noticed three young men standing with her. They had similar eyes. Eyes that noticed him.

Don't trust her. Don't trust any of them.

Muchoki studied the woman. What did she want? Why was she talking to him? What did she hope to get from him?

She smiled. A sense of peace came over him.

"Young boy," she said. A concern for him filled her eyes. "Why are you in the street?"

He wanted to respond. Wanted to answer her question. But he felt so drawn into her gaze. For the first time in a long, long time he didn't feel afraid. He put down his collection of bags. Releasing the weight relaxed his shoulders.

"I want to be in the street," Muchoki said.

One of the young men stepped forward. He crouched down to be at Muchoki's level. "Are you sure?" His soft voice reached into Muchoki, putting him at ease.

Who are these people? And why are they talking to me?

"This is all I have," Muchoki said, indicating the bags.

The women stepped closer. "What if you could have something better?" she asked, looking into him. Their eyes locked.

"How?" Muchoki asked. "Who are you?"

She smiled. "You can call me Mamma Esther," she said. "How does that sound to you?"

He wanted a hug. Wanted to sense what it felt like to have a mother again. He looked at the other three. The young man reached out his hand.

"My name is Kaleli. What's your name?"

"Muchoki."

"That is a wonderful name."

The other two men stepped closer.

"We want you to have a better life," Mamma Esther said. "We have a home with many children who come from the streets. We give them a safe place to sleep. They all attend school. They all eat good food. You know, we even give chapati. Do you like chapati?" she asked, laughing.

Muchoki felt himself smile. When was the last time that happened?

He pushed himself out of this dreamland. People don't just come up to kids like him in the street offering everything without wanting something in return.

They just don't.

Two thoughts fought within him. On one side, he sensed them to be the most unique people he had ever met. Genuine. Loving. Incredible. But the other side of him could not understand why anyone would reach out to him. Yes, he *wanted* people like this to exist. But wanting something to be a certain way is not necessarily the same as reality.

If something sounds too good to be true …

This is my chance.

A chance at what? Do you know these people?

I think I do. I can sense they are good people.

And that guarantees you are right? Use your head. You have nothing. Why would anyone want you?

I'm not sure.

That's doubt. And it is well placed. You are in the streets. People stay alive because they can take advantage of others. They are no different.

But they are different. I can ….

You can what? You can verify it? Impossible.

Muchoki looked in Kaleli's eyes.

"How do I know what you are saying is true?"

"Many years ago, a boy about your age was once abandoned by his family. He had to beg for food. He was thrown out of school. He had nothing. But he worked his way out of poverty, became successful, and then gave it all away to help street children. Boys just like you."

I've heard ridiculous stories before, but this one takes first place.

I believe them.

Of course you do. Because you want it to be real. That doesn't make it so.

"How do you know this story is true?" he asked.

Kaleli leaned forward. "Because that man is my father."

Muchoki glanced at Esther. She raised her eyebrows and nodded.

"There are many former street children just like you who live with us," Mamma Esther said. "They are part of our family."

Muchoki evaluated. Studied their eyes. Debated with his conscience.

It was time to decide.

CHAPTER 3

Their conviction won Muchoki over.

"Okay," he said, accepting Mamma Esther's outstretched hand. And the moment he felt his finger touch her palm, it seemed he had known her his whole life. He reached for his bags and lifted them.

Kaleli began to lead them over the bridge. "I think you can leave your bags behind," he said.

Muchoki considered, then let them fall from his shoulders. It felt both odd and good to abandon his only source of income. They got into the truck on the other side of the river. They drove off.

Muchoki didn't glance back. Slum life was a welcome departure from his mind.

As they bumped along the road, Muchoki studied the clean buildings and the well-dressed people.

The vehicle stopped outside a large black gate. A young man stood and opened it. His incredible smile hinted at a quality of life Muchoki had never seen. The vehicle entered and came to a stop.

Muchoki gasped. So many children. Colourful clothes. Clean. Playing. Laughing. An incredible house. Two stories. Trees filled with green leaves.

Kaleli opened the door. Muchoki stepped onto the cobblestone, gazed out at the happy children, and tried to absorb his stunning new reality. Was this place real?

Kaleli patted him on the back. He crouched down beside him. "You are home," he whispered. "You're at Mully Children's Family."

And the moment he heard the word *family*, an incredible comfort came over him.

They led Muchoki into the house. He took a shower. Changed into fresh clothes. Shorts that didn't have holes. A T-shirt with a clean scent. He hurried out to meet Kaleli, who took him to the backyard. Muchoki saw a flood of children. Some played. Some sat together talking. He recognized some from the street. Yet they looked altogether different. Vibrant. Relaxed.

Muchoki suddenly stood still. He felt unable to continue. Overcome by incredible music that filled his entire being. Where was it coming from? It felt so close. Like they were singing all around him. A children's choir sounded both powerful and gentle. Their voices captured his heart. The spirit with which they sang proved exactly what he needed.

Yahwe, Yahwe	Yahweh, Yahweh
Baba, tunakuimbia	O Father, we praise You
Yahwe, Yahwe	Yahweh, Yahweh
Baba, tunakuinua	O Father, we exalt You
Yahwe, Yahweh	Yahweh, Yahweh
Baba, tunakuchezea	O Father, we dance for You
Kama unapenda Yesu, sema Ameni	If you love Jesus, say "Amen"
Kama unapenda Yesu, sema Aleluya	If you love Jesus, say "Hallelujah"
Kama unapenda Yesu, sema Eeeeeee	If you love Jesus, say "Eeeee"
Kema napenda Yesu, sema Amen	If you love Jesus, say "Amen"
Teremuka, teremuka, aaha	Go down, go down, aaha
Teremuka, teremuka, aaha	Go down, go down, aaha
Teremuka, teremuka, aaha	Go down, go down, aaha
Teremuka, teremuka, aaha	Go down, go down, aaha
Panda, panda	Go up, go up
Panda, panda	Go up, go up
Panda, panda	Go up, go up
Panda, panda	Go up, go up
Ha … le … lu … jah	Ha … le … lu … jah

As Kaleli spoke with one of the other men, Muchoki turned to see a middle-aged man washing a young boy's feet. The man laughed as he placed red sandals on the boy.

"Now you look very sharp," the man said.

The little boy giggled. He hugged the man and hurried off to play with other children.

The man looked in Muchoki's direction. And when their eyes met, the man raised his eyebrows, smiled, and waved. He walked towards him. "Hello," the man said.

"Hello."

"I am not sure if I have seen you here before," the man said. He bent down to be at Muchoki's level.

"This is my first day."

"I am sure you must be very excited."

Muchoki nodded. "I didn't even know about this place," he said. "Have you been here long?"

"Me? Oh yes. Quite a while. Come, sit down." The man motioned to sit down at a nearby table. "And have you had something to eat?"

"Not yet."

The man called out to a young woman. A few minutes later she placed a plate of beans and ugali before him. The man prayed, and the boy began to eat.

"I am very glad you are here," the man said.

"Me too."

"I understand how difficult life can be," the man said. "And I want you to know that whatever you need, you can come and ask me."

Muchoki nodded in gratitude.

"What is your name?" the man asked.

"Muchoki," he replied in between bites. "Who are you?"

The man chuckled with such honesty Muchoki found himself beginning to giggle.

"Me?" the man asked.

"Yes, you. The man who is sitting right there," Muchoki said, pointing to the man.

They both laughed. Man and boy. Two kindred spirits.

"This one?" the man asked, indicating to himself.

"Yes."

"You want to know who I am?"

"I do."

"Can you guess?"

Muchoki shrugged his shoulders. A sense of awe came over him. His smile turned into wonder. He gazed into the man's eyes. And for the briefest moment, he thought he saw himself.

"My name is Daddy Mulli," he said. "I am your father."

The realization washed over him like rain on parched African soil. He suddenly felt as if he had entered a time warp and that Mulli was telling him something he had realized forever. Muchoki could no longer remember what it was like *not* to know Charles Mulli. Nor did he want to. It was as if Mulli had always been there.

Being together with Mulli uncovered a long-ignored hurt in his heart.

"I am happy to hear that," he whispered.

"I am happy to have you as my son," Mulli said. "And Mamma Esther is very happy also."

"Yes, Daddy."

Saying *Daddy* came out automatically. Like his heart was responding before his mind even needed to decide on anything to say.

Muchoki looked down to the ground the way shy children do when they want to ask something but lack the courage to make eye contact.

"How can I help you, Muchoki?" Mulli asked.

Muchoki raised his eyes. "I have two brothers and a sister and—"

"Oh yes," Mulli said. "They can come. They are most welcome at Mully Children's Family."

"Thank you, Daddy."

His mother felt incredible gratitude to MCF for taking on her children. She visited them often, feeling relief that Mulli could do for them what would be impossible for her.

Muchoki excelled in school. The other MCFers referred to him and his siblings as a family of geniuses. He sang songs with the other children on the way to church. But when they arrived, the looks of the church members made him feel unwelcome. It wasn't so much what the people in the church did as much as what they *didn't* do.

During the week, Mulli, Mamma Esther, and the MCF pastors and teachers taught the children to love God and to love their neighbour. Yet when they came to this particular church, they found the opposite to be true. Many did not like them. Did not approach them. Did not welcome them. And would not let their children around these former street children.

But when they returned to MCF, Muchoki had the unmistakable sense that like Moses at the burning bush, he too was on holy ground. He felt safe. Protected.

Why don't those people in the church like us?

At night, he wondered why he was so fortunate to be rescued and so many others in the slum were left behind. The images of those he once knew flooded his mind. And it made him question how he could be allowed to live here while others suffered.

I don't deserve to be here.

You got that right. How does it feel? Living the life of luxury while many others are eating out of the same garbage cans you did?

It isn't fair.

Correct again. You see how smart you are? You know why this is.

I don't.

Sure you do.

I am telling you, I don't.

You hear about it every day.

What?

Every, single day. You get the answer.

… God?

Three in a row! A family of geniuses.

God is responsible for this?

Who else?

But why? Jesus loves me, this I know—why is it His fault?

Let's be real. You shouldn't be here. You're bright. You're smart. Odds are that you would have made it out anyway.

Nobody gets out of the slum without help.

God picks you. Your number comes up. And many others who were just like you get to stay in the fear, the hunger, the danger. Nice to be on the right side of the lottery.

Muchoki rolled over in his bed, hoping a change in position would clear the thoughts from his mind. And to his surprise it did.

I shouldn't be here.

You are smart, Muchoki. Very smart. But be careful. Intelligence can't climb every mountain.

I don't understand.

Exactly. Do not lean on your own understanding. Just because you can't figure something out, doesn't mean there isn't a reason.

But I need to understand why I am here and others are not.

Why do you need answers?

Because I feel guilty.

You have been rescued. Blessed. Now what will you do with that? Spend it on yourself? Or will you work hard, live humbly, and use your skills to help others? Mulli can rescue many children. But what if each one in turn helps others?

But that old voice came back. And then there were three fighting inside his mind.

How nice for you. Sleep well. While others are suffering.

Don't be confused. There is a difference between guilt and compassion. Your guilt has been paid for on the cross. You've been set free. And part of being free means being free to give your life to the Lord and to serve others.

It still means I'm here and others are in the street.

So what are you going to do about that? Are you going to feel depressed? Or are you going to pour yourself into your studies so that one day you can help others? Everyone is given at least one talent. Everyone is given an opportunity to serve. How will you use yours?

Mulli brought Muchoki the news of his mother's passing. Muchoki in turn brought the news to his siblings. He struggled with moments of depression. Many times, he felt he would be swept under a tidal wave of hopelessness. He found it hard to study. Hard to pray. Hard to worship. He continued to perform at the top of his class. Success in school came as natural as sunshine. But nothing he did could rid him of the grief that gripped his soul.

"I think about her all the time," Muchoki said to Mulli. They sat together under the stars at MCF Ndalani. The sound of a choir practising filled the night air. Muchoki heard the music, but it felt distant.

"I can't stop thinking about her," he continued. "I dream about her. I feel so sad. I can't get over her. And then I wonder if it is wrong to *want* to get over her."

Mulli nodded. He understood. He always did. It seemed to Muchoki that Mulli could feel what he felt.

"There are times when life can overwhelm us. We feel defenseless. We feel defeated. We feel sad. We feel powerless. What I have learned in life is that prayer in the name of Jesus Christ changes things. It may not be in our time. It may not be in our way. But even me, I face many, many challenges. I get on my knees for many hours—sometimes even the whole night. Oh yes, from when the children go to bed, right through to the next morning. I pray to my Father in heaven. And He hears me. Just like He hears everyone who has asked forgiveness and put their trust in Jesus Christ alone. He gives strength to the weary and increases the power of the weak," Mulli said.

"Thank you, Daddy," Muchoki said, feeling the same deep connection he felt the first time he said those words to Mulli.

"We will pray about it, and it will go away," Mulli.

They prayed together. Muchoki's depression turned into a deep sense of gratitude for his mother. He found he could think about her without despairing. A protective net allowed him to reflect on her without being overcome.

He finished grade 12 at the top of his class. He breezed through university and earned a bachelor's in commerce, graduating among the very best. Mulli attended his graduation, where a CEO from a bank told everyone who got first-class honours to show up for work on Monday.

A shock of excitement raced through Muchoki. His mind struggled to keep pace with his new-found reality. He had journeyed from eating out of garbage cans in a slum to being offered a career in a prestigious bank. His path to success suddenly took off like a race car exploding down the track. Everything looked beyond perfect. He hugged Mulli. Congratulated his fellow graduates.

It never occurred to him that something could go wrong.

CHAPTER 4

It had all been going so well.

The bank posted Muchoki to the Kisumu office in Nyanze province. As a member of the Kikuyu tribe, Muchoki wondered what life would be like living in an area consisting mostly of Luos. Mulli asked Muchoki to work part-time for MCF. But Muchoki decided against it, choosing instead to gain experience with the bank. Plus, Muchoki considered the travel distance between MCF and Kisumu too far, making part-time work nearly impossible.

He moved to Kisumu. Found a good apartment. Settled in. The morning of his first day of work, he got up hours before the sun. He changed into his suit. Crisp white shirt. Polished shoes. He arrived at the bank, met the manager, and was shown his office. His very own office. He glanced down at the garbage can on his way to his desk. He sat down in his chair, trying hard to believe that a major bank had really hired him. The offer *was* real. He really *was* sitting here.

He started making loans to small- and medium-sized businesses. He loved meeting business owners, hearing their visions and helping them achieve their financial goals.

He met Isaiah, who became his good friend. He connected with others and found a local church. At first, Muchoki traveled long hours on weekends to visit MCF. But the distance took a toll on his energy levels, and he stopped.

Isaiah moved to Uganda, leaving a hole in his life. And for reasons that were not immediately clear to Muchoki, he found himself suddenly feeling lonely. When the working day ended, he felt an uncomfortable vacuum. Quiet evenings can be solace for some. For others, like Muchoki, the isolation felt like prison. To compensate, he poured himself into his work. He stayed longer hours and continued to succeed. He didn't speak the Luo language, so connecting with others wasn't as easy as it would have been with fellow Kikuyus. Given his history of living with siblings from a variety of tribal backgrounds, it surprised Muchoki how difficult it became to fit in.

Forming relationships with others became harder.

He would come home to his apartment. Sit there by himself. Fill his evenings with entertainment. It would distract him from his feelings, but only momentarily. No matter how hard he tried to avoid it, his loneliness would return.

Feels different, doesn't it?

I'll get through this.

At MCF, you had hundreds of brothers and sisters around you. A little quiet around here, wouldn't you say?

Work is going well.

But are you doing well at work?

Yes, my numbers are great. I am at the top of my department.

Sure, your sales are great. But are you personally doing well at work?

Of course.

Really?

I am there to do a job, and I do it well.

And when you come home, you get ready to have a fun evening with all your friends. How are they doing? Hello? Muchoki? How are your friends doing? You know, those many friends of yours?

Muchoki became uncomfortable being alone with his thoughts. Having his mind occupied with preparing loans and having conversations with business owners gave him energy. He lived off the thrill of work and the interaction with others. But when he left work, he felt life drained out of him, knowing it was time to return home to serve his prison sentence alone in his apartment.

Rescue came one day when coworkers invited him out to a club after work. He wasn't a drinker. Didn't even *want* to drink. But he wanted connection with others. Wanted to know he could talk and be listened to.

Muchoki wanted to belong.

He sat down at a table in the club with his coworkers, feeling the relief that comes with camaraderie. People. Community. Music. A tall waitress with long hair extensions approached the table. The others ordered drinks. She turned to Muchoki. He ordered a beer for the first time in his life, and then wondered why he had done that.

I'm in a club. This is what people do. They order alcohol. If you don't drink, they won't accept you.

That's ridiculous. Just change your order to tonic water.

They'll laugh at me.

They won't.

They will. And I will lose them.

If they laugh at you for ordering a non-alcoholic drink, do you really want to be with them?

I've ordered it. The decision has been made.

But why? This isn't like you. Why are you drinking?

So now you're an expert on alcohol? No alcohol for Christians? Is that it? Water into wine, remember?

You have a family history. There are tendencies built into you. Remember—

The clanging of beer bottles on the table interrupted his thought.

They toasted each other. He brought the bottle to his lips.

And took his first sip.

Pow. Something ripped right through him.

Oh, where have you been?

As if on instinct, he took a second swig right away. And he was rewarded with a deep relaxation that filled his body and, more importantly, eased his mind.

He laughed with the others. Felt confident with the others. Felt accepted by the others.

The first beer went down like water. That should have surprised him, but it didn't. Without being able to explain why, it felt natural. He downed the second bottle faster than the first. He leaned back in his chair, smiling at his friends.

And saw them smiling back at him.

Okay, you've had some fun. Two drinks. That's lots. Time to go.

Go? This is the best I've felt in a long time. This is fun.

I know you're smart in school and all that, but can I remind you of what happens when you drink more than you should?

Go away. I feel good again.

Because of what? What is making you feel good?

Stop.

You can't fill holes in a boat by adding more water.

He finished seven bottles. Seven. The room began to spin. He absorbed the sense of acceptance in being around the others. Nothing hurt. Not a single thing. Finally, life had fallen back into a good place again.

The clock struck midnight. They agreed to call it a night. He stood. Not good. Who was making the floor move like that? He returned to his apartment. Held the walls for balance on his way to his bedroom. Fell mostly onto his bed. Not bad aim, all things considered. His last thought before falling asleep was that he had gone through an entire evening without feeling lonely.

Felt good, didn't it?

It sure did.

Wonderful. We can do this again tomorrow.

Okay.

And the day after. And the day after ....

He woke to the sound of his alarm blaring. It felt distant. As if he were still dreaming. He opened his eyes to a blurry mess. His head pounded with such force, he felt as if his skull were about to explode. He sat up. Waited for his eyes to focus. Blinked.

What have I done?

His stomach felt awful. Like someone had poured gasoline into him.

He dragged himself into work. Red eyes and all. He greeted coworkers on the way to his desk. He sat down. Took in a deep breath. *Come on. Come on.*

With incredible skill, his mind snapped into shape, and he transformed right back into his usual self.

The drinking continued for months. He became a superhero of sorts. Dedicated employee by day. Compulsive drinker by night. With his friends. At the club. Beer after beer. Laugh after laugh.

You surprise me.

Why's that?

You are smart. Second smartest in the entire university class.

And?

You aren't smart enough to figure out what is happening to you.

I'm fine.

Would Mulli agree?

I would love to help at MCF, but I'm too far away. I can't work and drive all the way there on weekends.

But you could go to work and then drive to a local church that's only a few minutes away.

He took a long drink from his beer. *Maybe I should go back.*

Maybe? You love God. You love other Christians. Why is it so easy for you to down all these beers, but such a struggle to go to church? You love it there. You always did.

Another drink. This time, he gulped half the bottle.

I am fine.

Would Mulli approve of your lifestyle? Would Christ? You are loved. You are so loved. Your life can be so much better than it is.

I said, I'm fine.

What's worse? To be sinking, or to not know you are sinking?

The bank promoted Muchoki to Asset Finance in Nairobi. He settled into his new desk at his dream position. Bigger office. Bigger responsibilities.

He glanced out his window. Looked down at the street below. Street boys begged for money from a businessman, who turned them away. He watched in amazement. Had he really been there? Was that really him all those years ago struggling on the street? And now he sat all the way up here.

Success followed him at his new position. Bigger loans. Bigger clients. Everything kept getting better and better. And he would have continued ascending when two factors out of his control affected his performance.

First, the government imposed an interest rate cap, hoping it would help businesses. But with a lower lending rate, Muchoki's loans didn't bring in as much interest for the bank.

Second, the bank became risk-averse and required 100 percent collateral for all loans. An increasing number of Muchoki's clients were not able to comply and could not come to him to borrow money.

Muchoki operated in the top 5 percent in the country for his sector at the bank. But suddenly, his hands were tied. He could not perform nearly as well.

And it caused him much stress.

Stress? You call this stress? You used to live on the street. That was real stress. And what happened? God rescued you. If He can rescue you from the street, for sure He can help you now.

No. No—

No? You believe God can't rescue you?

Of course He can. But this is different than the street.

Different how?

The street wasn't my fault. My father left. My mother became an alcoholic, and I had to go to the streets to survive. God saw it wasn't my fault, and He helped me. But this situation with the bank is my fault.

How is it your fault?

I need to fix this myself.

God is available anytime for you. In any situation.

I have to take care of my problems on my own.

Muchoki came home to his Nairobi apartment. Even though MCF was only a short drive away, he felt ashamed of his drinking and chose to stay in Nairobi on weekends.

He grabbed a bottle of beer from the fridge and sat down on his couch.

You can get yourself out of this mess. Keep trying. You can do it.

I'm in real trouble with the bank. I need someone to talk to.

You have all the abilities you need within you. Just take a drink. It makes the loneliness disappear.

He did as he was told and drank the bottle. It calmed his nerves, but it did little to stop the thoughts from invading his mind.

See? You don't feel lonely, do you? This is your safe place. You can get through any day knowing I will be here for you. Guaranteed help at the twist of a bottle cap.

This isn't help. Do you remember when you had memories of your mother passing? Mulli encouraged you to pray, and it helped. The Lord is my helper. I will not fear.

Muchoki resolved the conflict in his mind with another bottle. Then another.

And another.

He felt as if his entire being had been turned to ice, making him unable to feel any of the harsh words playing over and over in his mind.

Evenings and weekends became filled with heavy drinking. He couldn't remember the last time he prayed. Or the last time he walked into church. Or the last time he showed up at the bank sober. Day after day, he came to work under a heavy cloud of fear and depression. And every evening and weekend he ran to his unfaithful refuge.

He lay back in his couch, aware that he was riding a bus headed for a cliff but unable to get off.

I need to stop drinking.

Stop? Why? It is helping.

It only delays me facing reality.

You have enough reality during the day. And look how hard you are fighting.

I have to get out of this mess.

And you will. The economy will turn around. Interest rates will rise. The bank will gain confidence in the economy and lower the collateral requirements. That way you will do better. Meanwhile, stay the course. And I am here to help. I am always here.

But it's not right.

You sure felt it was right when you started drinking with your friends.

Yes, but now it feels different. It feels like the alcohol controls me. I can't stop. I need to let it go.

I think you didn't hear me earlier.

I need to let this go.

I said I am always here for you.

I crave you as soon as I leave work. But as soon as I start drinking, I feel guilty. That needs to stop.

You're missing the point of what I am saying. I am always here for you.

You keep saying that. Now stop.

You let me in, Muchoki. But you can't kick me out. I am here to stay. Once in, always in. Like I said: I am always here for you. And I'm not leaving. Not ever.

Muchoki let out a long sigh. He wanted to pour the contents of the bottle down the sink. Wanted to finally be rid of it all. But still he clutched it tighter, as if it were his only rope preventing him from disappearing into quicksand.

Just one more sip. That's all.

He obeyed. Took a drink. While he was swallowing it, he heard the attack continue.

Pathetic. You are useless. How can you not resist something as simple as alcohol? I own you. I am always here. And no matter what you do, you will never get rid of me. We're best friends. Thank you for inviting me in. You will fail at the bank. You will end up back on the streets where you belong. You had your chance, and you wasted it.

The sound of his phone ringing pulled him from his thoughts. He didn't want to speak with anyone. Least of all not in this condition. He glanced at his phone. Noticed the caller identification. A strange combination of shame and love fought inside him. He reread the name to make sure he saw correctly.

Daddy Mulli was calling.

CHAPTER 5

What to do?

He's your father. He will help you.

Sure, he will. He will be so disappointed in you.

He won't be. He loves you. He understands.

Yeah, I'll bet. He understands that he gave you everything. You came from the slums. You had nothing. And he brought you out of all that. For what purpose? So you could become a man of God and give your life to serve others. And now look at you. A pathetic drunk.

Did Jesus throw away people who were at the bottom?

Go ahead. Pick up your phone. Get a few words out if you can. See how he responds to your incoherent slurring.

He glanced at Mulli's name again. It would click off momentarily. Now or never.

Don't do it. Don't answer the phone. Keep what little dignity you have left and call him back when you are sober.

"Hi, Daddy," Muchoki said. He closed his eyes and slumped his head down. It felt like Mulli was right there in the room with him, catching him in his state.

"My son, it is so good to hear your voice again," Mulli said.

Muchoki felt a painful sting of tears build behind his eyes.

Full circle, Muchoki. Well done. You've gone from one slum to another.

It's not that bad.

You're right, Muchoki. It's worse. In Langas slum, you had the will to escape but not the opportunity. Since then, you have been given every opportunity, but you have chosen to stay trapped in your new internal slum of alcohol. Hang up.

"It is good to hear your voice again too, Daddy."

A flood of guilt washed over him. *Daddy.* All he ever wanted was to make his daddy proud.

Didn't quite manage that one did you, Muchoki?

"I am concerned about you," Mulli said.

How? Muchoki opened his eyes, wondering if that would help him see the answer more clearly. How did Mulli know there was reason for concern?

How did he come by this information? He knew. Somehow, he always knew. Charles Mulli and his uncanny ability of knowing things.

What to say?

"Thank you for your concern, Daddy. I am always glad to hear from you."

Wow. Two whole sentences without stumbling. Not bad for a drunk. I commend you. But you don't think he actually believes you, do you?

"How is life going for you?"

"Fairly well."

"Is it?"

"It has its challenges. But life will always have challenges, right?" Muchoki said, forcing a laugh that convinced neither himself nor Mulli.

"I have solid intelligence that you are drinking a lot of alcohol."

Mulli's words pierced Muchoki. There would be no point trying to deny it. Besides, Mulli never spoke just words. He spoke truth. And the truth reached into Muchoki and yanked out the supports from under him.

He paused long enough to convey his guilt. He knew that Mulli knew. So then why was Mulli calling?

"I want to meet with you, Muchoki," Mulli said.

"Yes, Daddy. I will come to see you."

"Take your rest tonight," Mulli said. "I will come to see you."

"You have other things to do in Nairobi?"

"No," Mulli said. "I am coming to see you."

The rain poured down under dark skies making the late afternoon feel like midnight. It pelted against the window of the MCF Nairobi office. Mulli sat in a chair opposite Muchoki. A young woman carried in a tray with glasses of water. She placed it beside them and left, closing the door behind her.

At first, Muchoki felt both embarrassment and relief. He was embarrassed that he had sunk this low in life—and relieved that finally his problem lay out in the open, quieting those accusing voices in his head.

But as he forced his gaze to meet Mulli, he felt ashamed. Ashamed of how he had failed his father.

"I am glad to see you again, Muchoki."

"Me too."

"You did very well at MCF."

"Thank you, Daddy."

"You did so well in university. You performed so well in your work."

Here it comes, Muchoki. The words every son wants to hear: "But now you are a total and complete failure."

"I did."

"But things have gotten off track."

No, they haven't. You are in complete control. Tell him you are fine, and then find a way to get out of this meeting. Besides, it's time for a drink.

"They have."

Mulli glanced out the window. He squinted his eyes as if narrowing his vision could help him focus on what to say next. Mulli struggled to find the right words, something Muchoki had never noticed in his father before.

"Alcohol ruined my father's life," Mulli said in a tone barely above a whisper. "My father became violent towards me. He was awful."

He paused, visibly collecting strength for what he would say next.

"One morning I woke to discover my whole family had left me. I did not know where they had gone. Later, I found them again. I trusted God, and with much hard work under God's favour, I started businesses and made it to the top of the mountain of success."

Mulli paused, trying to absorb the impact of his own story.

"Addictions are emotional," Mulli said. "A person feels pain, anger, boredom, loneliness. And they stand at a crossroads. All people can feel this way. And it is in that moment when we make a choice. We either come to Christ with our hurt, or we run to alcohol, drugs, bad relationships, money … or violence."

Muchoki shifted in his chair, trying to shake the uncomfortable thoughts in his mind.

Why do I drink? What pulls me in? I was never like this at MCF. Not even in university. But now?

"My father continued drinking," Mulli said. "I warned him many times to stop. He recognized the damage alcohol did to his life. But he became powerless to stop it. Until, one day, he encountered the living God."

Nice, isn't it, Muchoki? But you already know God. Kind of embarrassing to be a follower of Jesus and to sink to this level.

Muchoki wanted to respond. Wanted to tell Mulli he would stop.

But you can't stop. You know that you can't. Drinking is like breathing. You can't go on without me.

Yes, I can. I can be rid of you. I don't want you anymore.

But you do. When alcohol slides down your throat, it reaches that part deep down inside. Soothes you. Comforts you. Where will you go when that disappears?

"You are loved, Muchoki. I love you. Mamma Esther loves you."

"I know, Daddy."

He wanted to start this all over again. Go back to university graduation. Resist the urge to cure loneliness. But how?

"Do you know why you drink?"

"It makes me feel better."

"But why alcohol? Why do you think you specifically go to alcohol?"

"Because it is accessible?"

"We can inherit things from our parents," Mulli said. "I don't mean money or possessions. We can inherit good attitudes or bad attitudes. We can also inherit ways in which we respond to problems. We can't blame them. We can't say, 'Oh, I am allowed to act this way because my parents were like this.' No. They are now *our* attitudes. And we must bring them to the cross."

"I don't understand."

"How did your mother deal with her problems?"

A chill ran through Muchoki. It was as if the rain had come in and soaked him. He swallowed. Had he turned into his mother?

"She drank," he said.

"Each of us needs to decide where we will go with our pain," Mulli said. "Either we turn to God, or we turn somewhere else. I don't just want you to stop drinking, Muchoki. I want you to rest in Christ's arms."

Mulli made sense. He always did.

"All right, Daddy. Thank you. I will stop drinking."

They hugged. Prayed. Talked about other things. The old days. The days ahead.

The rain settled. They said goodbye. As Muchoki headed out, he thought about his promise to Mulli. He felt renewed about the future that lay ahead. One without getting drunk.

Though some things are easier said than done.

CHAPTER 6

First, it was the breakup with his girlfriend of two years. He cared for her, and losing her sent him into a spiral of hurt.

Next, it was a mounting list of non-performing loans. He worked longer and harder but discovered it would be easier to draw blood from a stone than to draw money from a collapsed business. The lack of success filled him with shame.

Not to worry. All was not lost. There was still hope. Whenever Muchoki got into trouble, he could rely on old faithful.

He sat down on his couch in his apartment. The promise he made to Mulli rang over in his mind. *I will stop drinking.* That was a lie. Or was it? The intent was there for sure. He wanted to be free of addiction. Wanted his father's approval. Wanted to walk with God.

Inside his mind, he fought against competing thoughts. Each trying to convince him of the right path to follow.

You have a lot of problems.

Too many.

And you have to solve them.

I know. The alcohol helps me.

Does it? Does it really? What did Mulli say?

Each of us needs to decide where we will go with our pain. Either we turn to God, or we turn somewhere else.

That's all fine and good for real Christians like Mulli. But you aren't in his league. You have to solve your own problems. It's irresponsible to run to God for help when it was you who got yourself into this mess in the first place.

He paid for incredible amounts of alcohol. Paid for drinks for other women. The bills piled up. He ran out of cash. He borrowed money and took on large obligations. He sank deeper and deeper into financial trouble.

A loan officer in deep debt.

Lord, help me.

Help you? You chose to go into debt. You chose to become an alcoholic. It's your job to get out of these problems. Stop asking for help. Stop trying to shift responsibility.

Muchoki received word Mulli was looking for him. That should have been reason enough to see the man who had rescued him. But Muchoki did not return to MCF. He couldn't bring himself to go home. Couldn't face Mulli. Shame filled him to capacity. He spiralled into further drinking. Further depression. He would miss work. Come in late hungover. His boss came into his office one morning at eleven a.m. Just as Muchoki arrived.

Here you go, Muchoki. Time to get fired. Add that to your growing list of accomplishments.

She greeted him. Sat down in the chair across from his desk. Was this how people get fired? How did it go exactly? Her long black hair hung around her shoulders. Dark business suit. Angular cheekbones. Soft eyes. He glanced at her and then focused at nothing on his desk.

"You're missing work," she said.

"I'm sorry."

"There are many people who are looking to take your job."

"I believe you," Muchoki said. He glanced through the door window. So many people at their desks. He wanted to disappear.

"I want to see you succeed," she said. He met her eyes. "The bank believes in each of its employees. And that includes you."

He nodded.

"Three items I want to provide you. First, you need to report to my office every morning. This will encourage you to be on time. Second, we have a full-time pastor at the bank. I want you to see him. This will help you know that you can talk to someone about your life. It will encourage you to reach out to Christ with your problems instead of thinking you can solve them on your own. Third, I will connect you with friends who don't drink. Bad company corrupts good character. I want you to be surrounded with good people. How does that sound?"

It sounded good to Muchoki.

"I would like to invite you to come to church with me," she said.

He wanted what she had in her eyes. Conviction. A settled peace. No striving. No shame. He nodded again, indicating he would think about it. She stood. He thanked her. She left.

When she was out of sight he reached into his drawer. Pulled out a metal container. Took a swig of vodka.

He did well to control his staggering on his way out of the bank. It took him two tries to find the door handle. Crazy vision. So hard to see straight while under the influence. But he made it outside. Skilled drunk that he was.

He placed a call to his former girlfriend as he walked into a park. He could use some good news. But she told him to forget it. She hadn't changed her opinion of him. She'd had enough of him. Enough of his drinking. Enough of his excuses. When she hung up, his eyes darted around for a liquor store. Not finding one, he clutched his jacket pocket. Found his smokes. Sucked back on the nicotine.

Oh, that's good.

But it wasn't. It wasn't good at all. It was really, really bad. A chemical combination of depression, alcohol, and cigarettes blended together in just the right way to send him over the edge. He shifted in and out of focus. He stood there, his mind shutting off the controls to his muscles. His bones held him there as if he were one of those pretend skeletons you see in a specialist doctor's office. He thought he saw a street child in the distance searching through a garbage can. He began leaning over, his mind no longer able to send signals to keep him upright. He drifted off.

His body crumpled to the ground.

The sun had set. A passerby saw him lying there. She shook him, heard him grunt. Found his phone in his jacket. Saw the name *Daddy Mulli* in the call log. She called. Mulli picked up. She explained the situation. Mulli sent his son Dickson and others to help. They found Muchoki unconscious. Took him to detox.

Mulli spoke with the bank manager. They agreed on Muchoki entering rehab for three months. He lasted all but one month. His mind continued to distort reality. He had such a craving for his addictions. While being transported by the rehab facility, he opened the door as the vehicle was in motion and raced out into traffic. He returned to his old life. The bank pastor found Muchoki drunk in his apartment. The bank manager stood her ground. Muchoki could only come back if he finished rehab.

"What if I take him back to MCF?" Mulli asked the bank manager. "What if he completes rehab at MCF?"

"Three months?" she asked.

"Three months."

She looked at him. Saw his sincerity.

"Agreed."

As he drove onto the MCF Ndalani property, Muchoki wondered if he was in worse shape now than when he first arrived at MCF as a child. He looked out at the children playing football on the pitch. Had he really been like that at one point? Full of hope starting out? He saw other students walking to class for extra studying. That had been him. Top of the class. Top of the world.

And now he was re-entering at the very bottom.

All of that was nothing compared with having to sit down with Daddy Mulli.

The vehicle stopped. He stepped out. He noticed Mulli with his trademark leather cowboy hat approaching him with open arms. Mulli hugged him.

"Welcome home, Muchoki," he said. "Mamma Esther and I love you."

Muchoki felt a rush of tears race down his cheeks. He had wondered how this meeting would go. Wondered what Mulli would say. What he would do. What look he would give. But as Muchoki took in the unconditional love of his father, he sensed something he had not felt in a long time. Standing here with Mulli, Muchoki did not feel like a drunk. He did not feel like a failed employee. He did not feel like a failed boyfriend.

He felt like a son.

"Thank you, Daddy," he whispered.

Mulli led him to the eating area. Mulli walked to the back. "Come and see who is here."

Mamma Esther walked in. Her familiar smile revealed the joy she felt deep in her heart. She hugged Muchoki.

"I am glad to see you," she said. "This is your home. We are your family. And everything is going to be fine. I know you are concerned. I see it inside your eyes. But I know in my heart that you will be well. God knows you. And He lives inside you."

They sat down to dinner.

The MCF choir practiced in the distance.

They talked until late into the evening. The choir finished singing. Children headed to their dorms for the night.

"I know it is wrong," Muchoki said. "I don't want to drink. But I feel this unbearable compulsion. Even now."

Mulli nodded. He paused the way he often did to be absolutely sure he would not interrupt. When he was convinced Muchoki had finished speaking, he looked into Muchoki's sad, bewildered eyes and waited until they met his gaze.

"Every one of us is asking the question: Am I loved?" Mulli said, leaning forward. "Having the knowledge of God's love is the first important step. Then, as we take hold of His love, as we think about what the Bible says, His truth grows deep within us. It pushes out things from our heart that God has not planted. And we have the confidence that comes with being a child of God."

"I think it is easier for you, Daddy."

"Me? I am not a special person. I am normal like you. When I was younger, I was very depressed. I saw no hope for my life. But Christ changed me. He gave me real purpose. There have been many, many challenges. I tell you, so many. Even you. You have many challenges. But God has prepared you for a purpose. He does not simply make someone and then forget about them."

"I failed you, Daddy," Muchoki said.

Mulli waited. Allowed the quiet of the night to maintain an unhurried conversation.

"We are all accountable for our actions. Your birth mother turned to alcohol and other things to cope with her depression. You also did the same. But God forgives us. And we need to accept responsibility for our shortcomings. We can't blame someone else. We need to be humble before God and other people to walk the journey of recovery."

"I am embarrassed, Daddy."

"Don't be. Shame has no place in the Kingdom of God. The apostle Paul failed God miserably. But look how God used Paul. That does not excuse what Paul had done. But it does prove that no matter how far you fall, when we turn to Christ, we are immediately in the centre of His will," Mulli said.

"I don't see how that is possible for me," Muchoki said.

Mulli smiled. "It may surprise you how Christ will use your story to help others."

CHAPTER 7

R ehab proved to be an ongoing battle for his mind.
Part of him wanted to be free. The other part of him found ways to lie to himself to resort back to his old life.

Mulli spoke with all the streetside vendors outside MCF, asking them not to sell any cigarettes or alcohol to Muchoki. He also set up guards at various entrances to MCF to keep an eye out for Muchoki. Mulli had been through this many times before. He would rescue children from deplorable street conditions, yet sometimes their minds would continue play tricks on them and urge them to return to the very life they had left. Mulli and his team would search the streets for them. They would return with him to MCF feeling guilty and ashamed. He would restore them, assuring them of God's love for them. In some cases, the cycle of returning to the slum happened repeatedly.

And every time, Mulli would go out to find them.

Muchoki felt the same way. He felt like leaving. He woke up in a panic in the dark hours of the night. He felt his hands shaking. Sweat formed on his forehead. His entire being craved alcohol.

Get out! Get out of here! Get out now!

I don't think so. The guard dogs are out. They will get me.

At first light tomorrow, run out. Get to the street.

I can't. I can't do this to Daddy Mulli.

You can't survive like this. The alcohol will feel good. It will calm you down. How long can you stay like this?

His mind shouted at him all night, making him think he would go crazy without booze.

He sat down across from Mulli under the beautiful, sprawling trees along the Thika River. Mulli smiled at him, though Muchoki found it difficult to look into his eyes.

Muchoki's hands shook uncontrollably, like someone had hooked him up to a battery to make him do that.

"I am finding it …."

Muchoki stopped. What was he trying to say? He started again. This time he stuttered. "I am … finding it very …."

He gave up, exasperated. What was wrong with him?

"It is all right, my son," Mulli said. "Withdrawal symptoms take time. Your hands will shake. You will find it difficult to finish thoughts and sentences. You will have thoughts of running away."

You got that right. Get out of this place. This is no good. They are all trying to control you here. You need freedom. Make your own way in the world. Don't stay locked up here. Quit your rehab. Quit your job. Live on the streets where you had freedom to do anything.

"Your mind needs to be renewed," Mulli said. "As you study God's Word, His thoughts will replace your cravings."

That's impossible.

"This is why God's Word is so important," Mulli continued.

You don't need the Bible. You have to figure this out on your own.

"It is no different for you than for me," Mulli said.

"I don't think you …."

He had the thought in his mind. But then it left. Like someone had turned off the computer in his brain. Then, just like that, it came back on. "You and I are not on the same level," Muchoki said.

"Moses was a humble man. He led the children of Israel out of Egypt. He led them through the Red Sea, which God parted. What made him humble? Humble is not being weak. Humble is not necessarily being quiet. It is trusting in God. A humble person knows their strength is from the Holy Spirit living inside them. And we grow in our understanding of God by reading the Bible."

Mulli motioned for him to sit beside him. He pulled out a Bible.

"This is for you, Muchoki. You remember when you first came to MCF Eldoret?"

A sting of tears rushed out from him. Yes, he remembered.

"I asked you how I could help you," Mulli said. "And by the grace of God, I am going to help you again. I have a challenge for you. I want you to read the Bible every day. And I want you to spend time with Jesus while you are reading the Bible."

"I will try."

Mulli opened the Bible to Psalm 27. "I want to encourage you to memorize Psalm 27."

"Daddy, I can't. My mind …."

"I know. But remember, you were not always like this. It will not be easy, but within three months, you will see a dramatic change."

Mulli put many strategies in place for Muchoki. He followed a disciplined schedule of eating, sleeping, exercise, Bible reading, counselling, and helping others. He met regularly with Mulli. He began to finish his sentences and thoughts. His tremors slowed down. The battle in his mind quieted. He found moments of clarity with God.

"How is your Bible reading going?" Mulli asked as they met for breakfast.

"Sometimes I find it hard to understand."

"May I help you?" he asked.

Muchoki handed him his Bible. Mulli opened it to Psalm 27 in his English Standard Version Bible.

The LORD is my light and my salvation;
*   whom shall I fear?*
The LORD is the stronghold of my life;
*   of whom shall I be afraid?*

"This tells me that God is greater than any problem I face. The devil tries to make God small and problems large. But God reminds me that He is greater than the devil and greater than any danger or situation I will ever face. God is greater than alcohol. That is a fact. And as you think about this verse over and over again, the Holy Spirit will take this fact and make it real in your heart."

When evildoers assail me
*   to eat up my flesh,*
my adversaries and foes,
*   it is they who stumble and fall.*
Though an army encamp against me,
*   my heart shall not fear;*
though war arise against me,
*   yet I will be confident.*

"This encourages me that God is for me. God will pay back my enemies. I don't need to worry about getting even with someone. That is the Lord's business. No matter how bad a situation looks, I can know that God is with me, and He will protect me. My confidence does not come from wondering if I can win. It comes from knowing that Jesus has already won the victory for me on the cross."

*One thing have I asked of the L*ORD*,*
  that will I seek after:
*that I may dwell in the house of the L*ORD
  all the days of my life,
*to gaze upon the beauty of the L*ORD
  and to inquire in his temple.

"Everything I need is in God. My greatest admiration in life is not possessions or status. It is in being with God. And as you desire God, you will see you have everything in Him."

For he will hide me in his shelter
  in the day of trouble;
he will conceal me under the cover of his tent;
  he will lift me high upon a rock.
And now my head shall be lifted up
  above my enemies all around me,
and I will offer in his tent
  sacrifices with shouts of joy;
*I will sing and make melody to the L*ORD*.*

"Praising God builds our trust in Him."

*Hear, O L*ORD*, when I cry aloud;*
  be gracious to me and answer me!
You have said, "Seek my face."
My heart says to you,
  *"Your face, L*ORD*, do I seek."*

"God answers me when I call to Him. He does not hide fromme. I am designed for a relationship with God. Seeking God prevents me from seeking after other gods."

Hide not your face from me.
Turn not your servant away in anger,
  O you who have been my help.
Cast me not off; forsake me not,
  O God of my salvation!

"Even when we fail God, He does not abandon us. If we are faithless. He remains faithful."

For my father and my mother have forsaken me,
  but the LORD *will take me in.*

"You and I were both abandoned by our parents. But even when this happens, God will never abandon us."

Teach me your way, O Lord,
  and lead me on a level path
  because of my enemies.
Give me not up to the will of my adversaries;
  for false witnesses have risen against me,
  and they breathe out violence.

"Addictions are lies. They give false hope. And when you try to leave an addiction, it threatens you that you can't make it without it. As we walk with God, His truth dispels these lies, and we can walk in freedom—on a level path."

I believe that I shall look upon the goodness of the Lord
  in the land of the living!
Wait for the Lord;
  be strong, and let your heart take courage;
  wait for the Lord!

"No matter how difficult the situation, have confidence in God. Do not give in to fear. Reject fear, and constantly fill your heart with the truth of God's strength. Victory does not come right away. Continue trusting no matter what."

By the end of the second month, Muchoki found the courage to talk with other people at MCF and look them in the eye. By the end of the third month, he felt the way he did when he walked these grounds while finishing school. He smiled.

He felt the joy of freedom.

He walked across the concrete bridge that had replaced the old wooden bridge he used to cross over as a student. He saw Mulli as he worked at his desk under the shade. He motioned Muchoki over.

"You look very strong, my young son," Mulli said with a smile. It reminded Mulli of how the two of them laughed together when they first met.

"Thank you, Daddy."

"I have one other item I would like you to do."

Muchoki stood in front of the audience. The thought of giving his testimony to the MCF graduating class scared him. He wondered if the students would see him as a failure and dismiss him. He looked out at their hopeful eyes. So bright. Energetic. Had he been like them once?

Perhaps his story would help. Perhaps explaining that being at MCF doesn't automatically mean that life after MCF will be easy. Perhaps it would help someone avoid the path he took.

"I want to speak to you about working through failure," he started.

The room became quiet.

"Three times Peter said he would never leave Jesus. I felt the same way when I was here at MCF. No way was I ever going to let God down. But I did. I felt lonely. I wanted to drink to have friends. And everything spiralled out of control. I was at the top of my class here at MCF. It can happen to anyone."

He watched their eyes, wondering if he was correct in his assessment that he was connecting with them.

"Peter denied Jesus. But afterwards, Jesus told him to strengthen his brothers. Jesus was willing to see beyond Peter's failure. Even after Peter failed, Jesus gave him work to do. This is a message that spoke to me."

Muchoki said a short prayer in his mind and then continued.

"You need to decide now to stay close to God. To be part of a church. To serve God. To be careful who you choose as friends. It is very, very easy to drift off course."

Freedom came over him. Like it no longer mattered what people thought of him.

"On the one hand, you never want to fail. The consequences to you and others are enormous. But if you do fail, do not stay down and get depressed. Take your problems to God. Find a good friend or a good pastor to pour your heart out to. As followers of Jesus Christ, we don't just help others. We too need help. And when we find ourselves drifting, we need to be honest and have courage. To reach out to Jesus the way Peter did when he started sinking in the water."

The students clapped. To his surprise, many from that class and other classes came up to him to talk with him and to share their struggles.

He returned to work. He thanked his boss for not giving up on him, realizing people in other companies had been fired for less than what he had done. She had stuck with him even when she had every reason to boot him out.

He visited MCF regularly. Encouraged students. Visited with Daddy Mulli and Mamma Esther.

"You are doing very well," Mamma Esther said, pouring Muchoki a cup of tea. She sat down next to Mulli at the breakfast table. The covered roof and the partially opened wall protected them from the sun, allowing a gentle breeze to pass through.

"I am grateful," Muchoki said. "Thank you, Mom and Dad."

"Most welcome," Esther said. "MCF is your home. It will always be your home."

"You made so much time for me," Muchoki said, feeling the guilt that time spent on him could have been spent on others.

"You are our son," Mulli said. "And remember. Our God is an eternal God. There is always time."

Muchoki nodded, thinking that if he began to talk, he would begin to cry.

"Come for a walk with me to see the animals," Esther said.

"You love those animals," Muchoki said. "You see them every morning."

Esther thought. "God spared many animals on Noah's ark."

"Do you have a favourite animal?" Muchoki asked.

"It depends. Domestic or wild?" she asked with a laugh.

"Both."

"My favourite wild animal is the elephant," she said. "And domestic, I like cows and sheep."

Muchoki turned to his dad.

"My favourite domestic animal is the cow," Mulli said.

"Why?"

"Very practical animal. You can get milk and meat. You can take care of it. It can provide for the family."

"And wild?"

Mulli seemed stumped by the question. Muchoki leaned closer. Smiled. "Yes, Daddy?"

Mulli shook his head. "I don't think I have one."

"What? Impossible. You must have a favourite wild animal. The lion maybe?"

Mulli considered. Then shook his head. "No. No, I do not think so."

"Why not?"

"Why not? Isn't it obvious?" Mulli said with a laugh.

"Not to me it isn't," Muchoki said.

"Because you can't stay with a lion in the wild," Mulli said. "It will eat you up!"

Muchoki and Esther burst out laughing.

"You don't need to stay with the lion," Muchoki argued. "You can just admire it from afar."

"Yes," Mulli said. "From *very* far away."

Laughter filled the air. The atmosphere felt light. Like you could breathe without the threat of worry entering your mind.

"And you?" Esther asked.

Muchoki thought back to life on the streets. Thought of his rescue. His time at MCF. His start at his career. His re-rescue.

"My favourite animal is the jaguar," he said.

"Jaguar. Very fast. Why do you like the jaguar?" Mulli asked.

Muchoki took a sip of his tea. Oh, that felt good. It filled his senses. He felt the warmth of the morning heat. It was going to be a hot day.

"I love the jaguar because of its high level of endurance," Muchoki said.

PART 6
ZENDAYA

CHAPTER 1

Something didn't look right.

Zendaya gazed out the window of her Eldoret home. In the distance, she noticed people installing a fence on their private property. What was going on?

She opened the door. The morning heat blasted against her. Her grandmother shifted her attention from the field to Zendaya.

"Grandmother? What are they doing?"

Zendaya stood by her grandmother and felt her arm wrap around her.

"There's been a problem," Grandmother said.

"What kind of problem?" She saw her grandfather talking with a stranger out in the field.

Her grandmother sat her down on a small stool. "Your grandfather bought this land. It belongs to us," she said. "The man who owned this land before us sold it to your grandfather. But he didn't give your grandfather the title."

"What's a title?"

"It's a legal document. Something official that describes this property."

"So?"

"When Grandpa bought the land, he shook hands with the man and gave him money."

"Then it's our land. He paid for it."

"Yes, he paid for it."

"So then why are those people building a fence on our land?"

Her grandmother breathed in the hot morning air, wishing life could be as innocent as the way it existed inside Zendaya's mind.

"Grandpa and the man who owned the land made a deal. But the man is supposed to give the title to Grandpa. Instead, he kept the title. And the man sold the title to someone else. We don't own the land. Not legally."

A deep sense of anger ripped through Zendaya. "That's not fair! He paid the money. They shook hands. They made a deal," Zendaya said. She stood up. Placed her hands on her hips. "That man gave Grandpa his word."

Grandmother let out an exasperated sigh. She closed her eyes, trying to find a way to cope with this herself.

Zendaya clenched her jaw. Her eyes narrowed as she looked out at the fence.

"This is not right," Zendaya said. "It's not right."

The incredible heat inside the church sanctuary bothered none of the children for the ageless reason that children prioritize fun over comfort. When they are enjoying life, temperature issues tend to go away. Especially for Zendaya, who gleamed while competing in the church youth Bible trivia contest.

A short woman with a large smile looked out at the eager children. "The woman who continually banged on the judge's door wanted what?"

Zendaya's hand shot up so fast it caught even the woman leading by surprise. How many in a row would it be now? She nodded to acknowledge her.

"Zendaya," she said with the kind of gentle smile that revealed a contented heart.

"Justice!" Zendaya shouted. "The woman who continually banged on the judge's door wanted justice!"

"Correct again, Zendaya. Well done. The game is tied. Last question."

Strictly speaking, of the twenty children sitting at the front of the church only two people were tied. The remaining children resolved themselves to not winning. Again. All eyes focused on the hands of Zendaya and the girl beside her.

"Our God is our refuge and strength. And ever-present help in the time of?"

Zendaya's hand shot up like the water from Jacob's well. That was good and not so good. The leader acknowledged her. But the answer was still tucked away in Zendaya's mind.

"Zendaya?"

She swallowed. Hoping to buy time. *Come on. Come on.*

"The answer is …," Zendaya began.

Her stall drew a breath from the other contestants. Zendaya searched harder through every crevice in her mind until the answer came to the forefront.

"Trouble."

"Excellent!"

The others clapped. Again. For Zendaya. Again. Her nearest competitor's shoulders slumped. Zendaya gave her a playful hug.

"Sorry," Zendaya said.

Her competition waited, then smiled. "You couldn't let me win just once?"

Zendaya smiled back. "No."

The other girl rolled her eyes. The girls giggled and joined the rest of the children for choir practice.

TRANSFORMATIONS

Kama unafuraha na unajua	If you're happy and you know it
Piga makofi	Clap your hands
Kama unafuraha na unajua	If you're happy and you know it
Piga makofi	Clap your hands
Kama unafuraha na unajua	If you're happy and you know it
na unataka kuonyeshana	and you really want to show it
Kama unafuraha na unajua	If you're happy and you know it
Piga makofi	Clap your hands

The day after Zendaya's twelfth Christmas, the mood in Eldoret suddenly changed. The atmosphere of peace and joy celebrating Jesus's birth gave way overnight to uncertainty and fear. The contrast proved to be so stark it seemed as if all Eldoret had been transported to a different place. At first, Zendaya could not point to anything specific. Nothing definite. But she *felt* it. Sensed it. The elections approached. Tension filled the air, making it difficult to think of anything else.

Political parties divided themselves not so much along platforms as along tribal lines. Forty-two tribes existed in Kenya, and they generally voted in block. The Kalenjin stuck to one party. Zendaya's Kikuyu tribe to another. Eldoret stood in the Rift Valley, an area traditionally habited by the Kalenjin. Over time and through intermarriage, more and more Kikuyu came to Eldoret. Some Kalenjin saw the Kikuyu as advancing faster and further than themselves. And the economic divide between tribes acted like charcoal that grew hot in the cauldron of election.

Neighbours who used to be friendly to each other now became cold. Children who once played together found themselves in separate groups.

But the subtleties of questionable looks and odd feelings were made clear when outright threats reached Zendaya's ears. As she played in the front yard, she saw a Kalenjin man stop in front of their neighbour's home. She recognized him. He lived nearby. But his usual friendly face looked different, the way faces do when seething anger from the soul reaches out to consume the body. He screamed at an older man who was hunched over just enough to reveal he understood the stress of physical illness. The man on the street hurled a series of curses at him and issued a warning.

"If your candidate wins the election, we will burn your house!"

A shock raced through Zendaya. Had she heard that correctly? The newness of this intensity of fear made her feel as if she had suddenly been thrown off a cliff. She stood there. Unable to move. Her mind tried to process whether what she saw was real, or if it was something her imagination had created. The man on the street carried on. Zendaya hurried inside.

Grandmother finished cleaning the dishes.

"Why would he do that?" Zendaya asked. "Is he really going to burn down their house? Or is he just saying that because he is angry?"

Grandmother pulled Zendaya close and held her.

"I'm scared, Grandmother."

This was normally the time when Grandmother would respond to Zendaya's fears by saying, *That's all right, Zendaya. There's nothing to be worried about. Everything will be just fine.*

Zendaya waited to hear those words from her grandmother this time, too. Only they never came.

The next day, tensions increased. People became emboldened in their anger. People shouted at each other. Threatened each other. Zendaya tried to make sense of it. Where was all this coming from? Had people been harbouring these feelings for such a long time, only to have this election bring them to the surface?

She thought back to her Bible trivia competitions. Thought about the other girls she memorized Scripture with, including Kalenjin. Was their friendship not real? It certainly felt real. But had she been imagining things all this time?

Election day proved stressful and anxious for Zendaya and all Kikuyu. Even though Kikuyu had the upper hand in wealth, they were fewer in number compared with their Kalenjin neighbours. If things got out of hand—really out of hand—Zendaya wondered who would come to their aid.

They waited for the election results. Zendaya's family alternated between trying to convince themselves there was nothing to worry about and trying to find a way to rid themselves of the uncertainty that knocked at their hearts' doors.

Finally, the results came in. The candidate the Kikuyus supported won the national election. It should have been cause for celebration.

But it would soon prove to be a disaster.

A sudden explosion of unbelievable anger ripped through Eldoret. It was as if someone flicked a switched to turn everything into chaos. The moment the results were announced, Zendaya heard screaming in the streets. What was going on? Were they really coming to burn their neighbour's house? Would theirs be next?

Grandmother grabbed her hand. They hurried towards the door with the rest of the family. Panic filled their hearts. They wouldn't be safe in the house.

It was only a matter of time. Zendaya tried to understand. *We're home. We're safe here. Aren't we? Aren't we always safer at home?*

Grandmother glanced outside, wondering which direction to run.

What? We're not actually going outside, are we? We can't go out there. That's where the violence is.

"Grandmother?" Zendaya asked.

"We have to make a run for it," she said.

"We can't, Grandmother," Zendaya said, gripping her grandmother's hand.

"We're not safe here."

Zendaya felt hollow inside. Hope drained from her body. A stark, consuming fear filled its place. She looked out the window. Her mouth gaped open. Her heart pounded.

She saw fire and smoke in every direction. Everything had become engulfed in flames. Shouts of anger. People screaming in pain.

Grandmother opened the door. She pulled Zendaya's arm. The family raced out of the house into the night madness.

And ran down the street.

"Grandmother?" Zendaya cried.

"You must run faster."

"I left everything at home."

"That doesn't matter now," Grandmother said, turning down a corner.

Zendaya felt a blast of unbearable heat. Fires raged all around her. The roar of flames filled her ears. Billowing smoke filled her lungs. She coughed uncontrollably.

"Grandmother!" Zendaya screamed, but she could barely hear her own words.

Up ahead she saw angry throngs of people ravaging the streets with machetes. Bodies lay on the ground.

Smoke caused Zendaya's eyes to fill with water—a partial blessing that prevented her from being able to clearly see the carnage around her.

"You Kikuyus rigged the election!" someone shouted.

"There," Grandmother pointed. "The police station."

They ran down another street, hoping to avoid the main road. They turned a corner and hurried into the station.

Police officers with automatic rifles stood guard. They recognized their Kikuyu features and allowed them through. Inside the compound, Zendaya saw a crowd of people crying. She saw desperate faces, bewildered by fear, searching the crowd for other members of their families.

Zendaya's grandfather counted their family and confirmed all had made it this far.

Police ushered them into a bus.

"You are being taken to an Internally Displaced Persons camp," a young officer said. "Please remain calm."

Nice words. Really they were. But they came to no avail.

Zendaya's grandmother led them to vacant seats. They sat down. Zendaya tried to make sense of what she was seeing.

Mothers cried for their children, wondering where they were.

Children cried, looking around the bus for their siblings.

Zendaya clutched her grandmother's hand. She noticed a woman across the aisle staring off into space. The woman carried on an intense conversation with someone who was not there. She suddenly smiled and then managed a faint laugh, finding solace in a place other than reality.

Zendaya shrank back into her seat. She tried to remember a song from church. Any song. But the unbearable pressure of her surroundings caused words to fail her. She felt a deep fog creep into her mind, attacking her thoughts.

Where's God, Zendaya?

He … He is here.

Where? Can you show me? Is He in the streets? Is that where God is? With the murdering and burning?

She closed her eyes, hoping to turn this discussion off, but the conversation only grew more intense.

Zendaya? Can you help me with something?

Leave me alone. Go away.

You sing about God every Sunday. Can you sing me a song now?

I can't.

Sure you can. Would you like me to start you off? … If you're happy and you know it—

I don't want to sing right now.

But every time is a good time to sing to the Lord, no? Come on. Let's try again. If you're happy and you know it, clap your hands …. I don't hear you clapping.

I told you, I don't want to sing.

Fair enough. How about a Bible verse then?

I'm trying to remember.

Must be hard with all what you've seen. No problem. Let me help your memory. It goes like this: Our God is ….

It didn't make any sense. None of it. There was a world she remembered. A world where she played outside. Went to school. Sang in church about a God who loved her. But she had now been transported to a strange place far away. And she couldn't put those two worlds together.

Our God is ….

Hard to remember? Why is that, Zendaya? Why are the words so hard to remember?

Our God is our refuge.

And what? What else, Zendaya?

She swallowed, feeling the scratch of smoke particles in her throat.

Our God is our refuge and strength. An ever-present help ….

Yes?

An ever-present help ….

When is God your help, Zendaya? I'm dying to hear how this verse ends.

An ever-present help in the time of trouble.

I agree. One hundred percent. You can count on that verse all the time. He is your help and … Oh, wait. Except for right now. Things don't look so good. Where is God now? How is He your help in time of need now?

I ….

Yes?

I don't know.

How can you quote verses about God being your help when in reality you can see this is not the case?

Her mind struggled to find an answer. She searched but could not match the pieces of the puzzle.

I don't know.

Maybe God isn't who you thought He was. Maybe you're having trouble reconciling the God you sing about with what you are seeing in your beloved country?

Maybe there is something I am not seeing.

Or maybe you are realizing that it's all fine and good to sing and quote verses about something that has a wonderful way of existing inside the walls of a safe church or safe home. But which is not so good in the real world, where people actually have to live. Or die.

She leaned into her grandmother and wondered how to pray.

Wondered how long it would take them to get to the Internally Displaced Persons camp.

And wondered what life would be like when they got there.

CHAPTER 2

The hazy African sun began to rapidly disappear as the bus pulled into the Internally Displaced Persons camp. Darkness covered the land. Zendaya sat up in her seat. She gazed out in disbelief. A sea of white tents flooded the landscape.

"What is this place?" she asked Grandmother.

"This is home."

It didn't feel like home. Didn't look like home either. Zendaya saw an entire family cramming into one of the small tents.

How long are we going to have to stay here? And are we safe? Will they come after us here?

She saw military men standing guard with rifles. She wondered if it would be enough to keep out the disaster she had just witnessed.

The bus stopped, and Zendaya immediately wished it hadn't. She felt an uneasy sense of wonder come over her. *What's going to happen next? I don't want to get off this bus. I like sitting next to Grandmother. What will life be like in the IDP?*

But what choice did she have? She didn't want to go back to the city. Back to the violence. That only left the IDP and having to fit into a cramped tent in a white sea of confusion.

Can we just keep driving somewhere else? How am I going to continue schooling? Is this it? Do I stay here forever? How long before things turn back to normal? … Wait, will they? Will things ever turn back the way they were? Or is this the new reality for us?

She stepped off the bus. An exhausted relief worker wearing a uniform and an anxious set of eyes took their information, gave them cooking supplies and led them down a muddy path.

They passed an unending line of tents. Zendaya saw fathers, mothers, and children crying. Some people had become so overwhelmed with attempting to deal with the events that they could only manage to sit in their tents, trying to force themselves to hang on to the faint grasp of an unwanted reality. Men unpacked their meager handouts. Older children sat under the shelter of their tents, feeling the same uncertainty as Zendaya about whether being here was safe.

Zendaya's family of fourteen stopped. The relief worker gave out tent assignments. Zendaya entered a tent with her grandmother and some of the other members of her family. She sat down on a blanket. The adults discussed making food.

Zendaya rubbed her shoulders for warmth, feeling the uncomfortable combination of the chill night air and the burden of unbearable stress creep into her body.

"If it rains, do not touch the walls or the ceiling of the tent," her grandmother warned.

Zendaya nodded, unable to get words out.

"Otherwise, the water will come in."

The adults continued discussing.

Zendaya overhead conversations of other men in nearby tents plotting revenge. *We're going to get them back. We'll arm ourselves. They'll pay.*

Zendaya wrapped a blanket around her shoulders.

Why is this happening, God? Why did You allow this? Why did all those people hurt us? I feel like You have failed me, God.

She tried to steady her mind. Tried to find peace in the midst of utter confusion. Instead, antagonistic thoughts beat against her.

Where was God today, Zendaya?

She wanted to push that thought out of her mind. But it would not leave her.

What? No quick comeback? No smart rebuttal for an argument? No logical defence?

I don't understand what happened today.

Sure, you do. Look at all these tents. This is how your God works. He can't keep Eldoret safe from trouble, much less the whole world. An ever-present help? Can you really say that?

The Bible says it.

But look with your eyes, Zendaya. Please explain all this to the jury.

I ....

Yes?

I ....

Zendaya, please reconcile what you claim is in the Bible with what you are experiencing. Can you kindly explain that to the jury?

I ... I can't.

That's correct. So please then explain why you continue to hang on to these archaic and unsubstantiated beliefs in a God who can't live up to what He promises.

They had a supper of sorts. They went to bed. Zendaya kept her eyes open, wondering if the violence would spill over to the camp.

What if they come here? What if they follow us here?

She had seen the soldiers. Had seen their weapons. Still, she wondered if they could protect them. Wondered if there were enough of them. Wondered about her friends. Had they all made it through?

Fearful thoughts filled her mind.

Zendaya stayed awake the entire night.

Morning came as a welcomed change. They had lived through the night. That was something positive. She stepped outside. The early morning sun revealed the harsh bitterness etched on people's faces.

"Then how do we pay the loan?" a woman asked her husband.

There was no insurance. Banks would require people to continue paying their loans even though their houses and businesses had been burned to the ground.

Grandmother came to the tent carrying water. She did her level best to put on a brave face. But Zendaya recognized the psychological torment visible in her grandmother's eyes. Neither her grandmother, nor herself, nor anyone in the camp had any control over anything. They could decide nothing. They could move nowhere. Total loss of decision making. Total loss of planning. Zero ability to impact the future in any meaningful way.

The anguish of the loss of life shattered minds like a stone through a window. People grappled with the sudden shock of realizing a loved one would no longer be coming home.

Zendaya looked out into the distance and noticed a bus approaching with orange and blue colours on the side. The bus pulled into an opening not far from her. She walked closer. The bus stopped. A man stepped out followed by many bright faces wearing clean shirts and carrying food. As if pulled by a wave, people felt drawn to the bus.

Zendaya and her family joined the mass of people. She tried to gain a better look at the man. No uniform. He wasn't from the government. The group began offering food. As Zendaya and her family waited in line, she watched the man, curious about why he had come. The way he served food to people caught her attention. He didn't just put food on their plates. None of those serving did *only* that. He looked people in the eye. His expression conveyed he sensed their pain. He wanted to make eye contact. Wanted to meet them in their moment of distress.

Where did he come from? What is he doing here? Everyone is trying to get out of this place—I want out of this place—and yet this man and his people are running towards the problem.

Zendaya received her food from one of the other servers.

"Who are you people?" she asked.

A shorter girl with long braided hair smiled with the kind of smile that made Zendaya think she had known her for her entire life.

"We are Mully Children's Family," she said. "We have come to help you."

"And who is that?" Zendaya asked, pointing to the kind man.

Another wonderful smile. The kind that shone through her eyes. "That is Daddy Mulli."

"Daddy Mulli?" Zendaya asked. The girl nodded. "Who is he?"

MCF set up schools for the children in the camp. Zendaya joined the eighth grade, which consisted of 325 children. All in one class. Zendaya woke the first morning of school to have breakfast with her family. She attended class and had lunch provided by MCF. She tasted French beans for the first time and loved them. In spite of all the many children, Zendaya appreciated how MCF provided enough teachers so that each child could ask questions and receive encouragement.

Eva from MCF took special time to speak with Zendaya. She reassured Zendaya that MCF would pay for her critical grade 8 national exams that would enable her to study further.

After class the man she recognized from the food lineup came to the front of the class. He smiled and lifted two thumbs into the air.

"Ooo-aye," he shouted.

A few of the kids followed his lead and mimicked him.

"Have you ever heard that term before?"

The children shook their heads. Zendaya leaned into the aisle to get a better view. For a brief moment, she made eye contact with him.

"Ooo-aye means peace. Can you all say this with me?" He lifted his thumbs and laughed. "Ooo-aye!" he shouted.

The children thrust out their thumbs and shouted: "Ooo-aye!"

A sudden rush of joy filled the room. Zendaya felt as if a powerful gust of wind had blown through the massive tent. She studied his face. Not from her Kikuyu tribe. His features indicated the Kamba tribe. And what made matters even stranger, was that the other MCF people came from a variety of tribes. How was that possible? Why were they all working together? And why were people from other tribes coming to help her tribe?

"I am so glad to see each and every one of you. I know you have suffered so much. And that is very sad. I want to encourage you that even though we can't understand why things happen, we can still trust God," he said. "I want to know, have all of you had enough to eat?"

The children nodded.

"Very good. I want to tell you how much I admire you for all your hard work in school. There are many students in this class, and you are all doing very well.

"Each of you has been created by God. We are all human beings. It does not matter what tribe you are from or where you are from. We are God's creation, and He loves each of us. Human beings make distinctions between people. Rich and poor. This tribe, that tribe. This colour skin, that colour skin. But this is not how God sees us. He sees us as His creation. And He wants each of us to become His children through Jesus Christ."

He dismissed the students to their tents. As the hundreds of children began to leave, Zendaya walked to the front. Mulli noticed her. They introduced themselves and sat down on chairs. Members of the MCF team offered her a glass of water. Zendaya recounted her story to Mulli. As she spoke to him, she had the feeling she was the only person in the world.

"Thank you for trusting me to share your story. I am humbled," Mulli said. "My father beat me terribly as a young boy. One morning, I woke up to discover my family had abandoned me. I felt a huge anger in my heart. I was filled with hopelessness. But God in heaven is a Father to the fatherless. He will be your father."

"Did you ever see your father again?"

"Oh yes. I saw him many times. He is part of us now. I forgave him for what he did. That freed me completely. I want to encourage you to do the same. Forgiveness repairs us, and forgiveness can repair the country."

"I am a follower of Jesus," she said. "I believe the Bible and what it teaches about forgiveness. But if I am honest with you, I can't forgive the Kalenjin for what they did to us."

"I understand your pain, Zendaya. The Lord loves you. And Mamma Esther and I love you very much. Forgiveness comes with time. Stay close to the Lord, and He can help you."

"I am scared about my future. We have no money for studying. I don't know if I will even be able to finish school."

"Trust the Lord," Mulli said. "He is capable of helping you."

Zendaya studied hard. Long days at school. Long evenings in her cramped, cold tent. Many times, the rainwater would rush in, forcing her to sit up most of the night. She would show up exhausted at school. No matter. She had to push through. Tired or not tired, she had to study. At the end of the school year, she wrote her grade 8 exams. She finished first among all girls. Mulli approached her grandmother to ask permission for Zendaya to join the many children who were being rescued from the IDP camp to come to Mully Children's Family.

Zendaya's grandmother had come to terms with the reality that she would not have the means to give her granddaughter what she so greatly desired. The violence after Christmas had wiped them out financially. There would be no funds to send Zendaya to school. She hugged Zendaya goodbye. Neither felt any tears. They were both receiving exactly what they hoped for.

Zendaya said goodbye to her family and the friends she had made. After living in the IDP camp for so long, she was more than ready for a new home. The violence had ended. For some, the wounds were beginning to heal.

She boarded the bus for Mully Children's Family Yatta branch. She gazed out at the massive sea of white tents. She saw the exhaustion and despair etched on the faces of so many people gripped by the unforgiving realities of conflict. Her bus was filled to capacity. Yet there were still so many more who needed help.

The bus pulled away and turned onto the road. Zendaya sensed a rush of freedom and compared it with the worry she felt on her bus trip into the IDP. She whispered a prayer of thanks and turned her attention forward. She felt curious about the future. *If these people can take care of me before my exams, certainly they can take care of me after the exams.*

Mostly, she wondered what it would be like to be Daddy Mulli's daughter. And to have him as her father.

CHAPTER 3

It felt adventurous.

As the bus drove farther away from Eldoret, Zendaya felt more and more at home with MCF. She listened to other Kikuyu children share their experiences, and she shared her own. They discussed what life might be like at MCF. What they wanted to study when they finished school. For the first time in a long time, they could be optimistic about the future.

Hours later, they arrived at MCF Yatta. Teachers and counsellors greeted them as they stepped off the bus. Zendaya felt a warm rush of love pour over her. They received clean clothes, genuine hugs, and hot food.

She slept in a bunk bed, relieved that she was off the ground and free from the threat of water coming in. She slept relaxed that night. It was a feeling she had not had since her last night at home.

The following morning, she attended devotions. Children filled the church to capacity. They sang with such joy, such enthusiasm that it rivaled anything Zendaya had encountered before. She glanced around the sanctuary. Children clapped. They welcomed each other. It felt as if they had been together since birth. But as she studied the faces, looking not so much at their expressions, but rather their facial features, something shocked her. Amazed her.

Humbled her.

She recognized many tribes. Even Kalenjin. She looked behind and noticed many tribes from all over Kenya. Was every tribe in Kenya represented here? And yet they weren't segregated. It wasn't *that tribe over there and this tribe over here*. They acted as if they were all one. Children singing side by side *as if there were no tribes.*

How was this possible?

Zendaya knew very few people in this massive crowd. Only her friends from the IDP camp.

Yet she felt part of a family.

Part of a home.

The following day, she came to MCF Ndalani. The size of the campus amazed her. Football field. Schools. A church. Massive farms. A river for swimming. Dormitories. A dreamland. She settled into her dorm. Made instant friends with her new sisters.

She joined others in the crowded church. She sat down next to a new face. The Luo girl with a shy, infectious smile moved over to make room for her. "Welcome," she said.

After singing, the children erupted in cheers. They stood. Zendaya struggled to understand the commotion. But when she saw him take to the stage, it became clear.

"Ooo-aye!" Mulli said, giving a big thumbs up.

"Ooo-aye!" the children shouted back.

"That sounded amazing," he said with a laugh. "I tell you, that was really powerful!"

The children settled down.

"Each of you was designed for a purpose in life. But that purpose does not just happen on its own. You must plan and work hard. I want each of you to think about what you want to study—what you want to become—when you finish here. Each of you has unique abilities. And these abilities are developed through hard work. Study to show yourself approved. Do not just let life happen to you. Life does not just happen. You need to set a course. Yes, God may change it. But pray about the future, trust God, and work towards it so that what you achieve will be of service to God and other people."

Mulli invited Zendaya to join the Mission Choir. After practice one evening, he sat with her under a starry night while other students talked nearby.

"You are doing very well in class, Zendaya. Your singing is excellent. You are achieving many things," Mulli said.

"Thank you, Daddy."

Zendaya sensed a unique, personal connection with him. Somehow his relationship with her worked differently than relationships he had with others. Yet, she heard other people explain they experienced the exact same thing. How could so many people each believe they had a special relationship with him?

"Can you please tell me, what would you like to pursue for your studies?"

Zendaya felt her imagination step into reality. A hazy image came into view. The prospect of being able to go to university someday. The luxury of having a future with options. She looked down, a signal of her shyness about asking Mulli to make her dreams a reality.

"You are my daughter," Mulli said. "I want to know what is in your heart."

"I want to study international relations."

"You would do very well at that," Mulli said. His affirmation reached inside Zendaya. "Can you tell me why?"

"I love people," she said. "I love the world. I have not been to many places. But I would love to build relationships with foreigners."

She felt the peace that came with being able to express herself without needing to put up guards.

"You and your family have faced many challenges."

"You rescued me," Zendaya said. "You gave me hope."

"The Lord is doing a great work in your life," Mulli said.

"Something made possible through your obedience."

Mulli nodded. The evening became quiet. Oddly, people having conversations nearby suddenly could not be heard.

"The Kalenjin attacked Kikuyus in Eldoret," he said.

The mood changed. Her first instinct was to avoid going back there. To keep those memories shut out. Yet she sensed he had a reason to bring up her past.

"They should never have attacked us," Zendaya said.

"I know what you have gone through," Mulli said. "This is a good place. This is now your new life."

"A place where I can leave the past behind," Zendaya said, wondering where this was leading.

Mulli waited. The silence touched Zendaya.

"Have you forgiven the Kalenjin for what was done to you?" he asked.

The immediate answer she wanted to give was *of course*. The Bible taught forgiveness of enemies. But had she? She felt open before her father. She searched her heart to ensure she would deliver a truthful answer.

"I have. What they did to me was terrible. But I don't feel any anger towards them."

"May I ask, do you have Kalenjin friends here at MCF?"

The question pierced her heart. Just when Zendaya thought she had completed Mulli's line of questioning, she discovered he had a whole additional level to investigate.

Zendaya's eyes were opened to another aspect of forgiveness.

"I know Kalenjin people here at MCF. Honestly, Daddy, I do not harbour resentment against them."

"I believe you," Mulli said. "But I want to challenge you."

"Yes, Daddy," Zendaya said, tilting her head slightly.

"We need to be careful not to assign an entire group of people the actions of certain people within that group. We need to be careful to treat people individually. And not to think we know who they are because of what group they belong to. That is number one."

Zendaya nodded. She leaned closer, wondering what Mulli would say next.

"And the great test of forgiveness is choosing to love someone from the group that hurt you."

"I should befriend a Kalenjin."

"Unforgiveness is subtle, Zendaya. Our hearts can deceive us. We can forgive with our words and even our thoughts. But we also need to forgive with our actions."

"Meaning?"

"We need to see if we are building relationships with people from the group who hurt us. Or are we avoiding them while telling ourselves we harbour no resentment?"

The quiet night air seemed filled with thoughts.

She pondered his words. Thanked him.

"Good night, my daughter."

"Good night, Daddy."

She watched as he walked away, turned down a path, and disappeared out of sight.

Sitting by herself, she thought of his words.

She went to bed later that evening thinking about what he said.

The following afternoon, Zendaya caught up with a schoolmate after class. They knew of each other. Were used to greeting each other. But they hadn't talked. Hadn't *really* talked. Her name was Miriam. Miriam, the smart one in math. Miriam, the happy girl with long, braided hair.

Miriam the Kalenjin.

"How's math going for you?" Zendaya asked, taking the steps down out of the classroom. They walked out to the stone courtyard.

Miriam turned and smiled. Always so genuine. "It is going well. And for you?"

"Getting there," Zendaya said.

Miriam slowed, wondering if Zendaya would do the same. She did. Zendaya sat down on steps, wondering if Miriam would follow. She did.

"It's wonderful here at MCF, isn't it?" Zendaya asked, wondering how carefully she needed to choose her words.

"Being here makes me believe anything is possible," Miriam said, looking up at Mully Mountain. The special rock at the top of a mountain in the distance looked like it could fall at any minute. Yet it had stood there for generations, giving the illusion of defying gravity.

They paused, the way people do when they are getting used to each other's rhythm of communication.

"You are from Eldoret?" Miriam asked in a tone that conveyed she already knew the answer.

Zendaya raised her eyebrows, indicating *yes*.

They understood.

"Do you remember the first time you met Daddy?" Zendaya asked.

Miriam smiled. "I remember sensing this immediate connection to him."

"I felt the same way."

"Do you think all of the older children remember meeting Daddy for the first time?"

Zendaya nodded. "Every child's testimony is unique, and yet they share a common bond: *My life was going nowhere until I met Daddy*, they tell me," Zendaya said. "It's the one element that binds all of us together." She took in a breath. And for a moment a sudden realization came over her. "I can only hope all of us will also be bound together by our faith in Christ."

"The vast majority of us believe," Miriam said. "But we need to reach out to all our siblings and love them into the Kingdom. An everlasting family of brothers and sisters."

It struck Zendaya how much she agreed with Miriam.

"Some of us are getting together after evening devotions. Want to join us?" Miriam asked.

"I would love to."

"I need to get to drama club," Miriam said, touching Zendaya on the shoulder. They stood. Miriam began to walk away.

"Nice talking with you," Zendaya said.

Miriam turned, smiled, and shrugged her shoulders. The sun glistened off of her skin. "Me too."

Zendaya watched her leave. A new friend. She looked up at Mully Mountain. Wondered, *How is it possible for the rock to stay in that position?*

She thought about her future. About the direction she would take. She said a short prayer for guidance.

Her mind turning. Analyzing. Sensing.

What to do after school?

CHAPTER 4

Charles Mulli can be unpredictable. You are never quite sure what he will say or do.

Zendaya entered the packed-out church at MCF Ndalani feeling the buzz of all her siblings. Over seven hundred students and many of the staff filled the benches to capacity. But MCFers are famous for making room. So when Zendaya walked down the main aisle, a friend motioned her over. As if on cue, people parted to either side, cramming together even more to make an opening. Zendaya sat down.

Mulli designed the church to be in the shape of a cross. A main centre section with two sections off to either side. The children, former outcasts of society but now members of a family, stood and sang together, their voices resounding in the building.

When the singing stopped, everyone clapped in rhythm. Mulli stood. Despite all God had called him to do—all the rescues, evangelism, miracles—Mulli walked with a quiet, humble demeanour to the front. He greeted them with a classic *ooo-aye* and a thumbs up. The children returned the greeting.

"It is always a joy to be together as a family. Each of you is special to God. Each of you has been designed with a purpose. You are not here by accident. God created the world. And God created you. You are created by God to accomplish something on this earth. No matter where you have come from. No matter what has happened. You are loved by God. And you know what else? Me and your Mamma Esther—I think you know her? Do you? Can you tell me? Do you know her?"

"Yes!" the children shouted.

"You do? You know Mamma Esther? Are you sure?"

"Yes!" the children shouted again.

He turned to Esther and invited her to the front. "Your Mamma and I love you."

She joined him at his side. So many adventures. So many challenges. So many times they faced the Red Sea, and God parted the waters for them.

"*Bwana asifiwe*," Esther said, meaning "Praise the Lord."

"Amen, hallelujah, amen! Glory to Jesus!" they all shouted.

Zendaya felt the words enter her soul. Young children, older students, adults. Different tribes. One purpose.

Esther gave a word of encouragement to the children and sat down.

Mulli was about to start again when he paused. A hush came over the entire auditorium. He waited. Everything stood still in silence. What was going on, exactly? Mulli stepped down from the stage. He walked a few steps onto the floor and stopped. His eyes searched the entire student body.

People looked around. Who was he looking for?

Zendaya waited with the others. Is someone new coming to MCF? Why is it so quiet for so long.

"Zendaya," he said. "Stand up!"

A jolt ran through her. *Did he just say that?*

Mulli made eye contact with her. In that instant, she recalled seeing him for the first time at the IDP camp. He motioned for her to stand.

She got to her feet. Mulli walked towards her. Her mind started running through scenarios.

Okay, what have I done wrong? Am I not studying enough? Did I not volunteer for enough service opportunities? This isn't really the most ideal setting for a reprimand.

Zendaya felt everyone's eyes on her. *Can I please hide?*

Mulli was about to speak.

Here we go. What's he going to say? Why is he singling me out? Why here? Why now? Why not after?

"Zendaya, you are doing a great job."

Everyone erupted in cheers. Zendaya breathed a sigh of relief. People clapped. Really clapped. The way people do when they genuinely feel joy in someone succeeding and receiving praise—especially when it is not themselves.

"Thank you, Daddy."

"But I want to tell you this in front of everybody."

Yeah. Here it comes. The word *but* can be a tough one. It can send conversations in all kinds of directions. And it made Zendaya wonder where he was going with this.

Wonderful that he told me I am doing great. I am ever so grateful. So, what is the problem? Can we just stay on that note? Or better yet, can I just sit down? Would that be okay?

But as she studied his eyes, she saw there was no problem. Instead, she saw something deeper. A conviction in his expression. Suddenly the room went empty. They were no longer in a massive crowd. It was just the two of them.

Father and daughter.

"Forget about that international course you were thinking of."

His words shook her to the core. In an instant, she agreed. Something in her spirit convicted her. He was right. Whenever her father spoke, he used far more than words. He connected with the deepest part of her.

She watched him for any hint as to what he would say next.

"I want you to go into law."

A million things went off inside her mind at the same time.

Immediately, her thoughts raced back to when she was a young girl. She saw the fence being built on their property. She remembered seeing her grandfather being taken advantage of with their family land. Remembered how she argued with her grandmother about the injustice of it all.

She thought about the many students of MCF who had gone on to university. None of them had gone into law. Sure, in theory, she could be the first. But her grades, while good, weren't good enough.

It didn't make sense. Law? She could not find a logical path to reach the same conclusion Mulli had reached.

Still, he stood there with a burning conviction in his eyes.

Mulli sensed her wonder. He recognized in her the difference between doubt and curiosity. He saw into Zendaya. Saw her need for further help in understanding. Like Mary asking, *How can these things be?*

"I want you to go to law school."

This time when he said it, the vision solidified in Zendaya's mind and heart. It was as if he was receiving information from on high. Somehow, he saw what others could not.

"You have courage. You can do it," Mulli said.

And just like that, Mulli turned back and began addressing the crowd on a different topic.

Zendaya sat down. The room was there, but not for her. She was lost in her own world of wonder and amazement.

How did he know that? How did he know years earlier that I wanted to be a lawyer? I never told him. I never even hinted at it. But he knew.

Somehow, he always knows.

Zendaya approached Mulli at the French bean field at MCF Ndalani. He spoke with one of the field workers from the community. Zendaya thought the woman looked to be in her sixties—but so tough to tell when the harshness of life can speed up a person's appearance.

Zendaya overheard the woman express incredible gratitude to Mulli for allowing her to work and provide for her grandchildren. She served as the sole provider in the family. Her husband found full-time employment as an alcoholic. His job didn't pay well. But the benefits were great. For him. That left her with the task of taking care of the grandchildren on her own. Weather-beaten face. Eyes both exhausted and refreshed. She returned to her work.

Mulli turned to Zendaya.

"How did you know?" Zendaya asked.

Mulli walked with Zendaya under a bright blue sky filled with incredible islands of clouds. They spread out across the canopy giving the impression a person could jump from one to the other all the way from one horizon to the other.

"How did I know?" Mulli replied.

They turned onto a path to the main campus. A choir sang in the distance.

"What makes you know something with such certainty that you would call me out in front of everybody?"

"It's not a risk," Mulli said. "Not the way I see it."

"And?" she asked. "How do you see it?"

"God speaks to my spirit."

"God talks to you?"

"Oh yes."

"How do you know."

"When He talks, you know His voice. *My sheep know Me, and they hear My voice.*"

"I thought that meant the Bible."

"Of course. The Bible is authoritative. It is the written, infallible word of God."

"But God speaks to you about other things."

A worker carrying branches exchanged greetings with Mulli.

"When I was in business, God called me one day to sell everything I had accumulated and to dedicate my life to caring for the poor. Where did that command come from? It came from Jehovah God. And sometimes God gives me clear direction about how to encourage someone else. Like you for example."

"I never once told you I wanted to be a lawyer."

"But God told me," Mulli said. "A person must be very careful when they assume to share something God has placed on their heart. But if you are humble, then you know when you know. I don't seek it. But God gives me wisdom. And I know He will bring it to pass in your life."

"That's why you said so in front of all those students?"

"Of course. When you graduate from law, all the people who were present will remember the day I stopped the entire assembly and told people what God will do in your life. They will remember, and their faith will be strengthened, and they will glorify God."

"I don't think I will get into law school."

"I see it differently," Mulli said.

Zendaya smiled. "I had a feeling you would say that."

"I will send you to a private university. You will be the first at MCF to become a lawyer."

They crossed the footbridge. A collection of people waited to speak with Mulli. He bid Zendaya goodbye.

She thought about his words. Thought about being in the IDP camp in Eldoret. Next stop. Law school.

It all seemed so terribly far-fetched.

And yet, strangely enough, part of her felt it had already happened.

CHAPTER 5

Zendaya buried her face in her hands. If first-year law was difficult, then second-year proved to be even tougher. She breathed in, hoping that somehow the addition of oxygen might calm her down. It did not.

She sat at her desk, alone in her room, wondering how she was going to cope. The whole idea of law school had sounded so great in that auditorium when Mulli called her out in front of everyone. But here in the trenches, things became tougher. Harder. More real. What was that verse the apostle Paul said? Despairing even of life itself?

She felt overwhelmed. Like waves poring over her in rapid succession, sinking her further and further down.

Her phone rang. She picked up.

"Hello Zendaya," Mulli said.

"Daddy."

"Don't worry if law becomes difficult," he said.

That was both comforting and strange at the same time. She felt his presence. Needed his presence. But how did he know, at exactly this moment, when she was at her lowest, that she needed to hear from him? How many children had he rescued? How many other people and challenges were on his mind? And yet in spite of all of this, in spite of the crammed highway of issues running through his mind, he dialed her number. He sensed her need.

"It is challenging," Zendaya said, as a polite way of understating her case.

"It will be all right, my daughter."

She felt a sting of tears begin to form. Was it the stress of the classes? The affection of a father? Both?

"Thank you, Daddy."

"Prayer is always the answer," Mulli said. "Prayer comes from a place of humility. We cannot do everything ourselves. We need the assistance of God."

"I feel helpless."

"I also want to encourage you to fast. Remember the many times at MCF when we went without food as a whole family?"

"I remember."

"Fasting changes our concentration from our problems to Almighty God."

"I wish I had your faith, Daddy."

"But you do. You have Jesus. And when you have Jesus, you have full faith."

She felt a sudden lift. Like a once-wounded bird that suddenly remembers it can fly.

"I am preparing for exams and …."

She waited for the courage to continue. Mulli paused with his rare wisdom of knowing not to interrupt someone's thoughts.

"I am preparing for exams."

"You have studied very well. You have worked hard. Now you need to leave it in God's hands."

"I know, Daddy. But that is easier said than done."

"Trust in the Lord," Mulli said. "And use that verse over and over again to defeat the enemy."

"I will."

"May I pray for you?"

"Yes, Daddy."

"Our Father in heaven, I pray for wisdom for Your daughter Zendaya. I pray for courage. I pray for her to remember everything she has studied. I pray for your favour to be on her. Guide her and protect her, in Jesus's name."

She entered the oral exam room. A large classroom made impossibly larger by having only four people seated in the centre. Two men. Two women.

"You have beautiful hair," the taller woman with a motherly instinct said.

Zendaya smiled and thanked her.

They asked her numerous questions about a wide range of topics.

She called Mulli as soon as she received her results.

"I did well, Daddy!"

"Wonderful! I am excited for you. Very well done!" Mulli said with his trademark optimism.

"You called me at just the right time."

"You see how prayer works. Even when we do not see God working, we know He is active behind the scenes. God is always doing something. He may not be doing things the way we expect. But this is where trusting the Lord is so important. Even when we can't see something or understand something, God is still at work."

"It makes me wish I had more faith instead of doubting."

"True faith is calling on God in the midst of our fears. And you did exactly that. I am very, very proud of you, my daughter."

Her time in law school taught her to take notice of words. Their order. Their emphasis. Their meaning.

My daughter.

More than delivering the good news of her marks, she needed to hear the affirmation from her father about being his daughter.

Somehow he knew.

Somehow he always knew.

She finished law school. Finished her bar exams. Celebrated with Daddy Mulli and Mamma Esther. Lots of pictures. She found a position as a lawyer. Moved into her own place.

One evening, she sat at her kitchen table eating a late dinner after a long day.

Her cell phone chimed. Zendaya glanced at the name on the screen. A friend of hers. Why was she calling so late? Was something wrong?

"Hello."

"Zendaya."

Yes, something was wrong. Friends can sense it in each other's voices.

"What's happened?" Zendaya asked.

She paused. "I'm sorry to bother you," she said, with a slight change in tone to indicate her effort to fight back tears.

"It's no bother," Zendaya said.

"I fell."

Zendaya sat up. "Badly?"

"Bad enough."

"Are you in the hospital?"

"I fell at work. The doctors say it will be months before I can go back."

"I am so sorry."

"I ...." There was no use trying to hold the tears back anymore. Zendaya heard the muffled sound of crying.

"It's going to be okay," Zendaya said. "A fall at work is covered by their policy. You will get paid while you recover."

Her friend paused. "That's why I'm calling."

A sudden resolve filled Zendaya. "Meaning what?"

"They're denying any wrongdoing."

"What?"

"I asked them for help, but they—"

"That's not fair," Zendaya said.

"I agree, but ...."

"They owe you that money."

"I don't know what to do. I'm scared. I'm going to be out on the street."

"No, you won't be," Zendaya said.

"I can't make it more than a month."

"It's going to be just fine."

"How do you know?"

They sat in her friend's living room. Exhaustion filled her face. Her leg stretched out over another chair. Wrapped in bandages. A bad fall. A twisted knee.

"I'm telling you, they're not going to pay."

"Sure they will," Zendaya said. "They just need encouraging."

"I gave them this doctor's report." She handed Zendaya a medical report. Zendaya read it.

"It's clear."

"They don't care."

"They will," Zendaya said.

"How can you be so sure?"

"Most people, not all, respond to reason and logic. I will review everything. Their policy. The responsibility to pay. And I will send them a letter."

"I appreciate this, Zendaya. But I don't have the money—"

"You know better than that."

Her friend paused. Her eyes began to well up with tears. She nodded.

"You're going to smile again," Zendaya said. "Now leave this with me."

Zendaya said goodbye and walked to the door.

Zendaya dedicated her evenings after work to research and gathering facts. She crafted a letter referencing the law governing an employer's responsibility to care for workers injured at their place of employment. She thought back to her grandfather all those years ago. Their family land being stolen from them. She finished the letter.

Sent it off.

Her phone chimed.

"Hello," Zendaya said in her trademark optimistic tone.

"I'm sorry I missed your call," her friend said.

"I got a response."

"You did?"

"Don't act so surprised," Zendaya said. "Of course I did."

"And?

"They're going to pay you."

"What?"

"What do you mean, *What*?" Zendaya said with a laugh. "They're going to pay you right through your recovery."

"I … I don't know what to say."

"You could start with 'I knew you would pull it off, Zendaya.' Something like that."

A pause. Victory.

"Thank you," her friend said in a barely audible whisper.

"Sure thing. Bless you."

"You too."

Zendaya hung up. She glanced out the window at the setting sun.

Her grandfather would be proud.

Mulli and Mamma Esther, too.

Zendaya sat together with her parents at MCF Ndalani in the cool of the evening. The sun had set. A quiet and calm darkness covered MCF like a blanket, as if getting ready to tuck the whole facility in for the evening.

"I am very proud of you," Mulli said.

She heard a choir practising in the church. She smiled.

"You called me out all those years ago, and here we are. I am a lawyer."

"Of course," Mulli said.

Mamma Esther poured them all a cup of tea.

"You have an incredible way with people, Daddy."

"I love to be with them."

"He is very good with people," Esther said.

"Why is that?" Zendaya asked Mulli.

Mulli added some honey to his tea.

"Not too much honey," Esther joked. "Only a little bit."

She laughed. Mulli smiled and nodded. He pulled back the honey.

"Very good. I will only take this much. Is that okay?"

"It is good," Esther said.

"All right." He turned to Zendaya. He looked up, returning to his train of thought. "I allow people to speak, and I listen. I try to create a good environment for people to be themselves. I can hear them and their fears. When you *know* people's fears, you can help them *out* of their fears."

"I hope I can help people one day."

"You will."

Zendaya took a sip of her tea. She felt the warmth fill her. "How did you know?"

"IDP."

"The IDP camp?" Zendaya asked. "How so?"

"The IDP showed you how things can happen outside your control. We can't always control what happens. But we can respond to them. Do we respond with fear, or with faith? I think this will help you as you move into law."

"Everything felt so out of control there."

"And yet, it became a pivotal moment in your life. Remember where you came from. It is a serious mistake to reject your past. If you forget where you came from, you can become proud. You can think that it was you who got you out of that mess."

"I was a little girl in the IDP camp without hope."

"And now look at you. Do you understand?"

She paused, allowing her mind to process her thoughts. Still, she wondered where his questioning was leading.

"How do you mean?"

"I started at the bottom of the world. I rose to the top of the mountain. But no one thinks of me as a businessman. They think of me as a humble servant of God who was called to live out an amazing adventure rescuing children. And this story encourages people."

"You want me to be free to share about my struggles in the IDP."

"Few people can relate to success. But all of us can relate to failure, conflict, and challenges. You will go on to accomplish great things. I am sure of that. But your law degree will not sustain you. How you met Christ in the IDP camp will guide you. You felt hopeless. I remember it very well. But God will use your story to impact others. Even as He used my story to help others."

She hugged her parents and wished them a good evening.

Zendaya walked into the nearby church. The same building where she had sat all those years ago when Mulli called her out. The choir had finished practising. She was alone—rare in a family so large to find herself alone in a building as big as this. She thought of the packed learning situation at the IDP camp. She thought of meeting Mulli and how he invited her to become his daughter. She thought of the challenges she overcame at law school.

She said a short prayer of thanks.

All of this journey had been one big preparation.

But for what exactly? What would come next?

She walked out of the church into the cool evening air.

It was time for the next adventure.

PART 7
KARL

CHAPTER 1

The challenge was to beat out the dogs for food.

Karl Gatoto wiped sweat from his face. He breathed in the sweltering air, feeling it burn inside his lungs. The merciless inferno in the sky above Langas slum in Eldoret beat down on him. His eyes scanned the shacks on either side of the road for any hint of food.

Up ahead, Karl saw scraps in a small container outside a restaurant. He hurried as fast as his little five-year-old legs would allow. Would the food still be edible? How long had it been in the sun?

He heard a whimper and turned to see his competition. Had his older brothers stuck with him, he might have had a chance. But once again they had run on ahead, leaving him alone. Had he been running against another street child, he could have negotiated a way to share the treasure. Instead, a dog outran him and reached the garbage first. It sniffed through the leftovers, took what it wanted, and ran way.

Karl reached the garbage. The edible parts had been taken. The rest consisted of days-old rotten remains.

Karl exhaled. He sat down under a tree. Exhausted.

He leaned against the trunk, overwhelmed. His stomach ached, an ongoing combination of hunger and feeling sick. He looked around for water. His mind began to spin.

I need help.
No problem. Help is free.
I need a ….
You need what?
I need ….
What do you need?
I need an adult to ask me how I am doing.
That's ridiculous. Just go and talk to your mother.
I ….
You what?
I can't.
You can't talk to your mother?
I am too shy to tell anyone that I am sick.

You could go to the hospital and tell them.

I am afraid of hospitals.

Why?

All those treatments and injections are awful. I remember the vaccinations. It stinks like medicine in there. That's the last place I want to go.

Karl snapped himself out of it. Silly child. There were only two necessities in life. Food and a place to sleep.

Everything else was an out-of-reach fictional dream.

He stood, checked his balance, and struggled down the dirt road towards home. His eyes scanned the ground—the garbage bins near restaurants in particular. That's where the real treasures lay. Rich people visited restaurants. Rich people had others make food for them. Rich people could afford not to finish their plates.

Rich people meant leftovers.

There. Out of the corner of his eye he saw a waiter dumping food into a garbage bin. On instinct, Karl ran across the street. Not smart. A motorcycle hit the brakes and swerved to avoid him. The driver shouted at him as he sped off.

No dog this time. Not yet. Karl reached the garbage. Heaven. And to think the food was still fresh. He reached in and scooped up ugali, stuffing it in his mouth. Dogs had picked up the scent. They always did. They pushed for their fair share. Karl tried to angle them away. The dogs got up on their hind legs to reach inside the bin.

There wasn't much. Hardly enough to cover the palm of his hand. He would need ten times this amount for it to be considered a meal. He stepped back. It was something. Success of sorts. An entire morning scrounging the streets could not yield his one meal of the day.

He struggled towards home. His balance felt off. It took considerable thought to plan his steps. It felt as if the ground were shifting beneath him. His vision became blurry.

He blinked. Shook his head. *Just keep going. You can lie down when you get home.*

Such a strange reality to take this road back. It marked the line between slum life and that other place. He looked over. In the distance, he saw another world. Children in clean uniforms entered a school. They playfully pushed each other with the kind of health and vibrancy he could not relate to. They lived in the same city as he. They weren't *that* far away. And yet they were. They were as far apart as people can get on this earth. They might as well have been on a different planet.

And part of him wished they were.

Life proved hard enough to live each day with the sole purpose of trying to make it to tomorrow. Karl didn't need the extra humiliation of seeing a world where people enjoyed life. Where people had enough to eat. Where people could think about something other than survival. How was it possible to be so close to them and yet so far?

No matter. School was for others. School was for them. School was for those far removed from his reality.

Farther down, on *that* side of the road, he saw two boys laughing as they ate potato chips. He noticed how they reached for the chips inside of a bag. Not out of a garbage can.

What do potato chips taste like? I would like to have a bag of chips. I would like to sit and eat them.

It seemed crazy that two boys could have a whole bag for themselves. *Why do they need so much? Why can't they share?*

He turned the corner and headed down the alley to his place. He saw people walking the narrow path. Saw people outside their shacks cleaning clothes. No one looked at him. No one talked to him.

He had nothing to offer. And he had a lot of needs. He might as well not even have been there.

He reached home. Four mud walls. An iron sheet roof. Dirt floor. No tables. No cupboards. Blankets on the ground that served as beds.

His mother sat on a faded red blanket. Hunched over to the side. Sick again. He could always tell with that yellow haze in her eyes. He looked at her and raised his eyebrows to greet her. A weathered exhaustion aged her young face. Had she lived in a different part of the world, she would have easily exuded the joy of a happy, graceful woman. But people can't choose where they are born. And she did the best she could with what little she had been handed. The combination of a bad start to life and an absent husband left her bewildered and overcome. But she continued on, shouldering the responsibility of looking after Karl and his three older siblings in one of the worst environments Earth has to offer.

Karl never knew his father. Still, he sensed his loss. Sensed there should be someone else there. His siblings were still gone. Out looking for food. They often went without him. No point in having young Karl slow them down. A stabbing pain shot through his stomach like a knife. He squished his eyes together, hoping he could fall asleep and escape the pain.

"You found food for lunch?" she asked, as she struggled to her feet.

He nodded. But she knew better. Mothers always seem to know. She walked past him. He wanted her to stay. Wanted her to be free from having to work long days to keep her family going. Just a few moments. To talk together. Mother and son.

"Maybe you could tell me a story," Karl asked.

She stopped at the door. Returned to her boy. Sat down beside him. Ran her hand over his little head.

"What kind of story would you like to hear?"

"A story where you don't have to leave. A story where we can be together."

"I like that story, Karl."

"It can happen."

She managed a faint smile, exercising muscles she was unaccustomed to using. "Of course," she said, wondering how many generations in her family had hoped for the same future. Yet here they were: at the bottom, with no prospects of being able to escape.

She left. He lay down and rolled over onto his side. He heard people talking as they walked down the alley. Dogs barked. A ringing in his head signalled the beginning of a headache.

His thoughts drifted to God. He heard about God from his sister and mother. They had been to church. He wondered what God was like. Wondered if God had thoughts about him, the way he had thoughts about God.

Time took forever, the way it does for children. His mother returned at suppertime, though it felt much longer. She made a fire. Boiled water. The smell of potatoes revived him. He ate with his mother.

"Could I eat some more?" he asked.

She shook her heard. "That's for your siblings."

"Please?"

She stood. "Do not touch it. It is for them."

"Where are they?" Karl asked.

She had not seen them the entire day. That wasn't exactly unusual. They would often spend the day hunting for something to eat. But normally, they would have been back by now.

She left again. The hunger inside Karl became unbearable. He felt as if his stomach was shrinking to nothing. It screamed at him to eat something, but he was unable to answer the call. And the smell of potatoes only served to make the hurt that much worse.

The door burst open. Karl sat up. His mother's face had come alive. As Karl studied her expression, he saw something in her eyes he had never seen before. She looked ... she looked happy. His mother reached out her hand and urgently beckoned him to follow.

"Karl!"

He got up. Placed his little hand in hers. She led him out of their home and through the streets. She walked with determination. Desperation. What was going on?

"Mom, where are we going?"

Cars honked. Bicycles rang bells. People crowded the streets this time of day. Coming and going. The commotion of crowds. She negotiated through the mass of people.

Karl managed a glance up at his mother. He tried to process what he saw. And then he recognized it. At least he thought he did. So hard to make conclusions about something he was seeing for the first time.

He felt her grip his hand tighter. Felt her quicken their pace.

"Quickly, Karl," she said in a whisper that made him wonder if she was overwhelmed with what she had encountered. He had never seen her this way before. She *was* different.

His mother had energy. His mother had purpose.

His mother had hope.

CHAPTER 2

They stopped outside a large, black gate.

"Wait here," she said, crouching down and looking into him. Yes. Definitely. Her eyes seemed altogether different. Filled with curiosity and life. "And don't wander off."

She entered through the gate. It closed behind her. He touched it. Strange. Steel like anywhere else. But it *felt* different.

What is this place? Why am I here? And why do I have this unmistakable feeling that this is a good place?

A large wood pole stood near him with many black electrical cables hanging down. Electricity. How does it work?

He touched one of the cables. Then another. Moved them around.

A rustling behind him caught his attention. He turned to see a man walking with soft steps, as if he was trying to avoid waking up lions. The man stopped and looked out over Eldoret. Karl studied his face. The man exuded both love and concern. He had never known anyone to look out at Eldoret before, much less with this kind of intensity. Something weighed heavy on the man. He looked burdened by a deep sense of responsibility.

The man's gaze spanned from one side of Eldoret to the other. When he reached the end, he turned to see young Karl. The man smiled and let out a disarming laugh.

"How are you, young man?"

Young man. Wow. So many things for Karl to take in. A man spoke to him. And the man addressed him in a respectful manner. Who calls a child like him *young man*?

But most of all, someone noticed him. He wasn't invisible.

At least not to this man.

"I am doing fine," Karl said. Either his headache had left, or he was too engrossed in what all of this meant to notice it anymore.

The man looked over at the electricity pole. "What are you doing with the cables?" he asked.

"Just looking at them," Karl said, taking his hands off them.

"All right," the man said. "It's not safe to play with the cables. This is electricity. It's very dangerous."

"I'm sorry."

"You should step back and be careful not to touch them again." Karl moved away. He nodded.

"Who are you waiting for?" the man asked.

"My mother."

"Your mother. Where is she?"

"She is inside."

"Good. I am glad to hear that," the man said with a smile that caused Karl to wonder if the man knew something he didn't. "She will come back in a few minutes." The man crouched down. "I see you are very curious about things."

Karl wanted to smile. But didn't know how. He nodded.

"Remember not to touch anything. I want you to be safe." The man walked down the street.

And Karl was left with the feeling of a man who cared for him.

Time seemed to take forever until finally his mother reemerged. He felt a sense of accomplishment in resisting the urge to touch the cables.

"Let's go inside," she said, her smile the largest he had ever seen.

"What is this place?"

"Come and see."

The guard opened the gate. Karl's mother held out her hand for him and led him inside.

So many children. He recognized some of them from the street. At least he thought he did. They looked different now. Healthy. Clean. Happy. Like they came from *that* side of the street.

"Where are we?" Karl asked.

"Welcome to Mully Children's Family," his mother said.

A young woman introduced herself, hugged him, and explained MCF.

Karl was about to follow the woman to receive new clothes and wash up before supper when he turned to his mother. "Come mother."

Karl held out his hand. His mother knelt down and hugged him.

"This is your new home. I will come to visit you," she whispered. "God has answered my prayers. You have a great home." She looked into his trusting eyes. "You will have a father and a mother here. I want you to listen to them. And you will be able to eat until you are full, Karl."

"When will I see you again?" he asked.

"Very soon," she said. "Now go on."

He walked into MCF Eldoret and entered into a new world.

A boy took him to the back yard. Karl gave the names of his brothers, and the boy led him towards them. He ran up to his three siblings and hugged them. Together again. This time in a good place. He joined his brothers in eating a plate full of githeri. His brothers encouraged Karl to eat his beans and maize until he was full. The brothers watched, understanding where he was coming from.

Other children talked with him, making him feel at home. They took him to class, had supper with him and accompanied him to devotionals. That evening, he slept in a bed. Felt warm. Felt safe. Felt free from the pressure of having to find food.

Suddenly, his mind was free to think beyond survival.

The next Saturday he woke at six a.m. and joined other children in the courtyard. He saw the man he had seen earlier. This time, the man wore a track suit. Karl approached him.

"I did not touch the cables," Karl said.

The man looked over at him. "Very good young man. Are you ready for your exercises?"

"Are you the man who trains us?"

The man laughed. "Yes, I do that," he said. "I am also your father."

"Really?"

"Yes indeed. Get ready. We are about to go."

"Yes, Daddy."

It's been said every MCF beneficiary knows where they were and what they were doing when they first called Charles and Esther Mulli Daddy and Mamma. That was true of Karl. The moment he heard those words, they seemed as natural as leaves on a tree.

Mulli walked with the children to a playground. He led the children in stretching, exercises, and jogging. Following their exercises, they returned to MCF, where they had breakfast and cleaned the compound. In the afternoon, they piled into his pickup truck, and he took them river swimming at Two Rivers dam. They played football and other games and swam under the afternoon sun. On the trip back, the children sang the kind of relaxing, fun songs kids sing when the enjoyment of life is at maximum and the worries of life are left for another day. The kind of singing that happens when children get to be children. Karl joined in:

Gari iende	Let the car go
Ndio maana tunasema	That's why we are saying
Gari iende	Let the car go

Karl felt the wind rush past him. He felt what it was like to be free of hunger. To be without pain. He felt the comfort of family. Felt what it was like to enjoy life.

What it was like to have Mulli in his life.

He looked out at the countryside. Green trees. Crops growing in brownish-red soil. He relaxed.

Everything was looked after.

Karl sat shoulder-to-shoulder in the packed-out living room. The children sensed anticipation as they finished singing songs and waited for their Daddy to come to the front.

"I would like to tell you a story," Mulli said. "Who likes stories?"

Karl and the other children raised their hands. A hush fell over them. Karl focused on his father. Captivated by Mulli's love and passion for God and for them.

"Very good. Now I want all of you to know that this story comes from the Bible. Sometimes people make up stories. They think them up out of their heads, and those stories can be very interesting. But the Bible is different because the Bible is true. Everything that is written in the Bible is written by God in heaven who used people on the earth to write them down.

"A very long time ago, in a far away place called Persia, there lived a humble orphan girl named Esther. Her mother and father died. And her older cousin, Mordecai, took care of her. One day, the king of the land wanted to find a queen. The king arranged for young women throughout his land to be brought to him. One of those women was Esther. And he loved her very much, and she became queen.

"Esther belonged to the Jewish people—God's chosen people. Esther heard from her cousin that some people wanted to kill the king. Esther warned the king and saved his life. But there was a very bad man named Haman. Haman did not love God, and he wanted everyone to worship him. But Mordecai would not do so. So Haman decided to destroy all the Jews.

"Esther heard about this and became very sad. She had to gather courage—she had to be very brave—and she had to go and see the king. She fasted. She did not eat or drink for three days. When she stood before the king, she explained about Haman's evil plan. The king destroyed Haman. And Esther was used by God to save the Jewish people."

Karl felt the impact of the story. The way Mulli spoke reached inside him. Karl sensed God talking to him.

"Esther rose from nowhere to become a powerful person serving the king. God is in control of everything. Nothing is by accident. You are not an accident. You are here for a purpose. God created you for a reason. Your history does not define you. Esther took courage to help the Jewish people. And if you trust in God through His Son, Jesus Christ, He will use you to help other people. Our life is not about ourselves. Our life is about how God can work in us and through us to serve Him and to serve other people," Mulli said. "This is why you are here."

Mulli dismissed his children for the evening, knowing they felt the comfort of heading off to beds and not to the street.

The children felt a collective joy in hearing the story and sighed that it had already ended. Karl joined the boys as they headed to the dorm.

He could have listened to Mulli for hours.

His short legs struggled to climb to his upper bunk. Other boys helped him up. It felt adventurous to be sleeping this high. A welcome change as he became accustomed to not having to sleep on the ground and not having to go to bed hungry.

As he drifted off to sleep, he thought about Esther. Thought about her courage. Thought about how God chose her to rise to an important position. Thought about how for the first time in his life he felt connected to God. Like God wasn't simply some all-powerful being out there. He was present. He knew Karl. In the same way that Esther approached the king, Karl could approach God.

Was that how it worked? Could a kid from the slums really talk to God?

Karl wondered.

God? Can You hear me? Can You hear a young boy in Eldoret? Can You hear me the same way You heard Esther? I think You can. I know it. I know You can hear me. I know, God, that You are listening. Can I ask You a question? Is there something You wanted from me? Is there something You want to do with me? Is there a purpose You have for my life?

CHAPTER 3

Every child is gifted in at least one area with special aptitude. Sometimes, a special teacher will draw that out of a student. For Karl, that gifting became clear in his grade 3 science class.

Karl felt a connection with each of his teachers. His science teacher, in particular, exhibited a gentle personality to win Karl's affection and a command of science to ignite the curiosity inside Karl's mind about how things worked. The teacher required strict discipline yet combined it in a natural way with cracking jokes and smiling a lot, all of which earned him the respect of the students.

He gave Karl the responsibility of being a class monitor and also the school timekeeper, which came with a plastic watch for the job. Karl became fascinated by watches and couldn't wait to take it apart and put it back together piece by piece. Afterwards, he took apart every electronic item he could put his hands on and get permission to work on.

Karl's fascination with the world around him coupled with his hard work propelled him to dig deeper and learn more. He discovered how plants functioned. How they use the process of photosynthesis to transform the sun's energy, water, and carbon dioxide into oxygen as well as sugars to help the plant grow. He found the entire process ingenious. Behind the school classroom, his class germinated many seeds and watched them grow to maize, beans, and kei-apples. They watched them every other hour and sometimes dug out seeds and replanted them to monitor their progress under the soil. Karl led two of his friends to conduct many experiments, including generating hydrogen and carbon dioxide.

He discovered electricity is the movement of electrons. While he understood *how* electricity worked, no one seemed to be able to explain *why* electricity worked. Why did electrons in an atom's outermost shell not have a strong force of attraction to the proton? Why could they be pushed out of their orbit? Why not the other way around? Why did electricity work the way it did?

He loved studying animals. Loved land animals, domestic pet animals, birds. How they worked. How they were created differently from each other. Yet out of all the animals he studied, he did not have a favourite.

And out of all he studied, he loved the human body the most.

Karl did what all intelligent people do. He sought more knowledge. The more he studied the body, the more curious he became; the deeper he read, the more questions he asked. He found it amazing that from the top of his head to the tips of his toes there lived an entire universe, with nearly endless questions about how it all worked.

He read storybooks loaned to him by Grace Mulli, one of the daughters of Daddy Mulli and Mamma Esther. He read *Three Little Pigs*, *Chronicles of Narnia*, and East African publications. During the day and on holidays he snuck *into* class to read storybooks, Bible stories in various versions, and science textbooks for the grades ahead of him. All for fun.

He would study late into the evening. His teacher often came in to encourage him.

"You are doing extremely well in your studies," his teacher said with a smile. The young man could easily have found work at a higher paying school in Eldoret. He had even received offers from other employers. It would have been so simple. Just give Mulli his notice. Walk out. And make a whack more cash.

But he didn't.

He stayed.

Callings can be difficult to ignore.

I'll get paid in heaven, he told himself. He lived in modest accommodations, wore modest clothes, and inspired many, many children to develop their God-given gifts.

"You are a great teacher," Karl said in his classic soft voice. His words impacted his teacher, who felt the appreciation teachers feel when their work has not gone unnoticed.

"Praise God."

"You have a great way of explaining things. You understand science very well."

"A person grows in their understanding of science when they discover that it all points to a Designer."

"How do you mean?"

"If a car drives by, people will accept there was a group of engineers who designed that car. It didn't just happen by chance. A car has an engine, it has electronics, it has moving parts. It is sophisticated. There had to be a designer," he said. "The body is far more complicated than a car. A brain. A heart. Electrical signals. Thinking. Emotion. Feeling. Incredible details at every level. If something with lower technology like a car needed a designer, then it is reasonable to accept that the human body with higher technology must have also needed a designer."

"God is the engineer who made the body?" Karl said with a big smile.

His teacher laughed. "There are those who will look at the miracle of the body and think it is an accident. And there are those who will see the exact same evidence and respond to their Creator. Atheists and Christians can both do good science. But only the Christian has a true reason to understand why science exists."

The teacher moved on to other students. And it left Karl wondering what he meant.

Karl opened the door to the stores area. The large room normally contained heavy sacks of beans, rice, and maize, as well as crates filled with potatoes, cabbage or kale, tomatoes, carrots, and mangos. One of his responsibilities included sifting maize, beans, and other vegetables. He took the maize to the mill where it would be milled into flour before going to the kitchen to be used for ugali.

Mulli would buy food and have it delivered to MCF. Karl and others would distribute it to the kitchen for mass production of meals for the many children.

Food deliveries came at different times. There was nothing unusual about going a few days without any large trucks dropping off necessities. But what was unusual was seeing so much empty space in the food storage room.

It was odd. Spooky. It was almost as if Mulli had given orders to move all the food to a different location.

Only he hadn't.

Karl felt a sudden chill. Despite the hot afternoon sun, he felt cold. As if the image he saw of the near-empty shelves reached into his eyes and sent an icy message of fear through his body.

No matter. The deliveries have just been delayed. Sometimes things take longer than they should to get here. Nothing to worry about.

And he would have convinced himself of exactly that, were it not for a sense of concern wrapping itself around his heart.

He looked in and saw the last bag of maize—that felt strange. It was the first time he had seen that. No matter. Maize meant he would have his favourite ugali for supper.

Nothing to worry about. *The delivery truck will be here soon.*
Very soon.
Won't it?

The truck didn't show up that day. Not the next day either. Karl and two other boys used a wheelbarrow to deliver a sack of beans to the kitchen. Last one again. That feeling of uneasiness crept in deeper. He returned to the stores. It looked so vacant. Like the place had been robbed.

Is there even enough food for the rest of the week? What is taking that truck so long? Why don't we buy more food?

Karl stepped outside in an attempt to buy temporary relief from the sight of an empty stores room. Younger children laughed at a nearby water tap. So easy to entertain kids. He wanted to be like that too. Wanted to forget the impending disaster. But heaviness gripped him.

He saw Mulli in the distance, talking and laughing with the children as always. No sign of stress. No sign of panic. But Karl detected a tinge of concern. He wouldn't normally have picked up on it. And it made him wonder if the dwindling resources and Mulli's expression might somehow be connected.

Karl approached the stores door. He hesitated. Did he really want to go in? Maybe it was better to leave bad enough alone. He could pass by and not face reality. But facts are better than wishful thinking. So he opened the door.

And what he saw shocked him.

Only a few bags left. Was it even a day's worth?

Where is all the food? What is going on?

He took in a deep breath. Everything looked so out of place. Like a stadium that is normally filled with fans, but now stands empty.

A bell rang. That meant supper.

At least, it normally did.

Children gathered outside for supper prayer. Mulli came to the front. His face wore the marks of concern. He paused before speaking. The children glanced around for their meal. The kitchen cooked one pot that smelled of beans. The younger kids didn't notice. But the older ones did. Karl saw there wasn't nearly as much food for this meal as in other meals.

"We are going through hard times," Mulli said. Always straight to the point. From the very young to the very old, Mulli gave his children accurate information. There would be no point in shielding children from the realities of life. Creating a fictional world for children—offering a make-believe world where real problem didn't exist—would prevent them from believing in a real God who lives in a real world and deals with real problems.

A somber mood came over MCF. Young children hung on to their little, empty plates. Red. Blue. Green. Fun colours when the plates were filled with food.

"We have gone through our food," Mulli said.

It felt surreal to Karl. Did his dad really say that? Did God bring all these children out of the streets to have them stand here hungry?

"We have a small amount of food for supper. There only will be a cup of light porridge for breakfast tomorrow morning. And there will be no lunch. Supper will be at four p.m. … and will consist of a small ration of soup."

What? How do you go through a day of school without eating? And what happens the day after tomorrow? Are we going back to the streets? Are we going back to scrounging in the garbage bins?

Is this the end of MCF?

"You have always prayed," Mulli said. "Each of you has been taught to speak with Almighty God. Not just to speak *to* Him. But *with* Him. Prayer is a conversation. It is listening to Him and pouring out your heart to Him."

Esther stood beside him. "When we face challenges in life," she said, "we find out what we really believe. We can either trust in God and believe what He says, or we can worry and doubt what the Bible says. I want to encourage you today to have faith."

Her words inspired Karl to feel a sudden surge in confidence. How bizarre. Right behind him stood an empty stores room. Yet it didn't *feel* empty. He almost felt like opening the door again to make sure.

"You need to pray very hard," Mulli said. "Nothing comes without prayer. When you were on the street, you had to do whatever you could to eat. You had to beg for food. But we don't have to beg God. We need to ask God. God said, 'Ask and it shall be given to you.' Our God is our provider, and I want each of you to ask God for your daily bread."

Mulli led them in prayer. They each ate half a plate of food. Karl finished his and still felt hungry. He looked over at the smaller children. The laughter they expressed earlier was now replaced with questions.

They all went to bed hungry that evening. For Karl, it brought back feelings of life with his mother. He felt the same unwelcome gnawing in his stomach that wouldn't go away. He had gotten used to having food. How quickly the disappointment of being hungry came back to him. He rolled over on his side, hoping to make the pain go away. It helped momentarily. But soon, the hunger returned. He prayed a silent prayer.

Please give us food, God.

He closed his eyes.

And hoped sleep would take his mind off hunger.

His beloved science teacher continued talking, but Karl's mind kept wandering. Being hungry during class made it impossible for him to think of anything else. His eyes felt heavy. His stomach growled. Food. Food. Food.

Lunchtime came without lunch. Children didn't have the energy to play. Mulli led them in prayer. By suppertime, the rationed amounts were even less than the previous day. Bedtime came for Karl as a welcome relief from the pain. The following morning the pain became that much worse. He dragged himself out of bed. Got ready for the day. Everything felt in slow motion.

"The key is to have faith," Mulli said at suppertime. "We must trust God. We must reject the voice of the devil that tells us God will not provide. It is our job to have faith. It is God's job to provide in whatever way and whatever timing He sees fit. We cannot make demands of God. We cannot force God to heal or to give food or do something. We are to ask in faith.

"What is faith? Faith is believing God. The Bible says: 'We walk by faith and not by sight.' I love that verse. You can see we have no food. You have all been to the stores. You can visit the stores and pray while you are there. God answers prayer. Remember the people who gathered around Jesus. They had no food either. And what happened? A little boy brought bread and fish. How many? Can anyone remember? He brought five loaves and two fish. Jesus miraculously multiplied the food. And five thousand men as well as women and children ate until they were full. We have done our part. And now we watch and wait for Jehovah God to act."

Each morning, they heard the phrase run through the compound: *There's rationing today.* It served as a grim reminder that any portions would be decreased to halves and even quarters.

By day four, the hunger pains grew so intense that Karl's mind became consumed with the need to eat. He drifted in and out of the classroom. The teacher spoke, but nothing sank in for Karl. At breaktime, he bowed his head. He said nothing. He sat in the quiet presence of God. Instead of asking for food, Karl became filled with the conviction not only that God *could* provide, but that He *would* provide.

They sat down at the supper table. No more rationing. The rationing calculations become easier to make when there is no food to ration in the first place. Empty plates. Quiet faces. So many children. Everyone quiet.

Karl waited. How long before they would leave and go to evening devotions before bed?

Mulli stood and gave thanks for the food that both was and was not there.

Everyone became quiet. They waited in silence. Waited on God.

Waited on a miracle.

A knock at the gate.

The children heard commotion coming from the courtyard. Karl heard voices talking.

Older children ran to the gate. One of them returned.

"Daddy!" he shouted. His face filled with amazement, eyes big and bright. "Food!"

Karl and the children found a sudden burst of energy. They ran from the tables and hurried out to the front courtyard area. Karl saw a large truck. The back was filled with many sacks of beans and rice and maize and crates of fruits and vegetables.

Karl saw a middle-aged woman with short hair, wearing a dress skirt and blouse, speaking with a lot of enthusiasm to Mulli. She had the kind of fun personality that powers up a room. She studied the children, trying to absorb their sheer number. A sudden astonishment came over her. Like the sight of the children proved more than she could comprehend.

"You really are him, aren't you?" she asked Mulli. "The man who has rescued all these children."

"I am grateful for you coming."

She tried to reply but could not find the words. The younger children cheered. The older boys carried large sacks on their backs from the truck to the stores room.

"I'm grateful to be here," she whispered. She turned back to her truck and noticed the massive amount of food was nearly all transferred out to the MCF stores. She grabbed the side rails of the truck as if needing support to keep her standing.

"You have done a great thing here," Mulli said.

"It was on my heart to help," she whispered.

Karl grabbed a crate and carried it to the stores room. The boys offloaded their sacks and ran out to the supper table. Karl stayed inside the room. Sacks and crates of food crammed into every shelf, filling it to capacity. He touched one of the mangoes. He looked around the room.

Filled to capacity.

Mulli called them back to the table. The aroma of beans and maize filled the air.

"Our God has provided," Mulli said. "In His time and in His way. You have seen Almighty God act on your behalf. He touched that woman's heart to give food. And now we have so much to eat. May you always remember this day whenever you ask God for anything."

Mulli offered a prayer of thanksgiving.

Karl waited his turn and received a full plate of food. He finished and went back for seconds.

He ate until he was full.

CHAPTER 4

It was time to decide.

Mulli moved Karl from MCF Eldoret to MCF Ndalani, where Karl continued to excel in school. By grade 11, he felt the challenge of choosing what field to study after graduating. He planned back and forth between different options. He loved science and proved to be exceptional in it. But science is such a large field. How to narrow it down?

"Karl, I would like to talk with you," Mulli said.

Mulli's timing was perfect, as always. And as always, with Mulli, there was a knowing. In spite of hundreds of children plus many workers and friends, Mulli found time for people. Even though Karl never said anything, never even came up to Mulli with a *Can we talk? I am having trouble deciding what to do after grade 12*, Mulli sensed something on Karl's mind.

"Yes, Daddy," Karl said as he took the last bite of his ugali lunch. He cleaned up his plate as the other children hurried to play games on Saturday afternoon. Karl's mind travelled back to his time in Eldoret when they had nothing to eat, and all MCF fasted and prayed for food.

Mulli sat down with Karl under the protection of trees.

"Did you have a good lunch?" Mulli asked.

"Very good. Thank you, Daddy."

"And did you get enough to eat?" Mulli often asked this question of his children as well as people in his community feeding programs. The knowledge of hunger entered Mulli as a child, and it never left him.

"Yes, Daddy."

"Very good," Mulli said. "You are doing very well in school. Tell me, are you thinking about what you want to do after graduation?"

Karl sensed the security of knowing his father understood him.

"I am trying to think it through. But I am not sure what to do."

"It is a big decision. What you study after high school will have implications the rest of your life. What is important in making this decision, like any decision, is to be in prayer and to be careful. We need to be careful and not be impulsive. The Bible warns us not to make decisions in haste."

"I love science. But science is a big field."

"Very big. And you would succeed in many areas. So which one do you choose? I know that you love the Lord and that you are willing to serve Him wherever He sends you. Your heart is in the right place."

"But how do I decide between different options?"

"When I was younger, I loved being in business. God gave me many insights to make wise deals. There were many challenges. Oh, I tell you, so many challenges. But God granted success. And being in business is very good. God needs many good businesspeople. But for me, I sensed an undisputable calling to leave my businesses and dedicate my life to helping street children. Not every businessperson will receive this call because God does not give this calling to everyone. We each have our calling, where God says: Walk with me."

"Then how did you know for sure? How did you know you needed to sell everything to rescue children like me?"

Mulli nodded his head. He glanced up a moment as he processed his thought; then he focused on Karl.

"When you are searching for direction, when you are looking for a path to pursue, the thing that will reveal your purpose in life more than anything else is your service to humanity."

Mulli's words sank into Karl. Mulli waited, allowing Karl to absorb the weight of how to move forward.

"We live in a world where sometimes people struggle with decision-making because they ultimately want what is going to be best for themselves. I don't see it this way. Jesus came to Earth because He wanted to serve. The Bible says, 'For even the Son of Man did not come to be served, but to serve, and to give His life as a ransom for many.'"

"I remember this verse."

"Sometimes we think: This life—it is mostly for me. I am here to help people a little bit, but mostly this life is so that I can get whatever I want. You remember the Parable of the Very Wealthy Man? He made a lot of money. But he said to himself: 'I have done so well. I will make barns and rest easy.' God was not happy with that man. Why? Because he thought only of himself. Jesus talked about people who help the poor when He said, 'Even as you have done it to the least of these, you have done it unto Me.'"

Karl wanted to respond but found no words. They waited in silence until he finally managed: "Thank you."

"Of course." Karl stood.

As he walked away, he felt an unmistakable pull to become a medical doctor.

That's foolish! You a medical doctor?

It didn't take long. One moment, he was speaking with Charles Mulli about serving God by serving other people. And the next moment, his thoughts began to close in on him. He walked from the school back to his dormitory after a late evening of studying, struggling to sort out his thoughts.

What's wrong with becoming a doctor?

Nothing. There is nothing wrong with becoming a medical doctor … for other people. But you? You are from the slum.

Lots of people come from the slums and do all kinds of things. What difference does it make where I come from? Just because I am from the slum doesn't mean I am an idiot.

Have you ever thought of where you are going to get the money?

That was a challenge. That was a really, really big challenge.

I haven't yet.

Of course, you haven't. How much money will it cost to send you to medical school? That money could be used to help rescue other children. Is that fair? Is that right? Taking all those resources for yourself when they should be shared with others who can't even find food to eat? You know about being hungry on the streets, don't you, Karl?

It is a lot of money. Maybe instead of doing medicine, I should do clinical medicine. Still very good, but not as expensive.

A different voice spoke.

Don't give up. God's economy does not always work the way you think it does.

But it will cost so much money. And should Daddy really be spending all that on me?

Abraham and Sarah were old when God visited them. What did God say? He said: Is anything too hard for the Lord?

Karl kept medicine to himself and spoke to no one about his interest. He continued studying and completed grade 12 at MCF Yatta. One afternoon, Mulli called Karl and two girls, Keren and Grace, to one of the reservoirs. In an effort to defend against the devastating droughts that plagued the area, Mulli had dug massive reservoirs that served to store water for irrigation.

They stood with Mulli overlooking one of the man-made lakes. The incredible pool of water seemed surreal considering how nothing like it existed in the region before MCF arrived.

"You have all done very well in school," Mulli said. "I want Karl and Grace to study medicine and Keren to study nursing."

Mulli's comment shocked Karl.

What? How did Daddy know I want to become a doctor? How does he do that?

Karl performed a quick mental check to see if he had talked with anyone anywhere about his desire to be in medicine. He confirmed he had not discussed it. Still, Mulli knew.

Of course, he did.

Mulli always knew.

"You will make good doctors." He turned to Karl. "You are very smart and did so well. Still, your grades are not good enough for a government scholarship to do medicine in Nairobi."

See, Karl. Told you. Too much money. Go do something else.

"I know," Karl said.

But Mulli was way ahead of him.

"That's why I am going to pay for your school fees."

"Dad, medicine is very expensive. Maybe you are talking about clinical medicine? It's cheaper."

"No. I am talking about a Bachelor of Medicine. A Bachelor of Surgery."

"That is exactly what I want to do."

"The advertisements for the course have already been run in the papers. So, we are a little bit late for that. But I have spoken with Mr. Wesonga, and he has told me the next advertisements are for September. So you will go next September."

Karl's mind flashed back to struggling in the streets as a young boy. And now, here he sat on the cusp of attending medical school. Mulli seemed so sure. So confident that Karl would become a doctor. Grace, too. Mulli's confidence impressed Karl. But what impressed Karl even more, was thinking of Mulli's own situation. Mulli stopped school in grade 8 because he could not pay the school fees. Mulli never attended high school. Never had the opportunity to go to university. And yet, Karl found Mulli to be brilliant, wise, experienced.

And humble.

Willing to give opportunities to others that he never had.

Mulli spoke with Grace while Karl processed his new reality. Medical school. Yes, he had heard that correctly. All those days being sick in the slums with no doctor to help him. All those years with his mother being sicker than he. Suffering sharp abdominal pains and sometimes spending two or three days in bed. Doctors never offered a solution. And it had caused Karl to wonder if he could become a doctor. He could offer relief to suffering people who needed to take care of their children. Now, all these years later, his suffering—and his mother's suffering—had become a catalyst for a desire to serve those who were just as he had been.

"Remember the story of Esther," Mulli said. "Esther was someone you would never notice in life. She was a nobody. But she was already destined by God as the person who would save the family of the Jewish people. Your life is similar in that you were not a recognizable person. You are from the slum. From the very bottom. But God's plan is that you will change the lives of many people. You were put in this place of MCF for such a time as this. For a purpose. Even though you might not have seen it at the time. And even now, you may not be seeing the full picture of what is to come. God has a plan to work through you to bring change to the hopeless and the most underprivileged people."

"I hope I can live up to your expectations," Karl said.

"Leave the expectations aside. Remember the farmer who plowed his field. Keep your eyes on Jesus, and never look to your accomplishments."

Karl nodded.

"I love you *both*," Mulli said.

"I love you, too," they replied.

As Karl went to sleep that night, he thought about the path his life had taken. He thought about Mulli's incredible announcement. And how he now stood at a turning point that would catapult him into a new direction.

And he wondered what would become of it all.

CHAPTER 5

K arl studied an old picture of himself.

So young. So weak.

Was that really him all those years ago?

He graduated from medical school. His brilliant mind experienced the rare privilege of enjoying university. After all the congratulations and excitement of becoming a doctor—a kid from the slums no less, near the end of life, now a physician—he returned to MCF.

Returned home.

He sat alone in a small room. A folder open in front of him. His folder. The MCF intake file of one Karl when he was rescued.

The features were all identifiable, at least to him. He recognized himself the way we all can when we look at pictures of ourselves. He could clearly see the young boy even if others might not see an immediate connection between the old photo and the man now looking at it. They could be forgiven for not making the connection. When Karl arrived, he was frail, exhausted, and malnourished. Sick and at the end.

How strange to be here all these many years later, staring at who he had once been. The picture felt like a window. A special window. A place where he could reach in and tell the young boy that everything would be all right. That everything would come to pass. That he did not need to worry. That yes, something good would come of his life.

Something great.

And it occurred to Karl that maybe, just maybe, this was exactly what Mulli saw when they first met. Maybe Mulli did not just see a sick little boy. Maybe Mulli did not only see what *was*, but he also saw what *would be*. Karl wondered if that kind of insight was one of Mulli's many gifts. That he did not just see a struggling child but saw that child's future. Maybe he saw past what eyes could see.

Maybe Mulli saw with a special kind of vision.

Karl paged slowly through the pictures, the way people do when they are connecting with their past. He felt the weight of destiny. Without Mulli's intervention that face in the picture would have stayed right there in the slum. How odd to think that this little boy, a would-be medical doctor no less, could just as easily have remained uneducated and could have grown up in poverty and now be working endless hours in a slum, desperate to make enough money to survive just one more day.

He read the blood works in his medical report. Deficiency in minerals. Low red cell count, inferring anemia. On and on it went, describing a sick, malnourished kid.

Karl studied the file from an impartial medical perspective as best he could. He wondered if he would ever have managed to survive in the streets. Maybe.

Maybe.

"How are you finding your internship?" a senior doctor asked Karl.

They had already been working a long shift at the hospital. A short break in the medical staff lounge and they would be right back at it. Karl took a drink from his tea. Didn't look at his watch. Didn't need to. Or want to. He felt the kind of joy in the midst of exhaustion that comes to people when they are doing what they are designed to do.

"Challenging and rewarding," Karl said with a smile.

"You are doing well. Very well," the doctor said, adjusting his glasses. "Maybe too well." "Meaning?"

The older doctor was a master at *giving* advice, but not so good at *listening* to it himself. He carried more weight than he should. Drank coffee to such an extent it would have been more efficient to hook up to a caffeine IV instead.

"Did you always want to be a doctor?"

Karl laughed. "Those thoughts were beyond my reach."

"For a smart boy like you? Your parents must have seen it in you from the beginning."

"Yes and no," Karl said.

The older doctor didn't follow.

"I was a street child."

"Impossible."

"Wandered the streets. Dug around in garbage cans for food."

The older doctor's mouth dropped open. He put down his coffee. Leaned forward. Shocked. Amazed. Bewildered.

"I don't believe a word of it."

"I didn't have the courage to beg for food. I went to bed hungry. Was sick all the time. Until Charles and Esther Mulli rescued me."

He shared the MCF story. The normally talkative older doctor sat in silence.

"I sometimes wonder if my mother being so sick played some kind of a role in me becoming a doctor. Who knows how God uses the things in our childhood to prepare us to serve others in life? Often in ways we do not expect."

"I never ...." The older doctor stopped.

"You never thought a dying child in a slum could become someone who helps the dying?"

The older doctor sat in silence, processing. Then whispered, "It appears my faith is not where it should be."

Karl received increasing responsibilities. Hospital administrators noticed his strong understanding of medicine, his unrelenting work ethic, and his uncanny love for patients. Many learned more about MCF and admired how much Charles Mulli had accomplished. They promoted Karl to medical superintendent. No small feat considering he had only recently finished medical school. He earned the position ahead of eleven other interns and more than ten senior doctors. But promotion comes with challenges. And no leadership position is spared from dissent.

His posting proved to be the toughest yet in his career. The hospital faced many challenges both from within and without. Ironically, his struggles did not only come from medical issues in his patients. The dark clouds of struggles also came from resistance developed in senior staff who found themselves having to report to such a young doctor.

You're not the man for the job.

I was given this posting because of my excellence and dedication at work.

You should quit.

I'm not quitting. I am serving the most desperate in society, and that keeps me going.

Suit yourself. But here are the realities. The people who put you here just want to use you and dump you. They disguise their hatred with kindness.

Then I have to win them over.

With what? You don't possess the skills at this age.

I will not let them look down on me because of my youth. But I will set an example for them.

Optimism does not change facts.

Karl spent many hours on his knees. He did so for two reasons. First, he had no other option. And second, his father had modelled it. How often had Mulli told him that he was just a vessel. That a true relationship with Christ is not something that is simply handed out to people. Rather, it is offered, and it grows stronger through obedience and dependence expressed through desperate trust in prayer.

I can't see my way out of this, Father. So many are taking part in corruption and other things which You sent me here to stop. Some of them are doing great work. But they don't like that I am fighting their side incomes of corruption and their habit of showing up for a few hours and then disappearing to their private practices. Others seem to have questionable reasons for being here in the first place. Help me to rely on You. Deliver me, Lord. You are the God who shows me steadfast love. You rescued me from the streets. You will not fail me.

Karl never gave up. Never fought back. Didn't back down either. Over time, people acknowledged his work. Even applauded him for how he led the organization. Karl thought of when Mulli moved MCF to Ndalani. How the neighbours initially rejected Mulli because of the presence of street children. Yet with time, they understood his mission and grew to love him.

Karl came to MCF to volunteer his medical services on weekends. His younger siblings often came to him with their ailments. Other times they came to talk.

Or both.

Karl depressed the tongue of a ten-year-old boy complaining of a sore throat. He gave him lozenges.

"Will they taste good?" the inquisitive boy asked. He was short for his age, a symptom Karl recognized in children who are malnourished.

"They are not candies."

"All right."

"I have not seen you before," Karl said. "How long have you been at MCF?"

"A short while. Let me think. Two months?"

"Welcome. I am sure you are glad to be here."

"Very."

"You had a difficult past," Karl said.

The boy nodded.

"You are from the streets. It takes some getting used to when you leave poverty and come to a good and safe place," Karl said.

"How would you know?"

"I came from the streets too."

"You?"

"Yes, me."

"And now you are a doctor."

"I am."

"That is amazing."

Karl smiled as he shook his head. "It is not about what you become for your career."

"Why not?"

"You need to do your very best. But remember, you can serve God as a metal worker, politician, engineer, teacher, or mechanic. What matters most is serving God and serving people, wherever you are placed. Remember this. It is not simply about you. It is about glorifying God."

"Those are good words."

"They are our Daddy Mulli's words."

"We have a great dad."

"The best."

The boy's appointment was finished. But he glanced at the door, and seeing no one waiting, he pushed himself back in his chair and spoke with Karl with the kind of familiarity siblings have when the rules of time do not apply.

"How did you know you were supposed to become a doctor?" the boy asked.

"Two things. I was fascinated with the human body. And second, medicine is a great way to serve God and other people."

"How will I know what I am supposed to do?"

"What interests you?"

"How do you mean?

"God is our creator, right?"

"Yes."

"He took great care in designing you. You are not the same as other children. Similar in some respects, but not identical to anyone. You are unique. And the gifts and talents God has given you will help shape your direction in one way or another."

"I hope I will discover it."

"Sometimes, it is a profession. Other times, it is something outside your profession. The apostle Paul made tents. But he was best known as an evangelist. Daddy Mulli was successful in business. But he is best known for rescuing children."

"How will I know?"

"Tell God you are willing to do whatever He asks. Otherwise, you will end up on a path that might seem right to you, but will lead to nothing."

"It is a good job being a doctor?" the boy asked.

"An amazing job. But when I think of my profession, I don't think of a salary or owning a home. I think beyond that. I think of changing lives. You should too."

"I will," the boy said, edging off the chair. "Thank you."

"Most welcome."

Karl walked with the boy out of the MCF medical building. The sun had begun its rapid descent. A few more minutes, and the final shades of sunlight would give way to the peaceful African night.

"See you," the boy said.

"See you later."

Karl felt the boy's smile as he walked down the path towards the dormitory. He tried to keep it fresh in his mind as long as he could. But he knew the memory would not last.

Karl remembered the patients he lost more than the ones who walked out well.

He crossed over the bridge leading to Mulli's outdoor office in the courtyard, hoping to say goodbye to his dad before heading on his journey back. He saw Mulli talking with Mamma Esther. They waved at him, inviting him over.

Esther handed him a plate of mangos.

"I think you will need this for energy for your ride home," Esther said with a laugh. "They are picked from our farm just today."

Karl thanked her and sat down. They talked about the ministry, how his doctor visits had gone with the children, and his continued advancements in positions at the hospital.

"You are doing an excellent job, Karl," Mulli said. "You have really learned to put others ahead of yourself."

"I don't know how I can thank you," Karl said.

"There is so much to be thankful for," Mulli said. "I am so grateful for the endless stories that continue to amaze me. All the children. I think of so many. Paul and his skills in playing football. Keren as the chief nurse of so many hospitals. Moses serving as a pastor in the slum. Ruth on the national karate team and studying overseas. Muchoki who is coming back and stronger than ever. Zendaya a lawyer. And you, Karl, a medical doctor."

Mulli became silent. He looked up to the night sky.

"Everyone is a miracle," Mulli said. "All of you. Everyone who has come to MCF is a miracle. To think of where each of you has come from and where you are now," Mulli said. "Do you remember when you and I first met?"

Karl smiled. "Yes, I remember it well."

"You do?"

"Yes."

"Are you sure?"

"Very sure."

"Outside the black gate at MCF Eldoret," Mulli said.

How in the world Mulli could remember all these details from so many children continued to amaze Karl.

"I was playing with the electrical cables."

Mulli smiled in his quiet and humble manner. The music from a choir practicing in the distance filled the night air. Mulli spoke quietly. Almost in a whisper.

"This vision God has given me is so much bigger than me. One way I see the vision expanding is through our children. Children like you, Karl. I am so proud of you."

"Thank you, Daddy and Mamma."

"Esther has stood by me for so many years doing the work of the Lord. So many lives have been transformed," Mulli said. "Yes, there are unending challenges. And there will be many more challenges to come. But when I look back, just for a moment, I see how God is making everything work out as I walk this road with Him."

OTHER TITLES BY CASTLE QUAY BOOKS

CASTLE QUAY BOOKS

The Man. The Miracles. The Mission.

FATHER TO THE
FATHERLESS

The Charles Mulli Story

PAUL H. BOGE
Foreword by Bruce Wilkinson, *Dream for Africa*

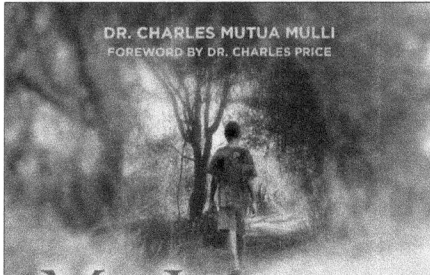

DR. CHARLES MUTUA MULLI
FOREWORD BY DR. CHARLES PRICE

My Journey
OF FAITH

AN ENCOUNTER WITH CHRIST
... and how He used me to spread His love to the poor

CASTLE QUAY BOOKS

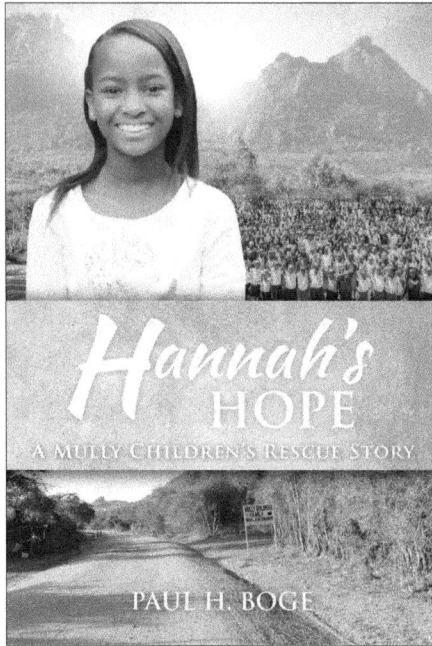

Hannah's
HOPE
A MULLY CHILDREN'S RESCUE STORY

PAUL H. BOGE

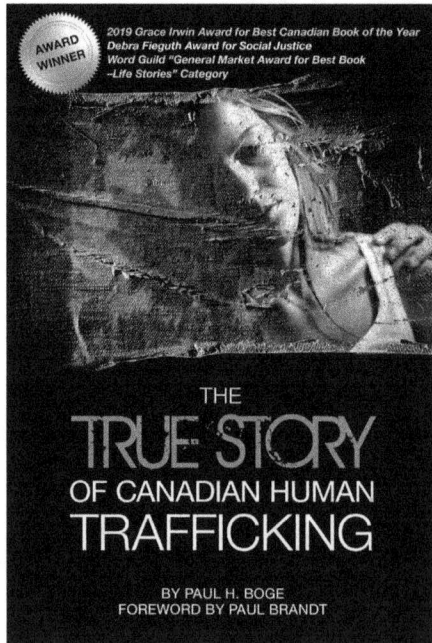

AWARD WINNER

2019 Grace Irwin Award for Best Canadian Book of the Year
Debra Fieguth Award for Social Justice
Word Guild "General Market Award for Best Book
—Life Stories" Category

THE
TRUE STORY
OF CANADIAN HUMAN
TRAFFICKING

BY PAUL H. BOGE
FOREWORD BY PAUL BRANDT

CASTLE QUAY BOOKS

THE **BIGGEST FAMILY**
in the world

Written by Paul H. Boge   Illustrations by Faye Hall   Foreword by Grace Mutua

CASTLE QUAY BOOKS